EDUCATING PROFESSIONALS

EDUCATING PROFESSIONALS

Responding to New Expectations for Competence and Accountability

LYNN CURRY

JON F. WERGIN

AND ASSOCIATES

Jossey-Bass Publishers • San Francisco

Substantial discounts on bulk quantities of Jossey-Bass books are available to corporations, professional associations, and other organizations. For details and discount information, contact the special sales department at Jossey-Bass Inc., Publishers. (415) 433-1740; Fax (415)433-0499.

For sales outside the United States, contact Maxwell Macmillan International Publishing Group, 866 Third Avenue, New York, New York 10022.

Manufactured in the United States of America

The paper used in this book is acid-free and meets the State of California requirements for recycled paper (50 percent recycled waste, including 10 percent postconsumer waste), which are the strictest guidelines for recycled paper currently in use in the United States.

10% POST
CONSUMER
W A S T E

Library of Congress Cataloging-in-Publication Data

Curry, Lynn.
    Educating professionals : responding to new expectations for competence and accountability / Lynn Curry, Jon F. Wergin, and Associates.
        p.   cm. — (The Jossey-Bass higher and adult education series)
    Includes bibliographical references (p.   ) and index.
    ISBN 1-55542-523-2
    1. Professional education.   I. Wergin, Jon F.   II. Title.
III. Series.
LC1059.C87   1993
378'.013—dc20   92-41686
                                                        CIP

FIRST EDITION
HB Printing   10 9 8 7 6 5 4 3 2 1   *Code 9323*

THE JOSSEY-BASS
HIGHER AND ADULT EDUCATION
SERIES

CONTENTS

PREFACE

The professions seem to be under attack everywhere. While the term *true professional* continues to be a mark of high praise, and the professions as a group continue to rank near the top in occupational prestige, public confidence in them has declined precipitously in recent years. Doctors and lawyers have been excoriated for their greed and lack of social conscience and even such helping professions as social work have been criticized for their lack of attention to the truly needy.

In truth, the criticisms are largely recycled. As long ago as the seventeenth century, the term *professional* was usually reserved for a member of the privileged class who chose to be paid for something that was more properly pursued with motives higher than money (Friedson, 1986). In the early part of the twentieth century, the public viewed professionals as monopolistic capitalists. And in the revolutionary political climate of the 1960s, the myth of professional expertise and the collegial autonomy of associations, licensing boards, and codes of ethics came to be seen more as forms of political than of quality control.

So the critiques of the professions as exclusionary guilds of highly educated and mostly well paid practitioners are nearly as old as the professions themselves. However, doubts about the adequacy of the education that professionals bring to their crafts are now emerging with greater urgency. Ever since Abraham Flexner's muckraking report (1910), which revolutionized medical education by grounding it in the basic medical sciences, one of the hallmarks of the professions, whether medicine, law, architecture, or engineering, has been the abstract systems of knowledge, usually scientific in nature, that constitute their foundations. But as Schön (1983, p. 14) has pointed out, "On the whole . . . professional knowledge is mismatched to the changing character of the situations of practice—the complexity, uncertainty, instability, uniqueness, and value conflicts which are increasingly perceived as central to the world of professional practice." Even if Schön overstates the turbulence of practice, the point remains that professional skill often has little to do with the systems of knowledge that form the basis of most professional school curricula. Abbott (1988) contends that the central public argument distinguishing the professions from other occupations, a posture protected and nurtured by professional schools, is that a strong theoretical education is necessary both to understand and to *do*. Even if this argument is specious, it still governs practice, and thus "irrelevant learning continues to be a central part of professional education" (Abbott, 1988, p. 68).

Purpose

Educating Professionals offers a comprehensive examination of how we need to educate professionals for practice in the twenty-first century, and why and how that education differs from the curricula of today. This book is thus a call for reform, and it is unlike most other books on professional education in three ways. First, it analyzes current and future professional practice from different social and educational perspectives and specifies how professional education must adapt to them. Second, it is cross-professional, identifying themes and issues common to the professions in a manner to which all people concerned with professional education can relate. And third, it is future-oriented, focused more on needs and needed changes than on the exposition of specific methods and techniques. Our goal is to have readers finish the book with a different way of thinking about professional education, a clearer sense of how it is (or ought to be) similar to and different from other forms of postsecondary education, and new ideas about how to modify current educational practice.

Audience

For whom, then, is *Educating Professionals* intended? First and foremost, we hope that the book will be read by those most able to change educational practice in our professional schools: deans, department chairs, curriculum coordinators, and faculty opinion leaders. Regardless of where the pressures for change originate, real change begins with the professional school faculty and its leadership. We hope that the book will also be useful to personnel in faculty and instructional development offices as a tool for generating conversation and debate, and to scholars and students of Western postsecondary education.

Before outlining the contents of the volume, we need to define more precisely what we mean by *profession* and *professional* and to indicate how our definitions frame the discussions in the chapters that follow. What constitutes a profession has been an issue of intense debate for decades, and any consensus on definition is difficult to establish. First, generally accepted meanings and the occupations those meanings define have changed over time. For example, through the end of the nineteenth century, the ranks of professionals included mediums and spiritualists. Furthermore, professional definitions have generally been framed and promulgated by the members of the groups themselves. Claims to special knowledge, distinctive ethics, or strong commitments to public service, for example, reflect rhetoric and ideology more than reality (Torstendahl and Burrage, 1990). Still, most members would agree that the professions encompass occupational groups that (1) share specialized skills requiring extensive systematic and scholarly training, (2) restrict access with rigorous entrance and exit requirements, and (3) because of their importance to society, claim high social prestige.

All of the contributors to this volume have taken pains to ensure that their discussions are truly cross-professional. We have adopted a simple organizational rubric first used by the Professional Preparation Project (Stark, Lowther, Hagerty, and Orcyak, 1986), which divides the professions into three clusters: the *helping* professions, such as nursing, social work, teaching, and the ministry; the *entrepreneurial* professions, such as journalism, business, and law; and the *technical* professions, such as architecture, engineering, and the military. Use of this rubric is not intended to elicit debate about how best to classify professions. Certainly, the categories are not mutually exclusive. For example, while medicine is here classified as a helping profession, few would argue that it is not also entrepreneurial; and law, here classified as entrepreneurial, purports to be both helping and highly technical. Our purpose, rather, is to ensure that the spirit of cross-professional inquiry is carried forward throughout each chapter and to avoid perspectives that are parochial or limited to one profession. Accordingly, each substantive point throughout the book is illustrated by examples from at least one profession in each of the three clusters. The result is a narrative that defines areas of concern across the professions and thus enriches the often implicit bonds between them.

Overview of the Contents

Educating Professionals has three parts. In Part One, the authors explore the broad social trends that promise to have profound effects on how professionals work: the social and political forces affecting professionals and their roles (Chapter One), the changing definitions of professional skill (Chapter Two), the effects of information technology on the very nature of professional practice (Chapter Three), and the increasingly strict demands for professional accountability (Chapter Four).

In Chapter One, Christine H. McGuire outlines societal pressures and expectations that are constraining and shaping individual practitioners and the professions to an unanticipated degree. Ilene B. Harris, in Chapter Two, characterizes the nature of professional practice using philosophical analysis and describes the concepts and approaches associated with the currently popular term *reflective practice.* Complementary roles of different types of knowledge and competence essential for professional practice are explored, and implications are outlined for the improvement of professional practice through new approaches to educational program design and instruction.

Joanne Gard Marshall, in Chapter Three, describes the changing technological environment within which professionals practice and draws implications for professional training and retraining. John J. Norcini and Judy A. Shea, in Chapter

Four, account for the growing pressures for recertification and relicensure of professionals as mechanisms to ensure competence in practice throughout careers. These pressures are traced to society's increasing expectations of accountability in professions. The authors describe conceptual and psychometric problems that must be resolved before the accountability objectives can be realized.

In Part Two, the authors analyze professional schools' emerging curricular responsibilities, assess how well the new challenges are being met, and suggest how professional education can become more coincident with changing practice requirements.

In Chapter Five, Sally Hixon Cavanaugh sets the stage with a wide-ranging critique of where and how professional curricula fall short of the new requirements. She urges several fundamental changes to help resolve the "education-practice discontinuity," including more practice-oriented learning, a larger role for program evaluation in curriculum improvement, and an educational research agenda that is more multidisciplinary in focus and more naturalistic in method.

In Chapter Six, Robert A. Armour and Barbara S. Fuhrmann propose a new definition for liberal education, one that has major implications for how we think about the skills and perspectives needed in today's society. Armour and Fuhrmann argue that liberal learning, far from being solely the concern of undergraduate education, is the underpinning of effective professional education as well, and they describe how liberal learning goals can be adapted for, and assessed in, specific professional curricula.

In Chapter Seven, David T. Ozar takes on professional ethics, long a part of the formal credo of every profession but often relegated to a peripheral role in professional schools. He describes the nature of professional obligation, debunks some common misconceptions about professional ethics education, and then sets forth sensible goals and educational strategies. Ethics can be taught, Ozar argues, and learned.

In Chapter Eight, Charles E. Wales, Anne H. Nardi, and Robert A. Stager consider the difficult task of teaching problem solving, long a mainstay of the professional's art. Their chapter is specific and practical and thus complements Ilene B. Harris's discussion of the need for greater attention to reflective practice in Chapter Two and Sally Hixon Cavanaugh's call for more practice-oriented learning in Chapter Five.

In Chapter Nine, Robert Rippey describes what professional education in universities could learn from professional education in corporations. Corporate settings, often highly suspect to the academic community, nonetheless offer intriguing models of education that are worth considering, and as Rippey points out, these models are often based more on established principles of teaching and learning than are the models found in academe.

All four chapters in Part Three echo the central theme of the book: the job of educating professionals for the twenty-first century requires stronger bonds between our systems of education and our systems of practice. The authors discuss three possible bridges between the education and the practice communities: more authentic measures of competence for professional practice (Chapter Ten), a more integrated system of continuing professional education (Chapter Eleven), and a broader view of faculty scholarship (Chapter Twelve).

In Chapter Ten, William C. McGaghie discusses possible revisions in the concept of and the attitude toward identifying initial levels of appropriate competence at the point of entry to professional practice. Nancy L. Bennett and Robert D. Fox, in Chapter Eleven, continue this line of thought in their discussion of changing expectations and structure to maintain professional competence throughout a practice career.

In Chapter Twelve, R. Eugene Rice and Laurie Richlin broaden the role of the academic, or university-based, arm of the professions. They suggest an expanded role that could more appropriately and more effectively sustain the four distinct purposes expected of professional school faculty: contributions to discovery in the profession, contributions to integrating professional knowledge, contributions to optimizing teaching and learning within the professional field, and contributions to professional practice.

In our final chapter, Chapter Thirteen, we offer a synthesis of previous chapters and speculate about the future. If public expectations of the professions and professional practice have shifted in basic and profound ways, what should the priorities be for change in professional education as we move into the next century? How likely is it that change will occur in the needed directions? Will the acknowledged irrelevance of much of what now passes for professional education remain as the last vestige of the traditional ideal? If so, what are the consequences for the professions and the clients they purport to serve?

Acknowledgments

For all concerned, participation in this book project was an example of its theme: it required critical examination of the gap between what we are comfortable with and used to doing and what is now required by our professional environments. Authors had to research professional domains other than their own; reviewers had to react from the perspective of multiple new audiences; and we, as the originators of the project, had to learn to articulate a vision of shared futures across professions that allowed consideration of shared solutions.

We thank the authors and the three reviewers, Sarah Dinham and two anonymous readers; they met the challenge to apply their expertise and vision to their own professions and others. We also thank Mary O'Farrell, who wrestled the words through the computer, and Lynn Luckow and Gale Erlandson of Jossey-Bass, who have believed in the multidisciplinary future of professions almost as long as we have.

February 1993
Lynn Curry
Ottawa, Ontario

Jon F. Wergin
Richmond, Virginia

THE AUTHORS

Lynn Curry founded Curry Adams & Associates, Inc., in 1990, after twelve years as an academic, concluding as Rosenstadt Professor of medicine at the University of Toronto. Curry Adams & Associates assists public and private sector executives, policy makers, providers, planners, and managers in health, education, and social services. In that capacity, Curry works with professional associations, educators, and regulators for a range of professions, including medicine, nursing, law, social work, and rehabilitation therapies.

Originally from Saskatchewan, Curry received her B.Ed. degree (1970) from the University of Alberta and her Ph.D. degree (1974) from Stanford University in education and psychology, with emphases in cognition and evaluation and research methodologies. She later received a diplomate (1982) from Bryn Mawr College in management sciences.

Curry founded the Medical Education Unit and the Research Section in Continuing Professional Education at Dalhousie University, and as vice president of the Canadian College of Health Services Executives, she established the measurement system for health care management competence assessment with related training programs. She also created Canada's first peer-reviewed journal in health care administration: *Healthcare Management FORUM Gestion des soins de santé*. She also served as vice president of the American Education Research Association (1987–1989), an international organization for professional research, where she was elected to represent the interests of researchers and educators in the professions.

Curry has executed over one hundred program design and evaluation studies in the health, education, and social service sectors and has published widely in the areas of general and professional education, program planning, design, and evaluation. She continues to be an active researcher in professional school curricula, professional behavioral change, and improvement of professional competence.

Jon F. Wergin is professor of education at Virginia Commonwealth University. He received his B.A. degree (1968) in psychology and his Ph.D. degree (1973) in educational psychology, both from the University of Nebraska. Wergin's primary research interests include evaluation and change in higher and professional education, and his scholarly publications have focused on clinical and program evaluation, faculty development, and cultural diversity. He is the author or coauthor of five books and monographs, including *Assessing the Impact of Continuing Medical Education Through Structured Physician Dialogue* (1987) and *Consulting in Higher Education: Principles for Institutions and Consultants* (1989). Wergin has been a consultant for more than two dozen colleges and consortia and has served for four years as external evaluator for the National Center for Research to Improve Postsecondary Teaching and Learning at the University of Michigan. From 1989 to 1991, Wergin was vice president of the American Educational Research Association for Division I, Education in the Professions. In 1992, he became a senior associate at the American Association for Higher Education (AAHE) in Washington, D.C., helping inaugurate the AAHE Forum on Faculty Roles and Rewards.

Robert A. Armour is assistant general secretary for the Board of Higher Education of the United Methodist Church in Nashville, Tennessee. Before his appointment to this position in July 1992, he was professor of English at Virginia Commonwealth University.

Nancy L. Bennett is director of educational development and evaluation in the Department of Continuing Medical Education, Harvard Medical School.

Sally Hixon Cavanaugh is currently director of an office of research at York Hospital in York, Pennsylvania, a large community-based teaching hospital with seven graduate medical education programs and a school of allied health, educationally affiliated with the University of Pennsylvania, the University of Maryland, and Pennsylvania State University.

Robert D. Fox is professor and director of the Oklahoma Research Center for Continuing Professional and Higher Education at the University of Oklahoma.

Barbara S. Fuhrmann is professor of counselor education and director of assessment at Virginia Commonwealth University. She has served as faculty fellow at the university's Center for Educational Development and Faculty Resources and is currently helping accreditation agencies integrate liberal learning outcomes into their guidelines.

Ilene B. Harris is professor of medical education at the University of Minnesota Medical School and College of Education.

William C. McGaghie is professor of community health and preventive medicine at Northwestern University Medical School, Chicago, where he is also associate director of the Office of Medical Education.

Christine H. McGuire is associate director and professor emerita, Department of Medical Education, University of Illinois College of Medicine, Chicago.

Joanne Gard Marshall is associate professor of library and information science at the University of Toronto.

Anne H. Nardi is professor and chair of the Department of Educational Psychology, College of Human Resources and Education, West Virginia University.

John J. Norcini is executive vice president for evaluation and research and director of psychometrics, American Board of Internal Medicine.

David T. Ozar is professor of moral philosophy and director of graduate programs in health care ethics at Loyola University of Chicago.

R. Eugene Rice is vice president and dean of faculty at Antioch College. He was formerly senior fellow at The Carnegie Foundation for the Advancement of Teaching at Princeton University, where he worked on the project investigating faculty scholarship.

Laurie Richlin is director of the Office of Research and Evaluation Studies at Antioch College, director of the Lilly Conference on College Teaching, West, and executive editor of *Journal on Excellence in College Teaching.* She received the 1992 Donald A. Gatzke Award for Outstanding Dissertation in Higher Education Administration from the American Association of University Administrators Foundation.

Robert Rippey is professor in the Center for Alzheimer's Disease, Southern Illinois University School of Medicine.

Judy A. Shea is project manager of a Patient Outcomes Research Team Study and senior fellow at the Leonard Davis Institute, University of Pennsylvania.

Robert A. Stager is professor of engineering at the University of Windsor, Ontario, Canada.

Charles E. Wales is professor of engineering and education and director of the Center for Guided Design, College of Engineering, West Virginia University.

EDUCATING PROFESSIONALS

PART ONE

Trends and Forces
Reshaping
Professional Practice

This first section outlines the important areas in which professional practice is being reshaped. Each of these areas represents fundamental changes in how individuals practice their professions.

In Chapter One, Christine H. McGuire outlines societal pressures and expectations that are constraining and shaping individual practitioners and the professions to an unanticipated degree. Ilene B. Harris, in Chapter Two, characterizes the nature of professional practice using philosophical analysis and describes the concepts and approaches associated with the currently popular term *reflective practice*. Complementary roles of different types of knowledge and competence essential for professional practice are explored, and implications are outlined for the improvement of professional practice through new approaches to educational program design and instruction.

Joanne Gard Marshall, in Chapter Three, describes the changing technological environment within which professionals practice and draws implications for professional training and retraining. John J. Norcini and Judy A. Shea, in Chapter Four, account for the growing pressures for recertification and

1

relicensure of professionals as mechanisms to ensure competence in practice throughout careers. These pressures are traced
to increasing societal expectations of accountability in professions. The authors describe conceptual and psychometric problems that must be resolved before the accountability objectives
can be realized.

CHAPTER 1

Sociocultural Changes Affecting Professions and Professionals

Christine H. McGuire

In the face of irrefutable evidence of precipitous and ongoing loss of popular confidence in, and strident public demands for regulation of, the traditional professions, it is ironic that those in other occupations continue to clamor for admission into what their practitioners perceive as the more privileged sanctuaries. Why should this be so? What is it that distinguishes a profession from other arenas of work? How have changing socioeconomic conditions altered the fundamental character of professional practice?

Changing Conceptions of the Professions

Under the headline "Is Graphology Emerging from the Kooky Closet?" Reibstein and Springer (1992) report that "for reasons buried deep in the stars, recent sightings indicate that graphology may be moving out of the kooky closet. Last year the U.S Labor Department gave it an imprimatur of sorts, promoting the job title of graphologist from the 'amusement and entertainment' category to 'miscellaneous professionals' (alongside Dianetic counselors and taxidermists)." Given such a proliferation of entries under the rubric "professions," one might be forgiven for wishing to imitate Aristotle's clarification of a similar definitional problem, when he implied simply that physics is whatever it is that physicists do. By analogy, can we say that the professions include all those occupations whose practitioners call themselves professionals? That this is not an entirely frivolous suggestion is supported by the view of Eliot Freidson, a leading student of the issue: "There is no single, truly explanatory trait or characteristic . . . that can join together all occupations called professions beyond the actual fact of coming to be called professions" (1983, p. 33).

Such a solution would have the virtue of restricting the scope of discussion by excluding not only production workers, but also persons in certain of the skilled trades and crafts (for example, plumbers, carpenters, and others) who rarely identify themselves as professionals. However, it would not eliminate many who pursue careers in sports, entertainment, politics, the arts, voluntary service, and the like for whom the adjective "professional" is used merely to distinguish the athlete, singer, artist, bridge player, lobbyist and others who "turn pro," that is, work for pay, from those who indulge in the same activities *exclusively* for the satisfaction of certain intangible rewards ("pure fun," "the joy of serving," and so on).

Rather than relying on self-selection and/or the reward structure, some authors have tried to define the professions by identifying the salient features that distinguish among the types of educational preparation required for alternative kinds of careers: vocational *training* versus professional *education* versus graduate *study* (McGuire, 1992). Advocates of this approach argue that the professions are distinguished from trades and crafts, on the one hand, by virtue of the former's reliance on theory, and from science and graduate study, on the other, by virtue of the latter's primary emphasis on the pursuit and creation of knowledge, not merely its "use" (Dinham and Stritter, 1986). This view leads its proponents to argue that professional education is unique in depending on a combination of basic science and "practical studies"; they equate the latter with apprenticeship, which they regard as "professional education's most important distinguishing feature," and which they contend provides the link between theory and practice (Dinham and Stritter, 1986, p. 952).

Thus engineering is distinguished from the construction trades by virtue of its reliance on mathematics and physics, and from these disciplines by its relatively lesser emphasis on pure research. Whether analogous statements can be made about some of the newer claimants to professional status is more problematic. Indeed, it may be the relative lack of a defined theoretical base of their own that characterizes vocations which Glazer (1974) terms the "minor" professions (for example, librarian, social worker) in contrast with what he views as the "major" (traditional?) professions (for example, theology, law, medicine).

Others see the nature of the evolution of a field of work as the unique characteristic that qualifies it for the appellation "profession." Thus Matarazzo (1977) argues that with the exception of the ministry, each of the other "learned professions" has evolved through more or less the same stages: random and haphazard entry of practitioners into the field, followed by their loose organization into voluntary guilds that soon begin to impose training and entry requirements, eventually enforced by the accreditation of training programs and the licensure and/or certification of practitioners. Matarazzo also notes that this credentialing process itself may become highly elaborated via recognition of subspecialties and imposition of requirements for documentation of continued competence by reexamination and/or evidence of participation in further education. The several elements (which Matarazzo regards as requisite) are perhaps most clearly evident in the health care arena, and in the medical profession in particular, but are also approximated to varying degrees in other fields as diverse as accounting, engineering, clinical psychology, social work, law, and public school teaching (McGuire, 1992).

The significance of this evolutionary development, as well as the importance of a theoretical base, in defining a profession are most succinctly summarized in the statement by Starr (1982, p. 15) that: "A profession is an occupation that regulates itself through systematic, required training and collegial discipline; that has a base in technological, specialized knowledge; and that has a service, rather than a profit, orientation enshrined in its code of ethics." With this definition, however, Starr introduces a new element, namely, a service motive, as an essential attribute of the professions—a position that many would question, especially in light of the current bitterly critical, antiprofessional climate (Halmos, 1973).

For example, Metzger (1987) notes that the intensified attacks on professionals which we are witnessing, a trend for which he coined the term "professionalism," increasingly include charges that the so-called quality controls professional groups exercise over selection, admission to training, and licensure to practice are merely thinly disguised attempts to maintain profitable monopolies. Others similarly attribute the expanding professionalization of work, that is, the growing tendency to classify increasing numbers of occupations as professions (Wilensky, 1964), to the desire of other callings for enhanced status, prestige, and monopoly power.

The prevalence of economic, as opposed to service, motives was particularly blatant in the U.S. business community in the 1980s when graduating M.B.A.s were not infrequently explicitly advised of the virtues of greed (Chapman, 1987). Nor was the economic motive very far below the surface in the bitter battles over turf (as controlled by licensure) that, since World War II, have been waged with increasing frequency in the courts, between members of the traditional professions and relative newcomers. In these cases the cacophonous rhetoric with which each group proclaimed its altruistic concerns for consumer protection and quality of service did little to disguise the basic economic interests of the contending parties. These views of the avarice of professionals were to some extent reinforced by the growing consensus among American scholars about the significance of power as the defining attribute of the professions (Johnson, 1972; Hall, 1983).

"While American sociologists have been obsessed with the problem of defining the professions, British sociologists have . . . been busy getting on with the business of studying the relationships between the professions and the larger society" (MacDonald and Ritzer, 1988, p. 255). It is to consideration of that relationship that I now turn.

Changing Conditions of Professional Practice

Given their variety, it is clear that no single generalization will apply equally to all the pursuits now embraced by the term *professional practice*. Indeed, in various important respects some of the professions are moving in precisely opposite directions. Consider, for example, the trends to restrict individual autonomy in medical decision making versus the increasing independence of social workers engaged in private practice. Nor are professions in different countries equally affected by current developments. "In analyzing the professions we are looking at historically and nationally specific events" (MacDonald and Ritzer, 1988, pp. 254–255). For the most part, the trends outlined below are most advanced in the United States, they are becoming increasingly influential in other of the developed nations, and, if at all operative, they are only beginning to impact practice in Third World countries.

　　Some authors believe that primary among these changes is the emergence of something new in the circumstances to which practitioners are required to respond—a problematic quality—that makes it necessary for the professional to balance competing values from different universes (Schön, 1983, 1987). This view implies that heretofore practitioners have been called on to treat only trial, or purely technical, problems a particularly naive, parochial, and misleading position, unsupported by data. Rather, I believe that changes occurring in the conditions of professional practice can be traced to three underlying causes: specifically, changes in the inherent characteristics of professions, in the ambient technology, and in the general socioeconomic conditions and in the cultural setting of professional practice.

Changing Characteristics of the Professions

Not only has the Renaissance scholar disappeared for all practical purposes, but his supposed successor, the self-employed general practitioner, is also rapidly becoming extinct in virtually all fields of endeavor. In my view this is due to a universal phenomenon: the inexorable, cumulative expansion in our knowledge base and the consequent specialization that inevitably demands.

The Knowledge Explosion

Unless interrupted by some catastrophe, the volume of our knowledge, by its very nature, increases at a geometric rate. It is reliably predicted that our scientific and technical knowledge base, now doubling about every five to eight years, will soon begin to double every year in some fields. True, the rate of expansion in the quantity of facts, concepts, and principles required for competent practice will differ among professions, depending on the nature of the theories that underlie each. Professions based on the "hard" sciences (for example, engineering and medicine) will be most affected, while those reliant on philosophy and/or theology (for example, the ministry) will be least impacted; others resting on the social and behavioral sciences (for example, law, teaching) will be somewhere in between, though even these are already encountering problems in "managing the burgeoning mass of data to be assimilated" (Freund, 1963, p. 697).

The Response: Further Specialization and Increased Division of Labor

Given the physical limits on human capacities to assimilate, organize, manage, retrieve, and utilize knowledge, institutional adaptations and/or technological developments are required if this expanding data base is to be employed for the benefit of recipients of professional services.

Until the relatively recent advent of small, high-speed, inexpensive computers capable of storing and processing vast quantities of data, modification in the institutional arrangements for providing competent professional service was the only feasible response to the problem. It is therefore instructive to observe the high correlation between the extent of specialization and the nature of, and rate of change in, the knowledge base underlying a profession. For example, physicians are increasingly restricting their practices to a single, small part of the body (the hand, the eye, the heart), or a single disease process (infectious diseases, endocrinology, oncology), and/or a single age group (pediatrics, adolescent medicine, geriatrics). Compare the proliferation of subspecialties in the health professions generally with the relatively limited specialization in the ministry, where changes in institutional arrangements have consisted primarily in the addition of ancillary services (for example, pastoral counselors).

The inevitable concomitant of increasing specialization is the further elaboration of the division of labor—a process that, during the Industrial Revolution, eventuated in the demise of the master craftsman. Some authors now predict that an analogous "deskilling" process and consequent erosion of control may overtake the professions (Shaw, 1987). Together with other socioeconomic developments limiting the autonomy of practitioners, it is predicted that this will lead to their "deprofessionalization" (Haug, 1973, 1975; Rothman, 1984; Fielding, 1984; Freidson, 1985; Reed and Evans, 1987) and ultimate "proletarianization" (Oppenheimer, 1973; Larson, 1980; Derber, 1982; Rothman, 1984; Whalley, 1985).

The Ambient Technology

Technological progress and its specific impacts on particular professions are discussed by Marshall (this volume); here, I shall briefly explore only two interdependent developments that have caused fundamental alterations in working relations and institutional arrangements in virtually all occupations: (1) qualitative changes in the speed, variety, and modalities of communication, and (2) a complete transformation in the techniques of managing data. Together, they have begun to reverse the century-long progress toward ever greater concentration of work in huge corporations housed in vast structures (the Pentagon being one of the most egregious examples), located in metastasizing megalopolises (for example, Tokyo, or for that matter, the almost continuous industrial corridors that spread along our own eastern and western coasts).

A professional no longer need be literally within arm's length of a colleague and/or a required resource: the corporate files of the chief executive officer, the attorney's specialized library, the architect's three-dimensional models, the physician's network of subspecialist consultants. With the imminent addition of satellite technology to present-day computers, it will soon be unnecessary even to have access to a conventional modem and modern telephone in order to establish immediate contact with almost anyone in the world, from almost anywhere on the planet. The epitome of this trend may well be the location of the headquarters for a leading investor newsletter in rural Montana—two thousand miles distant, both physically and culturally, from Wall Street. The portable personal computer, combined with desktop publishing capabilities and a simple fax machine, has made routine what was fantasy only a generation ago.

Truly, we have become a global village. But in so doing it is not alone the physical conditions of work and the breadth of access to information that have been altered by technology; of equal significance is the way we think about our work in at least two important respects: first, our expected response time and second, our imposed dependence on others.

With regard to the first consideration, an attorney recently remarked to me that, in his opinion, the fax machine is the most mischievous development that has occurred during his professional life. In response to my protests that the quick closing on a recent deal of major significance to him would have been impossible without the fax, he explained that its availability necessarily sets up the expectation of an instantaneous response, which is almost always contraindicated and which is especially harmful in situations that require thoughtful exploration of alternatives. In fact, he argued that such expectations have become routine and are adversely affecting his approach to client problems and the quality of service he can provide.

In essence, the current technological revolution is altering the physical and institutional arrangements for work to an extent that rivals quantitatively the changes in working conditions imposed by the Industrial Revolution. It has consequently modified in fundamental ways public and interprofessional relationships. The special status accorded professionals rests, in large part, on their monopoly of a body of "extraordinary knowledge of great social importance" (Hughes, 1959). However, this monopoly is seriously weakened by an enforced dependence on new occupations (for example, computer programmers, technicians, and electronics experts) to access specialized information, a dependence that is imposed by an esoteric, rapidly moving technology that further strips professionals of control over the nature, quality, and range of services that they are able to provide, thus exacerbating the pressures toward loss of autonomy (Haug, 1977).

Changing Socioeconomic and Cultural Contexts of Practice

I can here discuss only very briefly the most important trends in intraprofessional relationships, the organization and setting of professional practice, and the changing nature of control over professional behavior, all of which converge to diminish autonomy and public respect, and consequently, the status, prestige, and power of the professional (McGuire, 1989, 1992; McGuire-Masserman and Masserman, 1992).

From Collegial to Competitive Relations

The long socialization process which begins with entry into training has traditionally played a central role in governing intraprofessional relationships and in serving to establish and maintain collegiality. However, these relationships are being seriously eroded by the blatant competition inherent in the growing use of advertising by professionals. Daily, the public is exposed to paid pleas in the media, embodying carefully crafted and easily remembered toll-free numbers for immediate contact, implying that a particular law firm gets the biggest settlements for its clients, that the infants born at a particular hospital are the most beautiful, that a particular bank or brokerage house obtains the highest *and* safest returns (a patently impossible combination) for its customers, that a specified medical group has the most Nobel laureates and, by implication, the greatest therapeutic successes. Such advertising with its implicit claims of superiority denigrates colleagues (Freidson, 1985), jeopardizes productive collaboration, weakens traditional controls over professional conduct, and contributes to the destruction of public trust in professional ethics, wisdom, and competence.

From Entrepreneur to Employee

Though teachers have long since relinquished their reliance on payment for individual tutoring in favor of more dependable income from neighborhood schools, despite their characteristically bureaucratic controls (Frymier, 1987; Firestone and Bader, 1991), and clergy have abandoned circuit riding for the greater security of stationary chapels in which to serve an established congregation (Ibister, 1986), most Americans nonetheless cling to the nostalgic image of the self-employed, fee-for-service, neighborhood private practitioner. The stereotype of the professional as an independent decision maker does have some justification, in that American labor law has explicitly reserved for professionals an area of discretion and autonomy with respect to the conduct of their work, not accorded ordinary wage laborers (Freidson, 1985). However, whatever the earlier validity of this notion it has been brought increasingly into question as a consequence of the corporatization and bureaucratization of professional practice (see Rippey, this volume).

As national and multinational, for-profit corporations increasingly become major employers of professionals, who work in rigidly structured bureaucratic organizations with large support staffs of assistants, technicians, and clerks, it is inevitable that each person's knowledge of the ostensibly common task and objectives will become more circumscribed (Fielding, 1984), his or her responsibility more diluted, duties more often assigned and actions subject either to computer-driven protocols (Sullivan, 1984) and/or to managers who are necessarily subservient to the interests of owners and other diverse groups (McKinlay, 1982). Autonomy is consequently restricted, and power, prestige, and status correspondingly diminished (Freidson, 1985). This process increasingly alienates highly trained professionals and thereby contributes to their ultimate proletarianization (Oppenheimer, 1973; Larson, 1980; McKinlay, 1982).

From Informal Social Controls to Formal Regulation

Unfortunately, the image of the professional as a person whose daily work is strongly motivated by service and whose conduct is governed by the ethical and performance standards set by a voluntary association of colleagues (Starr, 1982; Matarazzo, 1977) no longer predominates in the public mind. Many actions once accepted as a means of quality control are now derided as economically motivated attempts to gain monopoly control over services (Metzger, 1987). Federal agencies increasingly require that the "discipline of the market" be substituted for more traditional controls (Bowie, 1988), business and market metaphors pervade journals offering advice to practitioners about office organization and management (Korcak, 1985), and consumer groups representing special interests lobby to require professionals to respond with specified and mandated solutions to a range of problems (Haug, 1975).

It is not clear whether this intensified commercialization of the professions merely reflects a general trend in Western society or represents a failure of traditional socialization processes to inculcate professional standards and values during training and/or a weakening of peer pressure in enforcing them in practice. Whatever the cause, it is apparent that ever greater reliance is being placed on formal administrative rules, governmental regulations, and court-imposed sanctions to control the behavior of professionals, to enforce standards in the quality of service they render, and to dictate their relations to each other and to the public they are pledged to serve.

These increasingly common "interferences" with professional decisions range from the generally accepted, through the questionable, to the hotly contested. The range spans, for example, building codes in incorporated communities, architectural requirements for restoration of landmark buildings designated for historical preservation, conflict-of-interest restrictions that prohibit attorneys from representing certain clients, the gag rule that prohibits health professionals from mentioning abortion in federally funded clinical centers, and court orders that mandate the treatment comatose and terminally ill patients are to receive.

While this substitution of formal regulation for compliance with voluntary standards has fundamentally altered the relationships of professionals to each other and to their clients, parishioners, patients, and students, the most serious intrusion in that arena is what can best be described as a *crisis of litigation in court actions* brought both *by* professionals and *against* them: aspiring students suing professional schools for admission, trainees suing credentialing authorities for licensure and/or specialty certification, practitioners suing potential employers and partners for jobs, compensation, and/or promotions, colleagues suing peer review groups over adverse reports, and, perhaps most damaging of all, clients, patients, and their families suing competent and conscientious providers for what they regard as unacceptable results. This burgeoning litigation not only impairs relationships with colleagues and clients, it also invites inappropriate governmental and juristic interventions in highly technical decisions and discourages many humanely dedicated young people from undertaking a socially valuable professional career.

The Convergence of Forces: A Reexamination of Trends

"All professions are organized around a comprehensive body of expert knowledge. It is this expertise—a resource not available to the public—that is probably the most fundamental factor in legitimizing professional prerogatives" (Rothman, 1984, p. 187).

In recent decades alterations in conditions both within and without the professions have weakened this essential monopoly of expertise. As elaborated above, these changes include expansion in the knowledge base, modifications in client populations, rise of consumerism, and increasing employment in bureaucratic structures that stress centralized authority and place restrictions on individual independence, initiative, and judgment (Rothman, 1984). The emphasis on specialization and standardization in these bureaucratic structures encourages routinization of tasks, which in turn facilitates "the incursion of other professions, semi-professions or would-be professions" onto the traditional turf of older fields of work (Reed and Evans, 1987, p. 3280). Further, by segmenting professional functions, specialization and routinization of tasks make it easier for the public to become knowledgable about an area of professional activity and thus strengthen consumer control. These trends are not independent; rather they interact, each reinforcing the effects of the other.

Reprise

Predictions for the future of individual professions strongly suggest that most, if not all, will continue to be faced by more external regulation, increased competition from outside the field, intrusion of newer occupations, louder public demands for more high-quality service at lower cost, and increasingly rapid and pervasive technological change that drastically alters practice (Podgers, 1980; Freidson, 1987). These continuing trends have given rise to four prevalent contradictions that represent current tensions in our society: (1) the professionalization of almost every service versus the deprofessionalization of almost every provider, (2) the exploding body of knowledge within a field *versus* the ever smaller slice of it for which any practitioner is held accountable, (3) the tightening of controls over the traditional (major) professions *versus* the opening of new avenues for initiative (private practice) in the newer (minor and para-) professions, and (4) the prestige and status accorded the abstract concept of an idealized professional *versus* the distrust and imposed controls heaped on actual practitioners.

Though the various professions are currently at different points on the several trend lines enumerated above and may therefore be affected in unique ways, the developments cited will eventually impact not only most arenas of professional practice, but also most areas of professional education both *directly,* insofar as they alter the competencies requisite for practice, and *indirectly,* via their influence on the size and characteristics of the applicant pool seeking entry to the professions.

CHAPTER 2

New Expectations for Professional Competence

Ilene B. Harris

What is the nature of professional practice? Is it fundamentally applied science, technology, or policy? Or is it fundamentally practical art and craft? Recent analysis and research across the professions has yielded new perspectives about the nature of professional practice, which counter the traditional view that it is applied science, technology, or policy. Schön (1983, 1987, 1991) has argued for a new epistemology of professional practice that characterizes it fundamentally as judgment and wise action in complex, unique, and uncertain situations with conflicting values and ethical stances. He argues, therefore, that, in addition to theoretical and technical knowledge, effective professional practice requires reflective and practical knowledge and competencies for dealing with problems in the "indeterminate zones" of practice, that is, the areas that do not yield to technical or familiar solutions. These competencies are critically important to the education and development of professionals in the current climate of rapid technological, cultural, and economic change.

This chapter characterizes the nature of professional practice and outlines the implications for professional education and the development of professional competence. First, I develop a conception of practice, using philosophical analysis, to provide a framework for understanding traditional and emerging views of professional competence, and their implications for education. Then, I review the concepts and approaches associated with the currently popular term *reflective practice,* including the landmark work of Schön, and research in the areas of cognition and analysis of expertise. In this context, I explore the complementary roles of different types of knowledge and competence essential for professional practice: reflective competencies, practical knowledge and competencies, and the specialized bodies of knowledge pertinent to each profession.

Next, I outline the implications of these views for improvement of professional practice through new approaches to educational program design and instruction. In this context, I propose deliberative curriculum inquiry as a strategy for curriculum design—for deciding what needs to be taught and how—that more closely mirrors reflective practice than do traditional approaches to curriculum design. I discuss traditions and institutional forms for education and initiation into the professions, with a focus on emerging forms of initiation that promote development of reflective and practical competencies. I then briefly discuss how the knowledge base for professional practice can be improved by analyzing and codifying the performance of master practitioners. I conclude with recommendations for changes in education for the professions based on these perspectives.

A Conception of Practice

Philosophical analyses are helpful to understand both traditional and emerging views of professional practice, and their implications for professional education. Specifically, Buchler's (1961) conception of method, Oakeshott's (1962) conception of knowledge, and Scheffler's (1960) discussion of rules and action suggest distinctions among types and aspects of practices. These distinctions are developed here through exploration of philosophical assumptions.

The possibility of guiding a practitioner, initiating a novice, or enhancing the competence of an expert—whether a chess player, poet, teacher, architect, physician, lawyer, or engineer—depends on the validity of two assumptions. The first assumption is that human experience is sufficiently regular and repeatable that one can learn from others' experiences. The second assumption is that in order to introduce a novice to the ethos of an activity or to improve the practice of a person already initiated, an order or method in the practice must be conveyed, as distinguished from random events.

Buchler (1961, p. 20) contends that although a "vast world of methodic possibility" exists, significant distinctions among methods or practices have implications for improvement of practice. These distinctions, according to Buchler, "are not exhaustive, but their possible combinations help to explain the differences that prevail when we speak variously of the art of surgery, the art of writing fiction, the art of management, the art of building, or the art of swimming" (p. 33). He elaborates on this point as follows:

> Whoever is said to act methodically (1) chooses a mode of conduct (2) to be directed in a given way (3) to a particular set of circumstances (4) for the attainment of a result. . . . The mode of conduct adopted may consist in (1a) established practice, in (1b) established practice modified by idiosyncratic technique, or in (1c) essentially idiosyncratic, private practice. Whatever procedure is adopted, it may be utilized (2a) strictly and in accordance with prescription, or (2b) loosely, variably, . . . with discretionary relationship to prescription, or (2c) uniquely in consequence of predominant reliance on insight. The circumstances under which the procedure is utilized may be (3a) definitely classifiable circumstances, or (3b) circumstances ranging from the expected

and classified down to the minimal circumstances that would allow the procedure. And the result toward which the activity aims may be (4a) an envisaged or familiar type of result, or (4b) an indefinite result accepted as such in terms of desirability, or (4c) a relatively novel result [pp. 32–33].

Buchler suggests, then, that practices can be distinguished by the extent to which they constitute established practice, utilized strictly and in accord with prescription, in definitely classifiable circumstances, toward a familiar type of result.

The possibility of guiding a practitioner also depends on the validity of the corollary assumption that the repeatable elements in human experience, that is, the methods, are *expressible,* although not necessarily in direct written or oral precepts. As Buchler (1961, p. 131) argues, "To claim . . . that a particular method is not subject to articulation is virtually equivalent to claiming that the method does not exist." As he notes, however, "A method is not always most intelligible in terms of direct, definite formulation" (p. 95). He argues, for example, that "there are indirect as well as direct forms of articulation. . . . The method of a poet . . . is articulated by its own products and by other products that reflect its influence" (p. 131).

The ability to formulate a practice or method only indirectly has major implications for how it may be codified, articulated, and taught. Oakeshott (1962) distinguishes among the types of knowledge needed for practice in terms of their potential for direct expression. He argues that every activity involves two types of knowledge, "technical" and "practical." By his definition, technical knowledge is susceptible to "precise formulation" whereas practical knowledge is not:

> Every science, every art, every practical activity requiring skill of any sort, indeed every human activity whatsoever, involves knowledge . . . of two sorts, both of which are always involved in any actual activity. . . . The first sort of knowledge I will call technical knowledge. . . . In many activities,

> this technical knowledge is formulated into rules which are, or may be, deliberately learned, remembered, and, as we say, put into practice; but whether or not it is, or has been, precisely formulated, its chief characteristic is that it is susceptible of precise formulation. . . . The second sort of knowledge, I will call practical, because it exists only in use . . . it is a characteristic of practical knowledge that it is not susceptible of formulation of this kind [pp. 7–13].

If practical knowledge cannot be precisely codified, how can it be expressed and acquired? Oakeshott (1962, p. 11) suggests that

> its normal expression is in a customary or traditional way of doing things, or simply in practice . . . the only way to acquire it [this type of knowledge] . . . is by apprenticeship to a master—not because the master can teach it (he cannot), but because it can be acquired only by continuous contact with one who is perpetually practicing it. In the arts and in natural sciences what normally happens is that the pupil, in being taught and in learning technique from his master, discovers himself to have acquired . . . knowledge . . . without it ever having been precisely imparted and often without being able to say precisely what it is. Thus, a pianist acquires artistry as well as technique, a chess player acquires style and insight into the game as well as knowledge of the moves, and a scientist acquires (among other things) the sort of judgment which tells him when his technique is leading him astray and the connoisseurship which enables him to distinguish the profitable from the unprofitable directions to explore.

The implications for guiding practice are clear. Only a part of the knowledge required for successful practice, that is, technical knowledge, is subject to precise formulation. Practical knowledge, know-how, artistry, insight, judgment, and connoisseurship are expressed only in practice and learned only through experience with the practice. Practices clearly vary in the extent to which they involve technical and practical knowledge in their conduct.

The possibility of guiding a practitioner also depends on the validity of a final assumption that an increase in a practitioner's understanding of a practice leads to improvement in that practice or, better, more successful outcomes of the practice. Yet, it is clear that improvement in practice depends on factors that go beyond mere tentative understandings. These factors include practitioners' personal choices, the relative proportion of technical and practical knowledge associated with the practice, the extent to which competencies are readily developed or require idiosyncratic talents, the relative difficulty of developing suitable training programs, the extent to which potential practitioners possess repertoires of relevant knowledge and competencies, and the feasibility of implementing the practice in particular settings (Harris, 1983).

Another way to distinguish among practices, in terms that have implications for the relationship between a practitioner's competence and realization of desired outcomes, is the extent to which practices can be articulated in precepts that ensure success if followed. Scheffler (1960) argues that the "rules" that can be formulated for an activity are either a "complete" set, which guarantees success if followed, or an "incomplete" set, which cannot guarantee success. Rules for spelling, for example, are complete. As Scheffler (1960, p. 70) observes:

> Consider a child trying to spell "cat" correctly, in writing. We might, in this case, formulate helpful exhaustive rules as follows: "First, (leaving a letter-wide space to the left) write 'C'; next, leaving no letter-wide space, write 'A' to the right of 'C,' on the same line; next, leaving no letter-wide space, write 'T' to the right of 'A,' on the same line

(leaving a letter-wide space to the right of 'T')."
The child may not, in fact, follow these rules, but
they are exhaustive relative to the activity and the
context in question since no child who follows
them fails in the attempt to spell "cat" correctly in
writing.

By contrast, the rules for other practices are incomplete:

Rules for lion-hunting (we may imagine) tell hunt-
ers what they ought to do in trying to bag lions.
Such rules cover the details of training, preparation, and the conduct of the hunt.... Let us
assume that the hunter's knowledge and skills are
excellent, that he interprets the rightness of conditions correctly, and that he follows this component set of rules . . . to the letter. It is still not
guaranteed that some lion will be bagged; the lion
may bound away at exactly the crucial moment.
Rules to follow in trying to win games are similarly
inexhaustive; one may follow all the rules of training and playing and still end by losing the game
[Scheffler, 1960, pp. 70–71].

Such incomplete rules, according to Scheffler, suggest how to
conduct activities so as to avoid failure and maximize the
likelihood of success, but they do not ensure success when the
practitioner is confronted with the uncertainties and complexities of actual practice.

Through this exploration of philosophical assumptions
associated with the possibility of guiding practice, distinctions
among practices have been identified that have important
implications for the task of guiding practitioners. Practices vary
in (1) the extent to which they consist of established competencies, as contrasted with idiosyncratic technique (Buchler, 1961),
(2) the extent to which they are utilized strictly and in accord
with prescription (Buchler, 1961), (3) the extent to which they
are utilized in definitely classifiable circumstances (Buchler,

1961), (4) the extent to which they aim toward familiar types of
results (Buchler, 1961), (5) the relative degree of technical and
practical knowledge involved in their conduct (Oakeshott,
1962), and (6) whether or not they are susceptible to formulation in complete sets of rules, precepts, or guidelines that
ensure success if followed (Scheffler, 1960). These distinctions
are not dichotomous but rather similar to points on a continuum. Their combinations can be used to characterize generic views of practices.

Practices that are established, utilized strictly and in
accordance with prescription, in definitely classifiable circumstances, and aimed toward an envisaged type of result, such as
producing automobiles on assembly lines, can be labeled *technologies*. In Oakeshott's (1962) terms, they require a substantial
component of technical knowledge. Moreover, in Scheffler's
(1960) terms, these methods can be formulated in complete
sets of rules that guarantee success if followed. It is noteworthy
that even these activities are not, in practice, subject to exhaustive articulation. A complete statement of written precepts for
producing automobiles on an assembly line would be so cum-
bersome to produce as to defy common sense or practical
wisdom. Moreover, in spelling, for example, skill in applying
rules is a knack that develops through practice.

Methods that can be classified as essentially idiosyncratic
private practice relying predominantly on insight, utilized in
circumstances ranging from the classified to the minimal conditions that would allow their application, and aimed toward a
relatively novel result, such as writing poetry or, in some aspects,
conducting scientific inquiry, can be labeled *arts*. In Oakeshott's
(1962) terms, they require a substantial component of practical
knowledge, utilized in the service of invention. These methods
are "modes of exploration," as distinguished from technologies, which are modes of "regularization" or standardization
(Buchler, 1961, p. 33). Principles can be formulated for the
technical aspects of arts, such as using color and perspective in
painting. However, the critical requirements for these practices
defy precise codification, since their products are assessed by

their originality and evidence of invention, rather than by their conformity to models.

Methods that can be classified as established practice modified by idiosyncratic technique, utilized loosely and variably, with a discretionary relationship to prescription, in a wide range of circumstances, and aimed toward an indefinite but desired result, such as cooking and carpentry, can be labeled *crafts.* These practices require significant components of both technical knowledge, which is subject to precise codification, and practical knowledge, which "exists only in use . . . in a customary or traditional way of doing things" (Oakeshott, 1962, p. 13). More specifically, they require know-how (or what Buchler, 1961, labels "tactics") for adapting precepts to the variable characteristics of materials and circumstances. In Scheffler's (1960) terms, the rules or guidelines that can be formulated for crafts are incomplete. They suggest how to avoid failure and maximize the likelihood of success, but they do not ensure success. For example, the master chef can specify for the novice nearly the exact quantities of ingredients and the fundamental techniques for producing a soufflé and warn against possible pitfalls. However, the experienced chef can neither envision nor prescribe for every difficulty that might confront the novice cook. The novice who intends to master a soufflé must develop practical knowledge of ingredients and techniques, which is expressed and learned only through observation and personal experimentation.

These different conceptions of practices—as technologies, crafts, and arts—are not intended as clearly distinct entities but rather as heuristic devices and metaphors for understanding the nature of professional practice and the implications for education. Moreover, any practice, such as medicine, nursing, law, engineering, or teaching, may be composed of different components, which can be viewed variously as technologies, crafts, and arts. The practices of interest in this chapter are those of the various professions. In the next section, I provide an overview of traditional and emerging conceptions of professional practice.

Reflection: A New Epistemology of
Professional Practice

Definitions of professional practice have tended to focus on the specialized bodies of theoretical and applied knowledge associated with the professions. For example, Starr (1982, p. 15) defines a profession as follows: "A profession is an occupation that regulates itself through systematic, required training and collegial discipline; that has a base in technological, specialized knowledge; and that has a service, rather than a profit, orientation enshrined in its code of conduct." He observes that this specialized knowledge rests on rational, scientific grounds. This definition suggests that the professions are applied sciences and technologies.

Specialized knowledge remains essential for professional practice. However, in the past two decades, scholars have formulated a powerful new epistemology of professional practice and associated approaches for professional education, encapsulated in the terms reflection and reflective practice, which suggest that important aspects of professional practice are practical arts and crafts. Subsequent to the publication of Schön's landmark books, *The Reflective Practitioner* (1983) and *Educating the Reflective Practitioner* (1987), the terms reflection and reflective practice have taken on the attributes of slogans— evocative terms used to broadly encapsulate ideas for reform (Harris, 1986; Nolan and Huber, 1989). Clearly, these terms are consistent with our common-sense view that professionals should be thoughtful (reflective); but those who wish to promote reform in professional education and practice must understand more precisely the new epistemology linked with these terms.

Schön's work, when integrated with research on cognition and on the development of expertise, yields assumptions and conclusions that constitute this new epistemology. Specifically, this work suggests that some of the most important problems in practice are characterized by complexity, uniqueness, uncertainty, and conflicting values. The goal of practice is wise action. Wise action may involve the use of specialized knowledge, but central to it is judgment in specific situations, with conflicting values about which problems need to be solved and how to solve them. An essential genre of knowledge used in practice is practical knowledge—"knowing how"—which is embedded in practical reasoning. It involves knowing-in-action, reflection-in-action, and reflection-about-action, using repertoires of examples, images, and understandings learned through experience. It involves using prototypes in memory of frequently encountered situations to construct interpretations of related situations. In turn, this knowledge is best learned through practice and through reflection on practice in the indeterminate zones of practice (Harris, 1989; Cervero, 1989). This characterization of professional practice suggests that it is fundamentally a practical craft or art.

These assumptions and conclusions, drawn from work in three investigative traditions, converge to support our popular wisdom and sense about the nature of professional practice, and they make fundamental contributions to our understanding of the nature of practice across the professions. Yet, this conception has not been at the core of most definitions of the nature of professional practice, which instead focus on the technological and specialized knowledge that sets the professions apart from other occupations and activities.

This new conception of professional practice is delineated here, based on an integration of Schön's work with research on cognition and the development of expertise. Schön's (1983, 1987) formulation of this new epistemology of professional practice is supported by compelling case rhetoric, that is, concrete examples accompanied by critical analyses (Harris, 1983). His work is grounded in important philosophical traditions, most notably Dewey's conceptions of knowledge and learning, and in analyses of practice and education for practice across the professions, ranging from the design-based such as architecture to the science-based such as medicine and engineering. Schön addresses four fundamental questions in his work on reflective practice: What is the nature of professional practice? What knowledge and competencies are needed, and how are they acquired? What possibilities exist for articulating and codifying professional practice? What modes of education and initiation are appropriate for professional practice? Through analyses and case studies across the range of professions, he addresses these questions both generically and concretely.

In responding to the first question about the nature of professional practice, Schön (1983) describes the dominant epistemology of professional practice, which he labels technical rationality, and substitutes for it the epistemology of reflective practice. According to Schön, technical rationality, which is associated with positivism and the hypothetico-deductive system of science, views professional activity as instrumental problem solving, the selection and adjustment of clearly applicable means to clear and unambiguous ends in stable institutional contexts. Means are chosen based on knowledge grounded in the theories, technologies, and techniques developed in the basic and applied sciences (1983, pp. 21–36). Schön observes that this model is embedded in the curricula of professional education, with students across the professions first learning the basic sciences, then the applied sciences, and finally the skills to apply this knowledge to real-world problems.

Schön argues that the epistemology of technical rationality does not adequately address either the types of problems that are central to professional practice or the knowledge and methods needed to solve these problems: "Increasingly we have become aware of the importance to actual practice of phenomena—complexity, uncertainty, instability, uniqueness and value-conflict—which do not fit the model of Technical Rationality" (1983, p. 39). The model of technical rationality assumes that scientific knowledge and technologies have clear and general applicability to situations of practice. However, most practice situations have elements of uniqueness or instability. Schön comments, "Even when a problem has been constructed, it may escape the categories of applied science because it presents itself as unique or unstable. . . . A physician cannot apply standard techniques to a case that is not in the books" (p. 41). Moreover, some of the most important problematic situations for professionals involve a determination of the *nature* of the problem, in complex situations with conflicting values and goals: "In real world practice, problems do not present themselves to the practitioner as givens. They must be constructed from the materials of problematic situations which are puzzling, troubling, and uncertain. In order to convert a problematic situation to a problem, a practitioner must . . . [make] sense of an uncertain situation that initially makes no sense" (p. 40).

Schön provides a powerful example of the problems confronted by professionals in the case of planning and engineering for transportation systems, a situation that illustrates both the complexity of problems as well as the conflicting ends: "When professionals consider what road to build, for example, they deal usually with a complex and ill-defined situation in which geographic, topological, financial, economic, and political issues are all mixed up together" (1983, p. 40). He adds, "Once they have somehow decided what road to build and go on to consider how best to build it, they may have a problem they can solve by the application of available techniques; but when the road they have built leads unexpectedly to the destruction of a neighborhood, they may find themselves again in a situation of uncertainty" (p. 40).

In responding to the questions about the knowledge and competencies needed for reflective practice and how are they acquired, Schön argues for the central role of knowing-in-action, learned through experience, reflection-in-action, and reflection-about-action. These three competencies account for the skill, and sometimes artistry, that practitioners bring to situations of complexity, uniqueness, and value conflict. Taking his cue from philosophers who developed epistemologies of practice, such as Polanyi (1967) and Ryle (1949), Schön characterizes knowing-in-action as the tacit knowing, the "knowing more than we can say," implicit in the spontaneous patterns of action demonstrated in everyday life and by skilled practitioners. It is composed of actions, recognitions, and judgments typically carried out spontaneously. Following Ryle, he observes that "although we sometimes think before acting, it is also true that in much of the spontaneous behavior of skillful practice we reveal a kind of knowing which does not stem from a prior intellectual operation" (1983, p. 51). For example, psycholinguists have observed that we speak in conformity with the rules of phonology and syntax, without thinking about these rules before speaking or even being able to readily describe them. Similarly for professionals, Schön observes that "the workaday life of the professional depends on tacit knowing-in-action. Every competent practitioner can recognize phenomena—families of symptoms associated with a particular disease, peculiarities of a certain kind of building site, irregularities of materials or structures—for which he cannot give a reasonably accurate or complete description. In his day-to-day practice he makes innumerable judgments of quality for which he cannot state adequate criteria and he displays skills for which he cannot state the rules and procedures. Even when he makes conscious use of research based theories and techniques, he is dependent on tacit recognitions, judgments, and skillful performances" (p. 50).

How do practitioners develop this practical knowledge? Essentially, practitioners learn through experience. Schön (1983, p. 60) suggests that "as a practitioner experiences many variations of a small number of types of cases, he is able to 'practice' his practice. He develops a repertoire of expectations, images, and techniques. He learns what to look for and how to respond. . . . His knowing-in-practice tends to become increasingly tacit, spontaneous, and automatic." More specifically, "A practitioner's repertoire includes the whole of his experience insofar as it is accessible to him for understanding and action. When a practitioner makes sense of a situation he perceives to be unique, he sees it as something already present in his repertoire . . . as both similar to and different from the familiar one, without at first being able to say . . . with respect to what. The familiar situation functions as a precedent, or a metaphor, or—in Thomas Kuhn's phrase—an exemplar for the unfamiliar one" (p. 138).

In addition to knowing-in-action, Schön views reflection-in-action and reflection-about-action as central to the "art" by which practitioners deal well with situations of uncertainty, instability, uniqueness, and value conflict. Reflection-in-action, which occurs in the midst of action, and reflection-about-action, which occurs in the tranquility of a postmortem or occasion for subsequent analysis, are stimulated by puzzling, interesting, or troublesome phenomena, by problems that elude the ordinary categories of a practitioner's knowledge and appear as unique or unstable, and by the need to articulate or codify the bases for practice, most typically by the need to teach aspiring practitioners. In reflection, the knowledge implicit in action is delineated, criticized, restructured, and embodied in further action through what Schön (1983, p. 63) labels "on-the-spot experiments." The specific objects of reflection vary across professions in relation to the situations of practice and systems of knowing-in-practice. Practitioners may reflect on the features that they notice in a problematic situation, on the frameworks that they have constructed in addressing a problem, on the tacit norms, appreciations, and criteria underlying judgments, on the theories and strategies implicit in patterns of behavior, and on the roles that they have constructed for themselves in institutional contexts. Schön argues that reflection is critical for expert practitioners in development, renewal, and self-correction of their practice; that reflection combined with demonstration, supervision, and codification of practice is a fundamental process for initiating novices; and that reflection eliciting the principles and approaches of expert practice may contribute to research-based knowledge about effective practice useful for guiding practitioners, what I have labeled "practice theories" (Harris, 1986).

In response to the final two questions about the existing possibilities for articulating and codifying professional practice and the modes of education and initiation appropriate for professional practice, Schön proposes the general concept of the "reflective practicum" as an institutional form and forum for development of reflective practice. In general terms, a reflective practicum provides opportunities for practitioners—often, novices and experts, and students and teachers—to reflect together on practice, using examples of practice in the form of cases or demonstrations. The practitioners reflect on their perceptions of the problems in problematic situations (problem frames), and on the theories, views, understandings, and criteria embedded in practice. They then bring these understandings to the surface and subject them to analysis, criticism, and reconstruction. They create what Schön labels "virtual worlds," situations that simulate, but slow the pace of, actual situations of practice in order to permit safe reflection on and analysis of practice (1987, p. 4).

Reflective practicums take very different forms in the cultures of different professions. Schön provides compelling examples of reflective practicums across a range of occupations, such as the master working with a novice on a design problem in an architecture practicum (1983, pp. 76–104), the psychotherapist working with a resident-in-training in supervisory sessions (1983, pp. 105–127), and the master teacher guiding a group of in-service teachers in reflection about their understandings in mathematics and the sciences, and the implications for their students' and their own learning (1987, pp. 3–6).

Schön's work on reflective practice, grounded in philosophical analysis and analysis of practice vignettes, is consistent with, and supported by, results of research during the past two decades in the areas of cognition and development of expertise. In cognitive science, schema theory describes how acquired knowledge is organized in the mind and how cognitive structures facilitate use of knowledge (Sternberg and Wagner, 1986). Schemata are prototypes in memory of frequently encountered situations. Ryle (1949), a philosopher, first introduced a fundamental distinction between two types of schemata: declarative knowledge ("knowing that" something is the case, whether facts, generalizations, theories, and so on) and procedural knowledge ("knowing how" to do something). This distinction has since been supported by analysis and research in cognitive psychology (Anderson, 1983; Shuell, 1986).

Research in cognitive psychology has demonstrated that procedural knowledge structures are learned principally *in* practice and, when activated by the problems or situations of practice, involve not only recall of information but also transformation of information for use in practice (Gagne, 1985; Lesgold and others, 1988). Further, cognitive anthropologists (Lave, 1988) and cognitive psychologists (Resnick, 1987b; Sternberg and Wagner, 1986) have argued that the knowledge used in practice—practical knowledge—is created and made meaningful by the contexts in which it is acquired.

Literature on professional expertise addresses questions such as What is the nature of professional expertise? and How do experts develop expertise? through systematic analysis of expert practice. Results of studies in this area are also consistent with the conceptions of practice articulated by Schön and are supported by research in cognitive psychology. Studies of expertise in a variety of professions, such as medicine (Dowie and Elstein, 1988), nursing (Benner, 1984), and teaching (Feiman-Nemser and Floden, 1986; Clark and Peterson, 1986), support the importance of practical knowledge, implicit knowledge, and know-how, as learned through experience in professional practice. In turn, a major difference between experts and novices is the extent of practical knowledge possessed by the experts (Gagne, 1985), based on their repertoire of experience with the complex problems of practice. In a comprehensive review of studies of professional expertise, Kennedy (1987) describes four different conceptions of expertise: as technical skill, as application of general principles and theories, as critical analysis, and as deliberate or reflective action. She identifies the conception of expertise "as deliberate action" as most consistent with the goal of wise action in complex situations.

The Role of Art, Craft, Technology, and Science in Professional Practice: Reflective Practice and Specialized Bodies of Knowledge

The importance of tacit knowledge and reflection in professional practice leads naturally to the following question: What is the role of specialized knowledge, theories, and approaches from the basic and applied sciences—the type of knowledge long held as the hallmark of professional practice? Critiques of Schön's work have focused on the importance that he assigns to practical knowledge in professional practice, seemingly at the expense of specialized knowledge from the basic and applied sciences (Harris, 1989; Fenstermacher, 1988; Shulman, 1988). Schön does appear to introduce a dichotomy between reflection-in-action and technical knowledge, but a close analysis of his work (Schön, 1983, 1987, 1991) demonstrates clearly that this apparent dichotomy is an artifact of conceptual and rhetorical emphases introduced to focus on a neglected aspect of practice. Nevertheless, Schön provides an incomplete view of the knowledge needed for professional practice.

While knowing-in-action and reflection-in-action are essential in professional practice, what informs reflection? Certainly experience, examples, observations, puzzles, descriptions, experiments, and "back talk," as Schön would say. In addition, the specialized body of knowledge associated with each profession must inform and guide and provide a repertoire for reflection (see, for example, Shulman (1987), for a detailed characterization of the knowledge base for teaching).

The body of knowledge generally available for each profession includes pertinent explanatory theories, doctrines (systems of values), applied theories, and practice theories (for a discussion of the roles of various genres of theories in guiding practice, see Harris, 1983, 1986). Explanatory theories, such as Piaget's theories of cognitive development or Dewey's theory of the relationship between knowledge and experience, provide persuasive explanations and frameworks for viewing problematic phenomena. Doctrines are rationalized and codified systems of values and beliefs about the means and ends of practice, and they provide frameworks for understanding and interpreting practices. Applied theories are principled structures, frequently grounded in explanatory theories, which suggest strategies and technologies for attaining desired outcomes of practice. For example, behavioral learning theory, an explanatory theory of learning, has spawned numerous applications, including programmed instruction, behavior modification programs, and behavioral counseling. Practice theories (Harris, 1986) result from analysis and codification of expert practice, in particular the practical knowledge embedded therein. These theories incorporate principles for potentially generalizable strategies and techniques, rationales for the strategies (personal explanations and doctrines), and decision parameters for implementing the strategies in practice.

What is the appropriate relationship of reflective practice, and its elements of knowing-in-action and reflection-in-action—the applied arts and crafts of a profession—with the specialized bodies of knowledge associated with each profession? Reflective practice and the use of specialized bodies of knowledge are entirely complementary. Each is essential for professional practice, especially in the indeterminate zones of practice. However, their relationship to each other is organized quite differently in the epistemology of reflective practice versus that of technical rationality.

Envision, for example, a complex situation of practice and the view of it that each epistemology suggests. Picture a physician meeting with an elderly patient dying of cancer, and his family, to decide on a course of action in the patient's care. In the epistemology of reflective practice, this physician would be viewed as using knowing-in-action, or tacit knowledge (with repertoires of examples, images, and understandings learned through experience with similar situations), and reflection-in-action, reflective competencies, in response to this complex situation in order to guide and organize the choices and uses of specialized bodies of knowledge. Most likely, this physician would scan her knowledge base in medical oncology, health care delivery systems, hospice care, medical ethics, theories of death and dying, family conferences, use of palliative techniques to reduce pain, and so on. By contrast, in the epistemology of technical rationality (as labeled by Schön), this physician would be viewed fundamentally as having expertise in certain defined specialized bodies of knowledge (such as those just noted), which she would use to organize responses to this situation of practice through applications and adaptations of this knowledge to this specific situation. In the complex situation described, the epistemology of reflective practice appears to provide a better model for understanding how this physician might access and organize her knowledge to guide her practice.

This situation does not call for the application of specific approaches or techniques to address clearly defined ends, but rather the convergence of multiple sources of knowledge to make judgments and take wise action, given conflicting values and ambiguous ends.

Examples from the Professions

Medicine, engineering, and law, despite their obvious differences, have long been regarded as prototypical professions. It is noteworthy that there is a body of literature and practice in each of these professions that echoes the views described above concerning the nature of professional practice and education.

The history of curriculum reform in medical education demonstrates swings in the pendulum that are consistent with the shift from an epistemology of technical rationality to an epistemology of reflective practice. As medicine took on professional status in the early twentieth century, the model for medical education originating at Johns Hopkins University lay firmly in the basic laboratory science disciplines; it included two years of basic science study, followed by two years of supervised experience in hospital wards where students learned to apply basic science knowledge to clinical medicine (Flexner, 1910). During the past thirty-five years, there have been significant reforms in medical education, tending on the whole to increase early curriculum emphasis on the problems of actual medical practice. This era of reform began in the early 1950s when Case Western Reserve University organized its preclinical curriculum around the study of organ systems through interdisciplinary presentations of the basic and clinical sciences and a patient-based introduction to clinical medicine (Williams, 1980). The majority of American medical schools adopted this curriculum model, and it remains predominant.

In the mid-1960s, McMaster University Medical School in Canada, and Michigan State University, went beyond disciplinary integration to implementation of a problem-based curriculum in which carefully chosen medical problems serve as the main organizational framework for learning the basic and clinical sciences (Barrows and Tamblyn, 1980; Barrows, 1985). This curriculum structure, widely known as problem-based learning, is associated with the "tutorial" learning format. In tutorials, small groups of students and their tutor work together to address medical problems presented in written cases and with simulated patients (that is, real patients with stable findings or individuals who simulate physical findings). They attempt to identify the problems in the case, formulate tentative hypotheses related to the problems, identify learning needs, access resources (such as text material, journal articles, and faculty experts), pursue the implications of their hypotheses, reformulate the problems and hypotheses, and so on. The members of the group and the tutor pool their resources in working together on problems, the tutor engaging in a process of learning along with the students.

This curriculum format has been adopted by a number of medical schools, whether as the organizational framework for their entire curriculum, such as the New Pathway program at Harvard Medical School, as a parallel track, such as at Bowman Gray Medical School, or in selected courses. The model has been held up as a beacon for medical education for the twenty-first century (Panel on the General Professional Education of the Physician, 1984). It is noteworthy that as medicine has become more secure in its professional status, it has increasingly found its focus for education in the problems of medical practice. The current reform movement in medical education provides guidelines for a curriculum organization and a learning format consistent with the development of competencies for reflective practice; in the tutorial, students learn basic and clinical sciences in the context of increasingly complex medical problems—a form of Schön's reflective practicum.

Moreover, a sustained body of research in medical problem solving (Dowie and Elstein, 1988) demonstrates that experienced physicians do not, in fact, address the problems confronted in practice in the way suggested by the model of applied science. Rather, they quickly formulate and confirm hypotheses based on their repertoire of experience with similar medical problems, a process consistent with the epistemology of reflective practice. This body of research also demonstrates that the superiority of experts over novices stems not so much from their superior general clinical reasoning skills but rather from their breadth and depth of experience in clinical reasoning with similar medical problems, in all of their complexity (Elstein, Shulman, and Sprafka, 1978). In turn, in reviews of the literature on expertise in medical problem solving, Berner (1984) and McGuire (1985) argue that the results reported in this literature call for a new view of expert clinical reasoning that can adequately account for the judgments that physicians in fact demonstrate in complex situations of practice. These complex situations include, among others, multiple interacting problems and conflicting values embedded in multiple practice situations.

In the field of engineering education, another of the prototypical professions, a controversy about the nature of engineering practice and its implications for engineering education mirrors the technical rationality–reflective practice debate. Engineering has traditionally been viewed as an applied science or technology. Truxal (1986), for example, argues that engineering is fundamentally a technology involving application of scientific knowledge to achieve specified human purposes. Engineering has also been viewed as fundamentally oriented toward design, an iterative decision-making process used to optimize human resources to achieve clearly specified goals (K. Smith, 1988, p. 319). K. Smith (1988) argues that these definitions seriously misrepresent the nature of engineering by failing to address the troublesome question of what constitutes a goal, problem, or need, and by failing to account for many engineering problems that typically involve the need for invention to address complex, uncertain, unstable situations. Smith prefers the definition of engineering practice offered by Koen (1984), who argued that the method of engineering is the use of heuristics to effect the best change in a poorly understood situation given the available resources. By the term heuristics, Koen means reasonable, plausible, but ultimately fallible approaches that suggest, but do not guarantee, a solution—the characteristic methods of crafts.

The normative engineering curriculum, like the normative medical school curriculum, reflects the view of engineering as applied science. According to K. Smith (1988), this curriculum consists of teaching the relevant basic sciences, teaching the relevant applied sciences, and then giving students a practicum in which they learn to apply science-based knowledge to the problems of practice. Smith argues, based on research and analyses in the areas of reflective practice and cognitive psychology, that engineering curricula should involve students in the problems of practice earlier in the programs in order to stimulate their interest and develop the problem-solving and lifelong learning skills needed by professional engineers. He recommends and describes several approaches that he uses in engineering courses at the University of Minnesota to decrease the disparity between the knowledge and skills traditionally taught in engineering schools and the knowledge and skills required by the professional engineer: modeling of professional activities, such as student involvement in building expert systems (Starfield, Butala, England, and Smith, 1983), reflective practica about engineering problems, and student involvement in cooperative learning situations (Johnson, Johnson, and Smith, 1991).

The practice of law has traditionally been viewed as a practical art and craft, informed by regulations, statutes, policies, precedents, and a repertoire of experiences applied to complex and uncertain practical problems. The normative education for the practice of law entails the use of Socratic pedagogy to analyze cases, which are the sole resource materials for students as they develop an understanding of the various areas of the law and the skills of legal reasoning. Analysis of cases typically involves, for students and practitioners, the ability to analyze pertinent facts and legal issues in the cases and to analyze the judges' legal reasoning. Typical law school examinations assess the student's ability to analyze the facts and legal issues in specific cases, set forth the applicable principles of law from case precedents, apply them to the hypothetical facts, demonstrate how those facts are analogous to or distinguishable from the reported cases, make the various arguments for the position of each hypothetical party, assess the persuasive weight of those arguments in the light of decided cases, and determine the likely result (Nathanson, 1989; Ogden, 1984).

This prototypical form of legal education mirrors some of the most essential skills of the practicing lawyer. Despite the virtues of the case analysis method, legal educators have argued that this method does not adequately prepare law students for the essential task of the practicing lawyer, namely, after the facts are gathered and the legal issues identified (through case analysis), to exercise judgment in surveying the client's options and offering authoritative advice about a course of action (Nathanson, 1989). Consequently, legal educators have developed the "problem method," which involves study and analysis of hypothetical or real client problems, guidelines for using the method in teaching, and a growing body of problem materials for use in virtually every area of the law (Ogden, 1984). According to proponents of the problem method, its goal is to simulate the kinds of situations in which lawyers actually find themselves and to help overcome the difficulties of transferring from an academic environment to a practice-oriented environment (Maggs and Morgan, 1975).

It is noteworthy that in legal education, as in engineering and medical education, scholars and educators have recently argued that undergraduate education, and the associated teaching strategies, should help students address the problems of practice earlier in their curricula, both to provide a richer context for learning substantive content as well as to develop the reflective and procedural skills required for the particular profession. These developments in institutions of professional education suggest a growing recognition of reflective practice as a viable description of professional competence.

Implications of an Epistemology of Reflective Practice for the Professions

Thus far, I have developed a conception of practice that helps us to understand traditional and emerging views of professional competence; I have outlined a new epistemology of professional practice, based on Schön's concept of reflective practice, along with supporting analysis and evidence from research in cognitive psychology and studies of expertise; I have discussed the complementary relationship between reflective practice and the specialized bodies of knowledge; and I have provided examples from across the professions. What are the implications of this discussion for professional education, codification of professional practice, and research about professional practice and education for the professions?

Implications for Curriculum and Program Planning

First, these perspectives of professional practice have implications for how we design educational curricula for professional education. The various fields of professional education have traditionally relied on the empirical-analytical paradigm for curriculum design, best known in the work of Tyler (1949), related work on educational objectives (Bloom, 1956; Krathwohl, 1964; Mager, 1962), and formulations of positivistic behavioral science evaluation and research methodologies (Campbell and Stanley, 1966). This paradigm has provided the field of professional education with a quasi technology for a linear process of curriculum design, including strategies for selection of educational objectives, selection and organization of content and learning experiences, conduct of evaluation, and assessment of concordance among the curriculum elements of objectives, instructional methods, and evaluation. This paradigm has also provided professional education with a framework for curriculum research in professional education (Dinham and Stritter, 1986). However, the paradigm only partially addresses the full range of problems confronted in professional education. These problems relate to education for complex practices, involving not only specialized bodies of knowledge but also reflective and practical competencies developed through experience with perplexing situations of practice and reflection on that experience. These problems also relate to the implementation of curriculum reform and changes in complex institutional settings, embedded in a social and political context.

In the field of curriculum studies, there is a growing body

of literature about curriculum design, labeled "deliberative curriculum theory" (for example, Harris, 1986; Reid, 1978, 1981), that addresses these problems. This literature, which focuses on the processes of reflective inquiry in curriculum design, virtually echoes in its assumptions and recommendations what Schön and others have outlined about the nature of professional practice, except that it is applied to curriculum practice, the practice of designing and studying curricula.

The perspectives of deliberative curriculum theory have their origins in three landmark papers written by Joseph Schwab at the University of Chicago in the late 1960s and early 1970s (Schwab, [1971] 1978a, [1969] 1978b, [1971] 1978c). In those papers, Schwab argued that curriculum problems are not fundamentally about how to apply theories, for example, learning theories, to instructional design. Rather, he viewed curriculum problems as practical problems about choice, action, educational policy, and practice in complete, unique, complex situations, in which belief systems play a central role. He argued that curriculum problems should be addressed by a method appropriate to issues of choice and action, namely, deliberation among stakeholders—morally engaged individuals—who bring to the discussion diverse perspectives about what to teach, why to teach it, and how to teach it and reach a consensus for a particular situation. Hearkening to distinctions made by Aristotle, Schwab viewed curriculum design as fundamentally a practical discipline addressing uncertain practical problems, akin to law and public policy, rather than a theoretical discipline, akin to mathematics and physics.

Schwab and others (Bonser and Grundy, 1988; Hegarty, 1971; Knitter, 1985; Pereira, 1984; Roby, 1985; Tamir, 1989) have characterized an array of systematic processes and "arts" needed for leading and participating in deliberations. The fundamental process that they characterize for arriving at curriculum decisions is a structure for deliberation: a systematic method for individuals, groups, or institutions to formulate and consider an adequate variety of alternatives—alternative perceptions and formulations of problems in situations and alternative solutions—directed toward decisions about what and how to teach particular students in a particular context. These investigators argue that deliberation, in properly constituted groups, is essential to curriculum decision making, for bringing together diverse sources of evidence and expertise, for educating participants through discovery of diverse perspectives, and for achieving commitment to decisions.

Given the purposes of deliberative curriculum inquiry— to make decisions for policy relevant to a given context, to educate stakeholders, and to achieve persuasive and political force for decisions—it follows that the most important curriculum deliberation takes place at local sites, involving those who "live in" or are strongly affected by the education setting. For professional education, this group includes administrators, practitioners, consumers, faculty, students, and a chairperson. Curriculum deliberation groups, so constituted, would, first, identify which curriculum problems need to be addressed in a particular situation and then formulate and weigh alternative solutions. They would bring to bear on their deliberations an eclectic array of practice experiences and theoretical perspectives, each with its own light to shed on wise action.

Heuristics have been developed to facilitate the phases of deliberation. For example, Hegarty (1971) describes the use of the nominal group technique, a structured group process approach developed in management sciences, as a means for expeditiously conducting the problem identification and solution phases of deliberation. Bonser and Grundy (1988) outline a structured process of deliberation that includes practitioner and researcher joint reflection, linked with group reflection. Tamir (1989) describes a process of preliminary data gathering, labeled preplanning evaluation, that is intended to inform and facilitate all phases of deliberation. These recommended processes of problem identification and problem solving, and of the eclectic use of experience and knowledge, are analogous to the practical reasoning that Schön has argued is essential to expert professional practice—in this context, the practice of curriculum design. The principles and methods of this program planning approach, with respect to professional education, are characterized more fully elsewhere (Harris, 1990, 1991).

Concretely, how does this process work in practice? Curry, Fried, and McQueen (forthcoming) provide an example in the field of professional education. They discuss how deliberative curriculum inquiry approaches, combined with the Tyler model, were used to structure the accreditation planning process of the University of Toronto master's degree program in health services administration. These planning processes were used to organize the program's institutional self-study, with the aims of planned and disciplined curriculum renewal, faculty development, and document preparation for accreditation. The process proceeded as follows. Discussions, led by an education specialist, involved all faculty, representatives from the field of practice, and data collected from students and recent graduates—the stakeholders who would have to live with the consequences of decisions. The deliberation began with a process of problem identification, through analysis of the present curriculum, based on accreditation body standards. There were repeated opportunities to reflect on problems and proposed solutions for the curriculum as a whole and for each component course. These discussions were propelled forward and documented with written arguments for change and exemplar curriculum materials. It is noteworthy that the process included familiar elements of the empirical-analytical model: consideration of objectives for the entire curriculum and specific courses, interrelation of objectives across courses, and alignment of objectives with teaching-learning experiences and evaluation approaches.

The results of this process were identification of specific problem areas in the curriculum and specific strategies to correct deficiencies. Justified decisions for action were documented in iterative written versions of curriculum plans, which included coherent arguments in support of intended plans, a review of alternatives considered, and rationales for choices made. These plans provided guidance for flexible curriculum implementations. Equally important, the process resulted in clear evidence of faculty understanding of and commitment to the curriculum. Overall, the process yielded justified decisions for action, developed through a process designed to educate participants and to obtain their personal and political support for curriculum renewal.

What are the implications of this view of curriculum planning for research about program planning for professional education? Researchers can devote more effort to developing and codifying traditions of deliberations, as exemplified in work reported by Walker (1971) and Atkins (1986). More effort can be devoted to studying curriculum deliberations, to studying the role of leadership in deliberation, and to studying methods for involving individuals with diverse perspectives, methods for formulating curriculum problems in concrete situations and generating alternative solutions, and methods for using an eclectic array of theoretical and practice-based perspectives to address curriculum problems in particular situations—in short, methods for reflecting on the consequences of deliberation and continuing the process. More effort can be devoted to developing and articulating traditions of practical reasoning in professional education, supported by case exemplars. Researchers can devote more effort to assessing the effectiveness of approaches to deliberation, approaches recommended based on practical wisdom. Such assessment may involve empirical studies of effectiveness with respect to deliberative processes and outcomes, as exemplified in work reported by Frey (1989) and Tamir (1989). Or, to be consistent with the epistemology associated with deliberative inquiry, such assessment may involve rigorous processes of deliberative reflection.

Implications for Curriculum Structure and Educational Methods

What are the implications of these views for education for the professions and improvement of professional practice? Clearly, professional schools need to devote greater attention to helping both aspiring professionals and expert practitioners develop and maintain artistry in dealing with the indeterminate zones of practice through processes of reflection-in-action and reflection-about-action. They need to create and support forms and forums for developing reflective practice. And, they need to help both novices and experts coordinate the processes of reflection with the other fundamental knowledge contributing to skilled professional practice—the pertinent basic and applied sciences and the values embedded in doctrines (Harris, 1986). Most fundamentally, professionals at every level of education would, to a greater extent, organize their learning in relation to the actual problems of practice, in various forms of reflective practica.

According to Schön (1987, p. 14), the idea of a reflective practicum is general; it would take very different forms in different professions. The main features of a reflective practicum are the following. First, people learn by doing, by dealing with complex problems of practice, together, in a virtual world representing but not identical to the world of practice; participants can try again and control the pace of their learning. Second, in a reflective practicum novices learn from experts, through reciprocal reflection-in-action and reflection-about-action related to demonstrations and exemplars of practice; in it, seasoned professionals may also learn with each other through reflection-about-action (Schön, 1987, pp. 13–14).

These ideas apply to curriculum structure and learning methods in each stage of professional education, from the initial preparation to the apprenticeship. If professionals are viewed as dealing with complex problems of practice by using reflection-in-action to organize their use of basic and applied science knowledge, then it would be desirable to provide more experience with problems of practice in the initial stages of professional education in the form of some type of reflective practicum. This view also suggests that professional schools develop and use cases and problems for analysis of increasingly complex situations of practice, particularly in the early stages of professional education, before students have extensive experience with actual cases. Case analysis is, in fact, a time-honored tradition in business and legal education.

The epistemology of reflective practice also has implications for the initiation of professionals into actual situations of practice, the apprenticeship institutionalized for most professions, as well as in continuing and lifelong learning by professionals. Schön's concept of the reflective practicum provides a powerful framework for viewing the potential for professional education inherent to apprenticeship—its purposes, its structures, and the relationships between novices and experts. The apprenticeship provides the scenario for exploring the principles and strategies embedded in and associated with skilled practice, through reciprocal reflection-about-action. This interaction has the potential to benefit both novices and experts. Schön (1983) provides compelling examples from various professions, including architecture, psychotherapy training, and teaching.

Medical education provides an example of the reflective practicum in institutions of practice involving formal initiation for novices and continuing education for seasoned physicians. In its traditions of clinical education for third- and fourth-year students and medical residents (medical school graduates in required postgraduate training), medicine has a prototypical reflective practicum. Clinical education, as well as patient care, is organized into teams in teaching hospitals, each including an attending physician, residents, and medical students. Students learn clinical medicine in the context of increasing responsibility for patient care. Concomitantly, they learn within the framework of traditions that institutionalize reflective inquiry, for masters as well as novices. Every teaching hospital has traditions of daily case-based conferences—attending rounds, morning report, grand rounds—during which master practitioners (including attending physicians and, in general, the department head and novices at various levels of education) discuss actual patient cases in relation to research and practice-based knowledge, thereby merging research-based and practical inquiry in the context of patient care.

Implications for Codification of Practice and Articulation of Practice Through Research

Knowing-in-action, tacit knowledge, knowing more than one can say, and reflection-in-action are the fundamental elements of reflective practice. Articulation of practice, whether in writing or some other form (such as demonstrations, written exemplars, or mutual reflection-in-action) is generally considered essential for guidance in development of skilled practice. Clearly, the different aspects of skilled professional practice have different sorts of potential for articulation and codification.

The aspects of professional practice characterized in the first part of this chapter as akin to technologies may be articulated and codified in orderly demonstrations or precise guidelines. Every professional practice includes technologies. By contrast, aspects of practice earlier characterized as akin to crafts or arts exhibit and require practical knowledge, knowing-in-action, and reflection-in-action, which resist articulation in orderly demonstrations or precise guidelines.

Yet, the education and development of skilled professionals require articulation of masterful practice, whether in written codifications or other forms. In general, development of professional practice through elicitation of knowledge about the practice also requires articulation of the practice, namely, making the tacit explicit. For example, as Lortie (1985, p. 58) comments with respect to problems in the development of teaching as a profession, "We do not find in education an equivalent to the centuries of codified experience encountered in law, engineering, medicine, divinity, architecture, and accountancy. . . . What meaningful record exists of the millions of teaching transactions that have occurred since the City on the Hill."

Codification of practice involves, essentially, articulating the understandings, assumptions, principles, and strategies of skilled practice. What are some of the potential modalities for articulation? Schön (1983, 1987) provides new perspectives on the articulation of master practice by exploring traditions of initiation into skilled practice in several professions and the fine arts. As noted earlier, he recommends the reflective practicum as a central component of professional education. He analyzes characteristic master-novice interactions in the practicum, labeled "follow me," "joint experimentation," and "hall of mirrors." In "follow me," the novice observes the master, and together they discuss the principles associated with the practice. In "joint experimentation," the master and novice work together on a problem and engage in mutual reflection-about-action to elicit principles and strategies for practice. In "hall of mirrors," the novice and master develop a professional relationship that mirrors the relationships in the professional practice that they seek to improve. Hall of mirrors is the characteristic master and novice interaction in the psychotherapy supervision session in which the relationship that the novice exhibits with the master may mirror the relationship of the novice with his or her client. This master-novice relationship may then provide the material for articulating the bases of psychotherapy practice. In analyzing characteristic master-novice interactions in the reflective practicum, Schön thereby provides important perspectives on the reflective practicum as a format for articulating the often tacit knowing-in-action and reflection-in-action of skilled professionals.

Another approach for codification is the development and use of cases in analyzing complex problems and dilemmas in practice. Elsewhere, I argued for the use of cases, accompanied by codified case analyses, as an essential form for codification of professional practice. The body of cases would include descriptions of practice (the cases) accompanied by formulation of principles of and for practice (the codified case analyses) and would thereby provide two important forms of discourse for codifying skilled practice: descriptions and principles (Harris, 1983).

Finally, formulation of practice theories, that is, the understandings, principles, and general strategies embedded in the practice of masters, is important for the development of professional practice. For example, there is an increasing body of research on teaching—the "teacher cognition and decision-making paradigm of research on teaching" (Shulman, 1986, p. 23)—that uses teacher reflection-in-action and reflection-about-action as a form of collaborative research with teachers, designed to elicit their decision-making approaches. The basic aspiration of researchers in this area is to identify teachers' constructs, implicit theories, and strategies for action. They ask questions such as, What factors do teachers consider in instructional planning? What qualities characterize teachers' thinking and decision making during instruction? What is the nature of teachers' perspectives, belief systems, and implicit theories about teaching and learning? This type of research, conducted by investigators such as Munby (1986), Russell (1986), Lampert (1984), and Elbaz (1983), holds great promise for guiding the development of professional practice.

Therefore, in addition to implications for education of professionals, the conception of reflective practice also has implications for research and codification of practice. Most fundamentally, this epistemology suggests the importance of systematically eliciting the general principles and strategies embedded in the knowing-in-action of expert practitioners and articulating this knowledge-of-practice in codifications for guiding other practitioners, both novices and experts. It is noteworthy that this conception extends the sources of knowledge for practice from university-based basic and applied science research to knowledge-of-practice emanating from analysis of masterful practice, conducted by researchers in collaboration with practitioners-researchers. Schön exemplifies this approach to research in his own work on reflective practice. In this work, he develops and communicates an epistemology of practice based on observation and formal analysis of vignettes of professional practice, across a range of professions, concentrating on episodes in which a senior practitioner attempts to help a junior practitioner learn to do something. In such episodes, one sees most vividly how articulation of practice may also guide it. As Schön (1983, p. viii) has observed, "Starting with protocols of actual performance, it is possible to construct and test models of knowing."

Conclusion

Recent analysis and research across the professions have yielded new perspectives about the nature and improvement of professional practice. A new epistemology fundamentally characterizes professional practice as judgment and wise action in complex, unique, and uncertain situations with conflicting values and ethical stances, in a social and cultural context. Given the current climate of rapid technological, cultural, and economic changes in the nature and context of professional practice, Schön's conceptions of reflective practice, supported by research in the areas of cognition and development of expertise, suggest new expectations for professional skills, namely, competence in reflective practice, with its elements of reflection-in-action and reflection-about-action.

In this chapter, I developed a framework for understanding traditional and emerging views of professional competence in terms of implications for education and codification of professional practice. I reviewed and characterized the concepts and approaches associated with reflective practice, including Schön's landmark work, and research in the areas of cognition and analysis of expertise. In this context, I explored the complementary roles of practical knowledge and specialized bodies of knowledge in effective professional practice. I then explored the implications of these views for improvement of professional practice through use of deliberative curriculum inquiry in program design, through restructuring of the normative curriculum to incorporate earlier experience with the problems of practice, and through research aimed at codification of the principles and strategies embedded in skilled professional practice.

How would education for the professions change if these perspectives were taken seriously? If accreditation bodies, licensure boards, professional schools, institutions of practice, educational policy committees, course directors, teachers, students, and consumers—everyone holding a stake in professional education—were to take these recommendations seriously, what would they do differently? With respect to the content and process of professional education, (1) education for the professions, at every level, should be organized to a greater extent around the problems of practice; (2) education for the professions, at every level, should provide opportunities for reflection-in-action and reflection-about-action among novices and experts; and (3) evaluation of students and practicing professionals must include, to a greater degree, assessment of performance in the complex situations of practice, appropriate to the practitioner's level of training. With respect to the process of educational change, they would design programs, using reflective deliberative processes, involving representatives of all stakeholders in a curriculum. They would engage in iterative processes of problem identification and solution, with a focus on particular situations. In the deliberative process, they would take account of conflicting values and give due consideration to political, social, and economic contexts. They would conduct curriculum deliberations with the explicit aims of reaching justified decisions, for a particular time, place, and set of circumstances; of educating participants through this process; and of securing personal and political commitment.

There is clear evidence in every field of education, including professional education, that repeated recommendations for curriculum reform have not been implemented because they were not adequately understood, they did not secure commitment from important stakeholders, and they were not adequately forged in terms of economic, political, and cultural considerations (Harris, 1987). The recommendations here are designed to address these problems. Thus, what would stakeholders do differently? They would systematically elicit and articulate the general principles and strategies embedded in the knowing-in-action and reflection-in-action of expert professionals, for use in guiding other professionals, both novices and experts; and, thereby, they would extend the sources of knowledge for practice from university-based basic and applied science research to knowledge-of-practice emanating from analyses of masterful practice.

CHAPTER 3

The Expanding Use
of Technology

Joanne Gard Marshall

The purpose of this chapter is to familiarize readers with new information technologies and to explore some of the implications of the use of these technologies for professional education and practice. These technologies are important because they have the potential to play a major role in creating the paradigm shift in professional education and practice called for by Curry and Wergin in the Preface of this volume. At the same time, the information technologies present major challenges to the nature of professional expertise and control of knowledge that must be acknowledged and dealt with if the professions are to survive into the next century.

Information technologies, which include a broad range of computing and telecommunications applications, are becoming ubiquitous in our home and work lives; however, as observers have noted in relation to earlier technologies, we are faced with the familiar dilemma of technological capability racing ahead of our social and political ability to deal with all of the issues raised by the new practices. In the case of information technologies in particular, the underlying long-range implications of technology use tend to be ignored by adopters, who often perceive the technologies as quick-fix solutions to the everyday problems of information gathering, storage, retrieval, and dissemination. Alternately, the technologies may be seen as simple time or cost savers.

Daniel Bell (1980, p. 43) has commented on the socio-logical truism that Americans and "moderns" in general are given to enthusiasm for technology and thus expect more or less instant results or gratification once a technological process is discovered. Certainly, this notion is reinforced by media advertising of information technologies, where each computer hardware or software vendor claims that their product is sim-pler to operate than their competitor's product. The unfortu-nate reality is that information technologies are not simple to understand and operate. Much hardware and software are still poorly designed, and documentation tends to be poorly written or sometimes even nonexistent. The rapid development of new versions of hardware and software means that new learning is constantly required.

One of the most distressing misconceptions occurs when difficulties in applying information technologies are narrowly interpreted as problems of learning to use equipment or soft-ware programs. The more fundamental and important prob-lems that must be addressed by professionals include such issues as integrating a new set of tools into an established work pattern and, for practicing professionals who value the indi-vidualized one-to-one client encounter, coming to terms with the routinization and control aspects of information technolo-gies. When the day-to-day frustrations of operating hardware and software and the more fundamental concerns are consid-ered together, it is easy to see why many professionals are being dragged reluctantly into the Information Age.

Educators must recognize the complex dynamics of the introduction of information technologies into professional practice and the fundamental changes that their use entails. They must work with both the faculty and the students to address the fundamental issues posed by the technologies as well as the practical implementation issues. In my experience, few, if any, professional schools are adequately addressing the learning and support needs of faculty and students in this area, and yet all professionals are being affected by the information technologies either directly or indirectly. Note that I have suggested that both faculty and students have learning needs. Many of today's faculty members are in a delicate position vis-à-vis information technologies because they did not grow up with them. Sometimes, past experience with an earlier version of a technology actually interferes with the user's ability to fully understand and move toward newer approaches. The task of finding the best way to assist faculty members and students to develop and redevelop their information technology skills is a major challenge.

When innovations in technology are introduced, adopters tend initially to use them to perform familiar tasks, perhaps in a faster, more efficient way. As the adopter becomes familiar with the technology, new ways of doing old things and even entirely new products or services tend to evolve. It is this innovation cycle that will potentially allow professionals to creatively use information technologies to make the paradigm shift suggested by Curry and Wergin.

At this point, I want to backtrack to present more detailed definitions and discuss the specific information technologies and how they can be used by professionals. With this common base, we can delve more deeply into some of the implications of technology use. Throughout these discussions, professionals will be able to find out more about the new skills that they will need for survival in the Information Age.

Information Technologies: Origin and Definition

Ide (1982, p. 36) has defined information in the broadest sense as any or all facts that are communicated, learned, or stored. Information technologies are defined as the means by which information is handled. In France, the word *informatique* originally meant the science of information; however, because of its close link with computers, *informatique* is now understood to mean the science through which computers store and process information. Based on this European usage, the English name for this new field has become *informatics,* and for its practitioners, *informaticians.* Bell (1980) described the emergence of information technology as a result of the integration and convergence of two separate technologies: computing and telecommunications. This integration has made it possible to develop information technologies capable of handling the gamut of information-related tasks, including finding, selecting, storing, organizing, modifying, and disseminating information. Reflect for a moment on the nature of the professions and their traditional claims to the acquisition and application of professional knowledge and it is easy to see why the emerging information technologies are of particular importance to professionals.

Historically, writers such as Machlup (1962) and Porat (1977) are credited with first describing the origin and development of the "information society." These authors take the general view that work in the modern world is increasingly involved in the manipulation of information. In this new knowledge-based economy, information and know-how, rather than labor and energy, are seen as the dominant forces in the production of goods and services in society. Dillman (1985, pp. 6–7) states that the essence of the Information Age is the massive increase in the number of technological capabilities, including aspects of communications, miniaturization, and the ability to select precise information from large electronic data bases. Again, once we reflect on the nature of the professions and the needs that their members have to quickly and efficiently retrieve information from their professional knowledge bases, the information technologies appear to be essential tools.

Another trend that deserves mention relates to the problems created by the ever increasing amount of information available to professionals. Vannevar Bush (1945) is usually cited as the first to write about the "information explosion." He did so in the context of the increasing difficulty that he personally experienced as a scientist trying to keep up with the work of his colleagues. Bush was responding to a situation created by the exponential increase in the number of scientists and scientific publications that occurred following World War II. This situation has shown no signs of abating, as new specialities are developed and increasing numbers of academics and professionals continue to feel the pressure of the publish-or-perish system of job evaluation. But Bush also had a vision for a personal electronic information system that he called Memex. Bush's thinking about the potential of Memex as a combined memory extender, information storage, retrieval, and communications device, as well as an analytical tool, was far ahead of its time. Only today are we beginning to see integrated electronic workstations that put his ideas into action.

As we think about the impact of information technologies, it is important to consider not only what is available now but also what may be available in the future. Such discussions of information technologies are often presented under the guise of computing, but it is dangerous to think of information technologies as related to computers alone. This view focuses on the machine and tends to ignore or put into second place the key elements of the effective use of computers, which include the content of the information system, the context in which it is used, and the way in which the information is communicated. Unfortunately, the popular media continue to focus on computers. As a result, readers usually find an update on information technologies in the popular press under that heading; for example, Worzel's (1992) report on computers in Canada's national newspaper, the *Globe and Mail*, provides a useful summary of expected advances in information technologies over the next ten years:

In one year:

- Multimedia (that is, computer-based presentations that combine two or more media such as text, graphics, video, and audio) will become more widely available for sales presentations and commercial training.
- Reference works such as encyclopedias and dictionaries will appear on compact disks–read only memory (CD-ROMs).
- Handwriting recognition by computer will become com-

mercially available and will become a principal input device for computer "clipboards" without keyboards.

- Data compression software and high-speed digital telephone lines will make videophones commercially possible without special equipment from the telephone companies.

In two years:

- Videoconferencing and videophones will be available to anyone who can hook together a videocamera, a computer, and a telephone line.
- Significant progress in speech recognition by computer will occur.
- Creation of computer-faked photographs and videos will be possible using ordinary desktop computers. These images will be impossible to distinguish from "real" photographs and videos.
- Virtual reality, or computer-generated environmental simulations, will become commercially available for training purposes.

In three years:

- Simple verbal programming will become available for business applications and a few high-end consumer products such as videocassette recorders (VCRs).
- Personal digital agents (PDAs) will allow computers to be used for automated customer service functions and responses to simple inquiries without human intervention.
- "Experts-in-a-box" will use neural-network software and PDAs to provide consultation and advice. People will start selling expertise on a royalty basis.
- Health practitioners will start using experts-in-a-box as diagnostic agents to increase productivity.
- Keyboard-free pocket computers will appear.
- Wireless communication will emerge for use with computers within an office.

In five to ten years:

- Speech recognition by computers will become more commonplace and more sophisticated.
- Increasing numbers of telephone inquiries will be handled by computers that speak with clients.
- PDAs will allow computers to filter and select information wanted from the global communications and information network.
- It will be possible to have "network friends" around the world whom one has never met in person.
- Individuals will carry their own computer-communications PDAs that are voice-activated, personalized, and capable of managing home appliances, office equipment, and other computers.
- Regulatory bodies (the Canadian Radio-Television and Telecommunications Commission and the U.S. Federal Communications Commission) will consider reducing the available bandwidths for television and radio to allow for increased use of mobile communications, including data transmission.
- Intelligent computers will be capable of creativity and problem solving beyond the abilities of humans.
- True robots will be under the control of intelligent computers.

Most of us greet these sort of predictions with a mixture of awe and skepticism. After all, many futurist predictions of the 1950s, such as three-dimensional television, personal helicopters, and ultrasonic laundries for vibrating dirt off clothes, seem as fanciful now as they were back then (Picton, 1988, p. A1). Voice-activated VCRs actually seem an attractive proposition for infrequent VCR-using parents like myself who have to rely on their teenagers to work bewildering remote keypad controls. Voice recognition would remove a major practical barrier to the use of information technologies by professionals who have never learned to use a keyboard.

Despite these potential benefits, professionals who read over this list of predictions for the 1990s will likely have a sense of unease. The predictions seem closer to reality than futurist predictions from earlier times because many of the predictions are based on the already widespread availability of the micro-computer. We are also witnessing the rapid adoption of tele-communications innovations such as the cellular telephone and the fax machine. Phrases such as expert-in-a-box probably represent the most disturbing prospect for many professionals because such electronic experts may appear to threaten the future need for professional expertise. But professionals should also pay attention to the fact that some of the innovations will change the way that information (for example, data about client encounters and outcomes) is collected and used and that this latter activity may well have a greater impact on professional practice in the short term than will expert systems.

Information Technologies and the Professions

Whether professionals operate in a solo fee-for-service setting, in a group practice, or in a large organization, all are bom-barded with opportunities to adopt new information technolo-gies. In the early days of computing, applications were limited to large-scale operations with substantial budgets for data stor-age and processing. Data terminals for telecommunications were separate entities, found most often in computing centers. Today, the same amount of computing power is available on an individual's desktop microcomputer, and, with the addition of a peripheral device called a modem, the microcomputer can be used for electronic communications.

A useful way to categorize and discuss information tech-nologies is by function: (1) document creation, (2) informa-tion gathering, (3) electronic mail and conferences, (4) data collection and analysis, and (5) simulation or modeling of reality. The purpose of this section of the chapter is to provide an overview of the capabilities of information technologies in a number of areas and to give examples of some of the ways that professionals are making use of them.

Document Creation

Even though document creation is potentially the end product of using information technologies for purposes such as information gathering and data analysis, it is frequently the first application adopted by professionals. Word processors may have originally been introduced for use by clerical staff, but many professionals have taken on the task of word-processing their own documents. While major document creation can be seen as central to the everyday activity of some professions, such as journalism and teaching, there are few, if any, professionals today who are not called on to produce written documents from time to time within their organizations or, more widely, within their professional communities.

Document technologies such as word processing, desktop publishing, optical scanning, and even, ubiquitously, photocopying are having a remarkable effect on professional practice. Heim (1987) has stated that the use of the word processor alters the way that we write, revise, and even think. These information technologies have made it faster and easier than ever before for professionals to create and distribute documents, both formally and informally. Furthermore, once a document exists in machine-readable form, it can be transferred to or modified for use in other documents. The introduction of word-processing software for microcomputers brought the hardware into the professional's office. Once the microcomputer was present, the adoption of other information technologies became possible.

Recently, word-processing programs have made it easier to incorporate nontextual forms of information such as graphics and numerical data into documents. This trend is reflected in a report in the *Financial Times of Canada* (Zeidenberg, 1991) proclaiming that, in office technology, the big news for the 1990s is integration. Essentially, the author was referring to the trend for previously separate software programs, such as word processing, graphics, and spreadsheets, to work together and for stand-alone microcomputers to be linked through local area networks. Not only software and hardware are integrating.

Zeidenberg (1991) discusses myriad information technologies such as the telephone, fax, computers, and copiers that are being linked in order to achieve lower costs and greater efficiencies.

The technology review from the *Globe and Mail* (Worzel, 1992) mentioned multimedia or the linking of computer-based technologies such as text, graphics, video, and audio. Another advance to watch for is hypermedia, in which computers make it possible for the content of documents to be displayed in a nonlinear way through hypertext links; for example, the reader of a hypertext encyclopedia could click on a word, and a linked definition of the word from an electronic dictionary would appear on the screen. Hypertext also allows for the presentation of information at varying levels of detail. This trend toward the integration of the information technologies and the essentially new technologies that are created by these mergers makes it particularly difficult to keep up-to-date with these innovations.

Information Gathering

Studies have been made about the information-gathering habits and learning preferences of professional groups such as physicians (for example, Curry and Putnam, 1981; Curry and Purkis, 1982), engineers (for example, Shuchman, 1981; Borovansky, 1987), and social scientists (for example, Roberts, 1977; Steig, 1981). While there appears to be much more written about some professional groups than others, existing research indicates that professional journals continue to be a primary source of professional information for most groups. Professionals, especially those in applied fields, also rely extensively on colleagues as information sources.

Information technology has a lot to offer at the information-gathering stage. A microcomputer with a modem can be used to do an on-line search of large bibliographical data bases that can potentially be located anywhere in the world. Another peripheral device for the microcomputer, a CD-ROM reader, is also available that provides access to large data bases locally without a telecommunications connection. For those who remember slogging through volumes of indexes and abstracts such as *Index Medicus* (for the health sciences literature), *INSPEC* (for the engineering literature), and *Psychological Abstracts* (for the psychology literature), these electronic versions offer substantial benefits.

Many universities are now making their catalogues available on line so that faculty can dial in from their offices and students from their dormitory rooms to search for a book location or a reference. Fully electronic journals such as the *Online Journal of Current Clinical Trials* are also an indication of the impact that information technology is having on methods of disseminating professional knowledge. An interesting aspect of these large electronic data bases is that even though they are primarily intended for a professional audience, they are publically available through electronic information services such as Dialog and Datastar. Anyone with a microcomputer, modem, telecommunications software, and the willingness to pay on-line connect charges can access these electronic storehouses of professional knowledge. This development removes the exclusive right to access their knowledge bases that professionals enjoyed at an earlier point in their history.

Specialized data base management programs exist for creating personal bibliographical data bases, and these systems could form an important part of continuing education resources available to professionals in the future. After doing searches on an on-line system or a CD-ROM, professionals can download citations into their own personal data bases and add notes or additional indexing terms to enhance the usefulness of the references.

The Hepatitis Knowledge Base being developed by the U.S. National Library of Medicine is an example of a new kind of electronic information source, called a full-text data base. The Hepatitis Knowledge Base is essentially a complete electronic textbook that is kept up-to-date by a ten-member consensus panel of nationally prominent experts in the field of viral hepatitis. Other electronic information projects in the medical area include the Online Mendelian Inheritance of Man data base at Johns Hopkins University and the Human Genome Project. The electronic environment offers many opportunities for professionals to develop new mechanisms for developing and disseminating knowledge and expertise.

Electronic Mail and Conferences

Professionals in many settings are now connected via their microcomputers and modems to electronic mail networks such as Bitnet, Internet, and CompuServe, to name a few. Electronic mail tends to be much more informal in style and content than traditional correspondence and, as such, lends itself very well to the informal information exchange preferred by many professionals. Messages can be sent on a one-to-one basis, or participants can sign up for shared electronic conferences. For example, on Bitnet, hundreds of special-interest electronic conferences have been created. These conferences essentially remove the barriers of time and distance among professional colleagues and create new professional communities. One of my students recently put a message about her assignment on the Bitnet MEDLIB-L conference for medical librarians and received advice from a librarian in Israel. The student was also encouraged to share the results of her assignment with other medical librarians via the electronic conference.

Electronic mail networks also have the potential to change communication patterns within an organization or a professional community. Electronic mail can lead to a flattening of the organizational hierarchy since it is often as easy to send a message to the company president as it is to one's immediate supervisor. On the Bitnet MEDLIB-L conference for medical librarians, an informal discussion among librarians about the implications of a decision by the U.S. National Library of Medicine (NLM) to provide direct access to the MEDLINE data base for members of the American College of Physicians resulted in an electronic response from a senior NLM administrator. In the past, such a response to the library profession's queries would have taken much longer, possibly requiring a wait for a forum at an annual meeting of the Medical Library Association.

Integration, previously noted as a trend in computer hardware and software, is also a trend in these electronic mail systems. Although interconnection will no doubt continue to be a problem, Internet, a "network of networks," is currently facilitating a great deal of communication among professionals and academics. Internet has interconnected many regional electronic networks such as SuraNet, PrepNet, and NearNet through a standard protocol known as Transmission Control Protocol/Internet Protocol (TCP/IP). In this electronic age, standards and protocols that allow different systems to talk to one another are of key importance. It is likely that these standards (or lack of them) will be one of the determining factors in the rate of adoption and use of the information technologies. A special issue of *Scientific American* (*Communications, Computers, and Networks . . . ,* 1991) discussed communications, computers, and networks in detail, telling its readers "how to work, play, and thrive in cyberspace."

One reason that professionals should pay particular attention to electronic mail systems is the 1991 passage of U.S. federal legislation authorizing the creation of the Federal High Performance Computing Program and the National Research and Education Network (NREN). NREN is a major American initiative to develop a high-speed, high-capacity, and broadly interconnected electronic network for research and education that will serve academia, industry, and government sectors. Under NREN, the National Science Foundation has the resources to expand and upgrade the existing Internet service and make widescale interconnection available by 1996. The availability of vast information resources through NREN will push the development of new electronic networks with greatly expanded capabilities relevant to both educators and professionals.

Data Collection and Analysis

Data collection and analysis is an important component of the work of many different professions. Accountants analyze financial data, social workers analyze client intake data, teachers analyze grade distributions, and lawyers analyze case law. A number of sophisticated statistical data analysis programs, such as SPSS and SAS, previously available only on large mainframe computers, are now available for microcomputers. Software for analyzing qualitative data such as written comments and interview transcripts is also available. Microcomputer-based spreadsheet programs provide accountants with an essential tool for auditing and other financial accounting tasks; but spreadsheets can be used for a variety of purposes by all types of professionals, for example, for personal financial planning or basic data analysis.

This analysis software makes it easier than ever before for professionals to systematically gather and use information from their practice settings. Yet, this activity also represents a departure from the focus on day-to-day client practice that has characterized the professional's workday in the past. In health care settings, some government offices and third-party payers are insisting that billing data be collected and submitted in electronic form, so that these agencies too can benefit from the resulting efficiencies and the overview of the professional services being provided to the population.

The use of advanced card technology, also known as "smart cards," is an example of electronic data collection being tried in Ontario, Canada. Similar projects are under way in other Canadian provinces and in the United States. In the Ontario pilot project, funded by the provincial Ministry of Health, community residents are being provided with smart cards, which are essentially plastic cards with microchips that can be carried by individuals. Each electronic card contains basic biographical data such as name, address, gender, and health care insurance number. The card also carries a health profile that includes a record of major illnesses, drug reactions, allergies, and blood type. Whenever the cardholder visits a participating physician, optometrist, pharmacist, laboratory, or hospital, the appropriate information is recorded on the card using special equipment. Some of the information regarding each encounter is also forwarded to the Ministry of Health for analysis.

The cardholders are able to read the card information on readers located at specific community locations. If they want information changed or deleted, they can ask their physicians to make the changes. The information on the card is coded for security purposes, and participating health professionals are given a decoder card for reading or changing information. The ultimate purpose of this service encounter system is to provide a means of collecting standardized information on client encounters throughout the health care system and to provide data for better planning and management of health resources and health outcomes. Given the government's recognition of the implications of this type of information technology for professionals, one of its aims in the project is also to provide a forum for discussion about the collection and dissemination of the service encounter data.

As professionals gather more information in their own practices, they also need to discover ways of organizing that internal information and finding it when they need it. For this purpose, the information technology of choice is data base management software. This type of program allows the professional to create a data base that is searchable using many different access points. For example, a psychologist might want to create a client data base containing the name of each client, his or her address, birth date, detailed notes of the consultation, referrals, time of next appointment, and so on. Using the data base, the psychologist could identify, for example, all of the clients who were counseled for particular type of problem, all of those who were referred to a particular agency, or all of those in a certain age group. Programs could be written to generate a practice profile on a regular basis, so that trends and changes could be noted for planning purposes. There are software firms that specialize in the development of customized programs of this type for practicing professionals.

Many professionals work in group practices or agencies, in which case the data base or information system may be developed at the broader organization level. Bronson, Pelz, and Trzcinski (1988, p. 37) have described the standard information systems components in a social service agency as follows: (1) a client information subsystem containing client intake and enrollment data, referral to and from other agencies, monitoring of services to clients, client progress records, client satisfaction measures, and so on; (2) an administration and financial subsystem containing general ledger and budgetary accounting, payroll and employee records, accounts receivable and client billing, accounts payable, and so on; (3) a personnel and case management subsystem for managing caseload, assigning staff to clients, allocating staff time to various functions, and maintaining personnel files and other employee information; and (4) a provider and resource subsystem for coordinating access to external resources such as funding agencies, volunteers and outside providers or facilities, outside consultants, agency vehicles, central supplies, and so on.

Simulation or Modeling of Reality

Computer simulation or modeling is among the most futuristic applications of information technology available now. A physician entrepreneur has set up a firm in Canada called Knowledge House Publishing that has used simulation programs to allow doctors to treat theoretical patients on their computer screens and to observe the results of their decisions. For architects, computer-aided design tools have revolutionized the design of buildings and landscapes. Such programs allow the architect to create a structure and to view it on the computer screen from anywhere outside or even inside the model. When the architect is finished, the computer program can even instruct a machine tool to cut a copy of the model. In science, computer-based modeling of biological and chemical activities can be used for synthesizing new pharmaceutical and agricultural products, thus reducing the number of animals needed for research purposes. Three-dimensional images of molecular structures are also possible. These graphics and modeling programs are being extended even further in a technology known as virtual reality in which the participant dons a helmet and gloves and moves through electronically simulated space.

Two more examples of the use of information technologies by professional groups indicate the leading experimental edge.

Social Service Profession

In Toronto, Ontario, Canada, the United Way, a major community funding body, has linked its agencies through electronic mail. This allows the coordinators at the United Way to communicate quickly and inexpensively with the member agencies. Informal mail messages as well as electronic documents and data files can be sent and received. The United Way is also investigating the use of electronic decision-making software, which allows the participants to share in the creation of a series of hypothetical "What if . . . " scenarios as a basis for deciding on matters such as the allocation of resources. This type of activity can be seen as an early step toward the development of a more sophisticated computer-supported cooperative work (CSCW) environment.

An expanded version of CSCW uses several information technologies to link people in different locations through voice, data, and video. In such an environment, participants can have meetings with each other and even work on the same documents together in much the same way that they would if they were all present in the same room. Mantei and others (1991) describe one such "media space," Computer Audio Video Enhanced Collaboration and Telepresence or CAVECAT. The CSCW workstations each consist of a personal computer, a television monitor, a television camera, a pair of speakers, and a microphone. A video board allows the display of images from up to four different remote sites so that the participants at each site can see video images of the other groups' members in the corner of their computer screen as they work together.

Legal Profession

The legal profession provides a different picture of the use of information technologies. Law is a text-intensive profession that relies extensively on research into legislation and case law precedents. As such, lawyers can benefit greatly from the use of information technologies. A variety of commercial legal data bases exist for searching legislation and statutes in both the United States and Canada. Some of these search systems have been enhanced with news data bases and other features, such as making the U.S. or Canadian federal budget available in electronic form as soon as it is made public.

Legal data bases were among the first to be available as full-text data bases, that is, as electronic files containing legislation or case law in its entirety, as opposed to a bibliographical citation of the original document. Full-text data bases are now increasing in number in many fields. Within a law practice, lawyers can use data base management software to store and retrieve their own previous legal research (and that of their colleagues) for cutting and pasting into new documents. Other popular applications include accounting, time management, and billing.

In recent years, large full-text data bases have been created for litigation support in major legal cases. One of the first such cases in Canada involved the *Ocean Ranger*, an oil rig that sank in a storm off the coast of Newfoundland. Hundreds of documents were brought forth in evidence in the case, and the lawyers used optical scanning and data base management software to locate relevant information in the documents when it was needed in court.

The idea of a lawyer striding into the courtroom with a notebook computer instead of a briefcase is a reality for some members of the profession today. One of the major legal data base companies in Canada has made access to its services available free of charge to judges and law students, which would appear to be an ingenious way to encourage the other, potentially paying members of the profession to take advantage of the technology. Other companies, such as the California-based Dialog Information Services, have developed programs for introducing on-line searching into the schools and have provided free access time to graduate library and information science faculties.

New Challenges for Professionals in the Information Age

The previous section of the chapter provided background on the major information technology applications of interest to professionals and examples of their use. At this point, the reader would be wise to step back and consider some of the broader implications of these technologies. Several of these issues were introduced at the outset of the chapter and are expanded on here.

One of the reasons that information technologies have a great appeal for professionals is that the applications are designed for knowledge workers. Professionals are essentially purveyors of expert knowledge. They are the ones who make the handling of human dilemmas routine through the application of their expertise, dilemmas that can involve such diverse aspects of life as the client's health, social or financial well-being, or the relationship of these factors to the law.

Information technologies can be thought of as intellectual technologies that expand the mind's ability to gather, store, retrieve, analyze, and use an ever changing and increasing knowledge base. In comparison to traditional industrial technologies, information technologies are much more flexible and adaptable. This feature offers a creative opportunity for professionals to tailor their applications and to be creative in their use. The challenge for professionals is to be sufficiently knowledgeable about the technologies to recognize the potential and the limitations and to guide the development of systems that offer the maximum benefit for themselves, their clients, and society in general.

The benefits of information technology will not necessarily be easily achieved. They require a significant financial investment by the adopters, and, perhaps more problematic, they require an investment of time for planning, learning, and making use of the products of information technology. Professionals in the field of information science can help professionals and educators develop information technologies, but the involvement and support of the professionals who will use the technologies are also required. Are professionals ready to make this commitment of resources or will they continue to have a limited vision of information technologies as peripheral to their major activities? Are educators willing to retrain themselves and to think more broadly about how information technologies can be integrated into the professional curricula?

There are frustrating and often unfamiliar problems that are encountered with the new information technologies. For example, software programs or telecommunications applications frequently have "bugs" that can be time-consuming and difficult to work out. The use of microcomputers for increasing numbers of applications sometimes creates compatibility problems or the need for new, more high-powered hardware. Adopters sometimes find that they have the same problem with information technologies that they have with popcorn, that it is difficult to stop consuming! The term technostress has been used to describe some of the anxieties that new and unfamiliar (and even familiar) users experience with the new technologies. At least part of this stress may be engendered by the feeling of "technodependence" that inevitably accompanies the adoption of complex technologies. Although we would like to demonstrate the direct benefit of using information technologies, this is often difficult because the technologies often change what we do as well as how we do it.

Naisbitt (1982, pp. 14–16) and Zuboff (1982, p. 148) have commented on the impact of information technologies on the pace of work. Zuboff speaks of the increase in the volume of information transactions made possible by the immediate access to information and the consequent compression of time that results. Naisbitt refers to the situation as the collapse of the information float. When we mail a letter through the postal system, we know that it will be a few days before it is received and a reply sent. Before voice mail, if it was not possible to speak to a person on the phone, there would be some time involved in waiting for that person to return the call. The time required for these traditional information transactions gave us more time to think about our actions and craft a careful approach or response. The convenience of pressing the reply option in the electronic mail system, of sending a fax that we expect will receive priority treatment, or of leaving an extensive message on a voice mail system is very seductive. But the end result is that when information is communicated more rapidly, the pace of activity picks up, or at least the expectation increases that action will be immediately forthcoming. This in turn increases the communicators' feelings of information overload. Perhaps the new information technologies present a danger for professionals, who need time for thought and reflection, by making them too accessible and too pressured to respond in short time frames.

Another phenomenon of note in the new technological environment is the trend toward the direct use of information technologies by the person who will ultimately produce or use the information. For example, a few years ago typing (or keyboarding) was often the task of a secretary; now, word processing is often taken on by professionals themselves. Recently, there has been a move by vendors of on-line search services to encourage professionals such as physicians, social workers, and engineers to search electronic data bases directly rather than to request a search through a librarian intermediary (Marshall, 1990). Data analysis programs on the microcomputer are now menu-driven, and a professional does not necessarily need a programmer or expert to perform many tasks.

The signs of the end-user society are everywhere, from automated teller machines to self-service gasoline stations, and they have been especially noticeable in the phenomenon known as end-user computing. Sometimes we even pay more to do transactions ourselves, just to avoid waiting in line. This is a somewhat strange turn of events in a society that has been built on principles of the division of labor; but information technologies have the potential to simplify many tasks for the novice user, at least to the point where the end user is able to achieve some level of success. Whether end-user access to complex information technologies is the most cost-effective way of obtaining information from data bases is a question that has not yet been answered, but it seems certain that this trend will persist as the information industry strives to enlarge its market.

The phenomenon of the end-user society has implications for professionals in another way. Professionals can be end users of information technologies, but clients of professionals may, in turn, become end users of expert systems that codify professional knowledge and make it accessible in electronic form. The consumer movement has challenged professional control over decision making, particularly in areas such as women's health and the environment. Part of this challenge has involved consumer access to professional sources of knowledge, such as professional journals, indexes, abstracts, and data bases. It seems likely that consumers will also want some type of access to electronic expert-in-a-box systems, if only to allow them to obtain a second opinion. Professionals may find that the informed consumer is, in fact, a much better client, and in such situations there could be a more positive and mutually participative professional-client relationship.

Earlier in the chapter, I skirted around the question of the impact of the expert-in-a-box possibility for professionals. For many practitioners, the idea of augmenting or perhaps even of replacing human professional expertise with a machine may appear potentially threatening to both their livelihood and sense of personal worth. The impersonal electronic expert also seems to counter traditional professional norms and values, which call for a more direct professional-client relationship. It is possible that the use of electronic experts in concert with human experts is, in fact, a practical and desirable development. Will professionals welcome the quality control provided by an expert-in-a-box? Could the use of such an aid decrease the risk of malpractice? Could this tool improve the accessibility of professional expertise in underserved areas? Perhaps future professionals will be routinely expected to codify new expert knowledge in a way that can be deployed through these experts-in-a-box.

Another issue that needs debate relates to the increased capabilities offered by information technology for recording and analyzing client contacts and outcomes. Such a system has many advantages for evaluating efficacy and monitoring service delivery costs, but it also raises the thorny issue of control over professional work. Zuboff (1982, p. 147) has noted that remote supervision, automatic control, and greater access to subordinates' information all become possible in computer-mediated work. She also suggests that in many settings management employs these capabilities without sufficiently considering the potential human and organizational consequences. Presumably, a balance needs to be achieved among the professional's right to autonomy and the rights of the clients, third-party payers, and society to ensure efficient and effective service. This balance needs to be discussed and agreed on in the context of the use of information technologies.

A recurring theme throughout this chapter has been that professionals need to take seriously their learning needs with respect to information technologies. The convenience and speed of information technologies are very deceptive. They give the impression that all the user has to do is "plug and play," when, in fact, considerable understanding and skill are required to use the technologies effectively. Initially, educational institutions and professional groups who were concerned about acquainting their members with information technologies saw the issue as one of gaining computer literacy. More recently, as researchers have explored the changing nature of work in an electronic environment, they have realized that the new learning must go much deeper than merely learning how to use a computer and a few software packages.

Zuboff (1988) has pointed out that computer-mediated work is more abstract and demands new conceptual skills. The knowledge bases of intellectual workers, a category to which professionals belong, are increasingly being stored and retrieved in an invisible electronic form. In earlier times, a group of professionals had a physical symbol of the size and scope of their knowledge base in the form of the major printed indexes and abstracts, such as *Index Medicus, Sociological Abstracts,* or *Engineering Index.* Today, these printed tools still exist, but they are often searched as electronic data bases where no concrete representation of their content is evident to the searcher. Other data bases such as AgeLine, produced by the American Association of Retired Persons, and ABI/INFORM, a business data base, have no print equivalents. Researchers have suggested that to use electronic information systems effectively, searchers need to develop mental models of information systems that will give them an understanding of content and data base structure (Borgman, 1986; Huston, 1990). It will be the combination of a knowledge of the information technologies and of the content and structure of the information contained therein that will enable professionals to use these new tools effectively.

How will professionals learn to use information technologies? Will the various professions develop their own informatician specialties, such as the fledgling medical informatics? Will a new information profession emerge to meet the need for information systems development and education in diverse settings? Even if these informatician specialists emerge in the professions, how will average members of the profession learn about information technologies and use them effectively in their practice?

Librarians have come up with a concept known as information literacy that could be very helpful to professionals as they strive to come to terms with the new skills needed in the Information Age. Moreover, librarians are willing to work with professionals in their efforts to achieve this goal. In 1989, the American Library Association Presidential Committee on Information Literacy published its final report. In a discussion of the report's implications, Rader (1990, p. 20) points out that information literacy extends the process of learning information skills so that it becomes a part of lifelong learning.

Information-literate people are able to organize information searches, evaluate information, and build their own data bases and know how to manage electronic files. They understand the nature of information, its sources, and its modes of delivery. Information literacy is seen as a skill that will enable people to handle information critically and productively, no matter what the source. Ideally, the acquisition of information literacy skills should start in the earliest grades, but keeping up with information technologies will no doubt continue to be a lifelong task. Librarians and other members of the information professions need to work with educators and in the professional community generally to promote the notion of information literacy and to develop educational programs and support services that will help the various professions optimize their use of the new information technologies. As one example of an information literacy initiative, the Centre for Computing in the Humanities at the University of Toronto organized a two-week course for faculty members and graduate students that covered word processing and file management; bibliographical management and note taking; desktop publishing; electronic mail; on-line resources on CD-ROM and Internet; text retrieval, indexing, and interactive concording (which is of particular interest to humanists); data base management; and spread-sheets.

Information technology has given humanists impressive new ways to analyze texts using computer programs such as TACT and WordCruncher. Greek and Latin texts, previously only available in rare book collections, are now available on CD-ROM as *Thesaurus Linguae Graecae* and *Thesaurus Linguae Latinae*. The various professions need to think through the applications of information technology that are relevant to their fields and develop similar programs at both the basic and continuing education levels. Professional associations could play a leadership role in bringing such information literacy programs into existence for the benefit of their members.

This discussion of the implications of information technologies for the professions has only brought up some of the major issues. It was meant to ask more questions than it answered because it is the responsibility of the professions to identify the relevant questions, debate the answers, and make a plan of action. The rapidly changing world of information technology is both exciting and daunting for professionals, as it is for other members of society. Although professionals are being called on to change and adapt to an increasingly sophisticated technological environment, there are also many opportunities for professionals to adapt these technologies to their own creative purposes.

Zuboff (1982, p. 143) states that new conceptions of work organization and behavior will emerge from an interaction among the demands of the new information technologies, the social organization of that technology, and the responses of the men and women who work with the new systems. In this process, there are opportunities to influence the design of information systems and their application. As these technologies develop and are used, it will be important for professionals to critically identify the disadvantages of the applications as well as their advantages and to optimize the benefits that they can provide to clients, to professional practice, and to society.

CHAPTER 4

Increasing Pressures for
Recertification and
Relicensure

John J. Norcini
Judy A. Shea

Over the past fifty years, the focus of licensure and certification in the professions has been the assessment of readiness for practice. Through their requirements and evaluation procedures, licensing and certifying bodies have defined the scope of practice and assured themselves and the public that individuals have attained the desired level of competence. This process has been successful in setting initial standards for the professions.

In many professions, however, multiple pressures have forced an expansion in focus from initial licensure and certification to recertification. These pressures can be thought of as arising from three sources: (1) the expansion of knowledge that underlies the practice of the profession, (2) the culture of the profession, and (3) the individuals (patients, clients, and so on) to whom the professionals provide service. Although these distinctions are somewhat artificial, and most are not new, in combination they create an atmosphere conducive to recertification.

The strongest pressure to recertification derives from the rapid expansion and changing nature of knowledge. This has led to a need for both lifelong learning and an evaluation process that supports it. Innovations in telecommunications, information storage and retrieval systems, and expert systems may soon make continuous learning a manageable process (Marshall, this volume).

Within the culture of the professions, there are also pressures for recertification. While some of the motives can be viewed as age-old strategies to maintain turf and control, most of the professions have a genuine desire to maintain, if not raise, standards. Teaching is an example of a profession striving to improve its practices in light of growing discontent with the achievement levels of students. Along with teaching, professions such as nursing desire to increase their visibility and elevate their status. Also, concepts from the corporate world, such as competition and productivity, are moving into the professional arena, which has traditionally been viewed as a comparatively supportive and collegial environment (Rippey, this volume).

Finally, the public is demanding accountability throughout the careers of many professionals. In contrast to the past, consumers of services show a desire to be more educated about the decisions that affect them. In all but the most rural areas, they have ample opportunities to shop for alternative providers, and they are more likely to challenge the recommendations of professionals. Moreover, when individuals are unhappy with the outcomes of professional practices, as described by McGuire (this volume), they increasingly resort to legislation and litigation to resolve differences. Such a trend dictates that professionals "prove" their ongoing competence.

In combination, forces such as these have led many licensing and certifying bodies to consider relicensure and recertification programs. In this chapter, three goals for a prototype recertification or relicensure program are offered. In order to fulfill these goals, a complementary evaluation component is described for each. The components are justified in terms of what they contribute to the assessment of competence, and some of the different types of evaluation methods for each component are described. The gaps between available and ideal methods of assessment are thus identified.

New Demands for Relicensure

Throughout the chapter, examples from medicine, law, and computer science are used to show how the prototype recertification program could be put into practice. Medicine plays a primary role because, in contrast to most other professions, it has a long-standing and intricate system of mandatory licensure that confers privilege to practice, followed by voluntary but popular certification in its specialties. Since it is a relatively wealthy profession and it has its roots in the scientific method, it also has a history of studying different methods for evaluating competence. Physicians have come under pressure to document continued competence, to provide more cost-effective care, and to ensure that the small number of dangerous, unscrupulous, or impaired physicians are removed from practice. Consequently, several medical specialties already have recertification programs with serious evaluation components (candidates for recertification can and do fail). These programs serve as the profession's means of improving the quality of patient care and establishing its accountability to the public (Benson, 1991).

The process for earning the privilege to practice law is, in many ways, similar to medicine. Once a person is admitted to the bar, they retain the rights and privileges of the profession for life except in the unusual circumstance of disbarment. Although law does not have a formal, periodic relicensure program, the profession has long been interested in continuing legal education (American Law Institute–American Bar Association Committee on Continuing Professional Education, 1984). State bar associations and commercial vendors regularly provide educational opportunities in the form of lectures, seminars, and video instruction. In addition, several journals, such as the *ALI-ABA CLE Review and Practical Lawyer,* are specifically designed to support continuing education (American Law Institute–American Bar Association Committee on Continuing Professional Education, 1990). In 1988, the American Bar Association adopted a Model Rule for Minimum

Continuing Legal Education (MCLE) that was designed to give states guidance on implementing MCLE programs (Gillers and Simon, 1991). By 1992, thirty-eight states had adopted mandatory MCLE (Alexander Hart, director of the Office of Courses of Study, American Law Institute–American Bar Association, personal communication, March 11, 1992), though there is considerable diversity in the amount and content of required education and in the stringency of documenting MCLE activities (Brooks, 1991). With the MCLE requirements, the legal profession has laid a groundwork that could be useful to relicensure programs.

Within the field of computer science, a voluntary certification and recertification program is offered by the Institute for Certification of Computer Professionals (ICCP). In recognition of the widespread impact that computers have on many facets of life, the certification program was developed in the 1970s by eight professional societies (Eggert, 1991). The purposes of the program are to establish high standards, to measure knowledge appropriate for different facets of industry, and to create a system whereby consumers can verify the qualifications of computer professionals. In addition, certified professionals must adhere to a code of ethics and standard of conduct. Certificates are offered for the certified computer programmer, certified data processor, and certified systems professional. Candidates must pass a broad core examination as well as examinations in two of nine subspecialties. Unfortunately, initial certification is not yet popular among practitioners.

Recertification is required for computer professionals who obtained certification starting in 1986. The purpose of recertification is to help the professional keep abreast of new developments and to support personal learning. Recertification requires 120 hours of continuing education every three years. These hours can be earned by engaging in activities such as university courses, vendor courses, paper authorship, and self-study. Records of continuing education activities are kept by the ICCP.

Goals of a Recertification Program

The assessments used in recertification or relicensure programs should provide a complete picture of the competence of the professional, and they should have three goals (Norcini and Dawson-Saunders, forthcoming). First, some aspect of the evaluation should warrant the competence of the individual as demonstrated in actual practice. Ideally, this goal would be achieved by an assessment of the outcomes of professional activity. Second, the evaluation should warrant that a practitioner has the potential to respond appropriately to a wide range of problems, even though not all situations are commonly seen in practice. Achievement of this goal entails an assessment that simultaneously gives evidence that the certificants retain their original knowledge base, including the rare but important occurrences, and are also knowledgeable of recent advances. Third, though perhaps not equally important in all professions, recertification and relicensure should warrant the interpersonal and moral characteristics of the practitioner. This goal can be achieved by reviewing credentials and by collecting the opinions of peers and clients.

Regardless of exactly how each component is evaluated, the process must be consistent with *Standards for Educational and Psychological Testing* (American Educational Research Association, American Psychological Association, and National Council on Measurement in Education, 1985). This will ensure the fairness and quality of the evaluation.

Component 1: Assessment of Practice Outcomes

The first and probably most important component of a recertification program is an assessment of practice outcomes. This is an answer to the central question, "Did the professional achieve the appropriate result?" For physicians, practice outcomes might refer to the end result of medical care: Did the patient get better? For teachers, it might refer to the end result of the educational process: Can the student read? For engineers, it might refer to the integrity of the structure: Did the bridge stand? Equally challenging questions could be set forth for attorneys, pilots, computer scientists, and others. Clearly, the broadness and importance of the question will vary within and across professions. Regardless of how the central question is posed, there are a number of limitations to current methods for assessing practice outcomes. Until some of these problems are resolved, Kremer (1991) has recommended that the gap be filled by using process-related outcomes measures, that is, assessments of the quality of the process used by professionals to achieve outcomes.

Justification for the Assessment of Outcomes

In many ways, outcomes are the ultimate criteria; they provide measures of the consequences of what is actually done in practice (Relman, 1988). As such, they are probably the most attractive form of evaluation for both the public and the practitioners. To the public, they provide direct evidence that the practitioners are or are not achieving appropriate results. To the practitioners, assessment of outcomes offers the opportunity to be judged on their results, rather than on how those results were obtained.

Outcomes assessment avoids many of the problems associated with traditional measures of competence because it is a measure of what actually happens in practice. Conventional measures place the professional in an artificial (testing) situation and assess responses to hypothetical questions. Thus, they reflect the potential to perform rather than actual performance. In addition, it is expensive to develop the tailored examinations that are needed given the varied and unique practice patterns that develop over a career. Outcomes assessment permits recertification in what the practitioner actually does in his or her professional activities rather than in the total discipline.

Methods of Evaluation

Methods of evaluation that focus on the results of practice behaviors take two forms: outcomes assessment and outcomes-related assessment.

Examples of Outcomes Assessment in Medicine. Medical research
has focussed on outcomes as criteria for quite some time.
Common studies compare patient outcomes for two or more
alternative diagnoses or treatments and traditionally concentrate on mortality and morbidity as the end points of interest.
Although such studies have provided much of the knowledge
base in clinical medicine, recent work has broadened the
definition of outcomes so that it includes other important
clinical end points such as the functional status of patients,
patient satisfaction, and cost-effectiveness (Lohr, 1988; Kaplan,
Greenfield, and Ware, 1989; Wennberg, 1990). Moreover, interest is shifting to an examination of the influence of the
individual physician in the context of a complex health care
system.

A data base built as part of the Medical Outcomes Studies
(Tarlov and others, 1989) illustrates these developments.
Groups of practitioners were randomly sampled from different
systems of health care (for example, health maintenance organization [HMO] and private practice) in three cities. The
practitioners' patients who had relatively common conditions
(diabetes, hypertension, coronary heart disease, and depres-
sion) were evaluated at the start of the studies and then followed over a two-year period. The information collected about
the patients over the two years included demographic data,
clinical status, functional status, general well-being, and satisfaction with care. At the same time, information was gathered
about the characteristics of the system of health care (for
example, HMO versus private practice) and the practitioner
(for example, work load, job satisfaction, and specialty). Finally, data were gathered on the process of care; included were
technical aspects of care (for example, medications prescribed,
tests ordered, and hospitalizations) and interpersonal aspects
of care (for example, counseling and communication).

Although this data base has not yet been explored in
detail, early results are encouraging. A study by Stewart and
others (1989) illustrates the use of outcomes measures beyond
traditional morbidity and mortality indices and establishes
their sensitivity to different medical conditions. It is noteworthy

that after removing statistically the effects of a number of indicators, enough of the variability in outcomes remained unexplained to lead the authors to suggest that medical care, and thus individual physicians, may make a difference even in chronic conditions where a cure is not possible.

A study by Wells and others (1989) using this data base illustrates the effect of other influences on outcomes measures. Specifically, the functioning and well-being (adjusted for a range of background and health status variables) of depressed patients were compared by the type of professional who treated them. Depressed patients with another medical condition who visited mental health specialists had worse functioning than those who visited medical specialists. Conversely, depressed patients without another condition who visited mental health specialists had better functioning than those who visited medical specialists. While these findings are not surprising, they do indicate the usefulness of outcomes in examining differences among types of professionals and the treatments that they offer.

Gaps Between Ideal and Available Methods. The appeal of outcomes measurement is apparent, but there is considerable distance between defining important outcomes and being able to measure them. In medicine, the intricacy of the delivery system is coupled with the fact that outcomes are usually determined by a very complex set of events. Until more sophisticated methodology is developed, the use of outcomes assessment for recertification has serious limitations (Epstein, 1990). In medicine, the vast majority of the research has been done in a hospital setting. Often the patients are acutely ill or particular procedures are involved (for example, surgery), making appropriate outcomes relatively clear to define. In contrast, the bulk of medical practice is in an ambulatory setting. Many problems are chronic, thus good outcomes are difficult to define, and significant follow-up is required to document an effect. Studies like that conducted by Wells and others (1989) need to be extended to other conditions that are frequently seen in the ambulatory setting, and standards for what constitutes acceptable patient outcomes are needed. The Patient Outcomes Research Team Studies recently funded by the Agency for Health Care Policy and Research should help fulfill some of these needs (Raskin and Maklan, 1991; Wennberg, 1990).

Second, as suggested above, the professional is rarely the sole reason for any particular outcome. In medicine, whether or not a patient gets better is a function of myriad factors. Clearly, the patient's problem and the initial severity of the condition are important. While these may be documented, other potential influences such as the patient's willingness and ability to comply with the doctor's orders, the resources available to the patient and the physician, and the performance of other members of the health care team also contribute (Dawson-Saunders and others, 1989). This problem is exacerbated by the fact that physicians tend to specialize in certain areas of practice and thus may manage a group of patients whose outcomes are not particularly promising compared to the average. Therefore, it is important to identify those factors likely to influence outcomes and then adjust the measures so that they reflect only the influence of the physician. Obviously, these issues can be extended to many other professions like social work.

Finally, virtually all of the work in the area of outcomes has been done with a large number of physicians but only a small number of conditions. This general design has allowed collection of enough cases to thoroughly describe the conditions and to permit adjustment for factors, other than the physician, that affect outcomes. For evaluation of the individual physician, as would be required for recertification, considerable work remains. It is necessary to evaluate physician performance from several perspectives. First, one must determine how many cases are required to achieve a reproducible estimate of a single physician's outcomes. Second, work in other areas of physician evaluation has indicated the importance of broadly sampling different kinds of cases, so this factor must be explored for outcomes (for example, Elstein, Shulman, and Sprafka, 1978). Third, as described above, accurate measurement requires development of adjustments to outcomes for a number of different conditions.

Outcomes-Related Process Measures of Care in Medicine. Because
the gap between ideal and practical methods of outcomes
assessment is so great, Kremer (1991, p. 193) has recommended
that "process measures known to correlate with patient outcomes could serve as standards for judging physician performance in recertification programs." In other words, it would be
a useful first step to look at the process of care provided by the
practitioner and decide whether it was good enough, rather
than looking at the outcome of the patient.

Of course, the most difficult aspect of this form of
assessment is deciding what constitutes appropriate treatment.
In a publication sponsored by the Institute of Medicine, Lohr
(1990) suggests a four-step process for developing quality-of-
care criteria. First, a thorough review of the literature, relevant
to the problem, is undertaken to define current practice patterns. Second, experts are convened to review that literature
and to develop the criteria (that is, an answer key). Third, the
criteria are pilot-tested. And, fourth, the impact of the criteria
on patient care is monitored. Kremer (1991) cites several
studies and reviews of attempts to validate process criteria
against outcomes. Some (for example, McAuliffe, 1978) found
little relationship between process and outcomes whereas others (for example, Kahn and others, 1990; Rubenstein and
others, 1990) demonstrated a relationship. Additional work is
needed, but on balance these studies provide support for the
use of process measures related to outcomes.

Once the process-related measures are defined, another
notable issue is deciding how to collect appropriate data. At
least two medical certifying boards (Leigh, 1987; Munger and
Reinhart, 1987; Solomon and others, 1990) take as input the
physician's medical records or charts concerning one or more
patients. These are evaluated in some fashion (by computer or
as part of an oral exam) to determine whether the quality of the
records, the care, or both has been appropriate.

Extensions of Outcomes Assessment to Law. This component of
recertification asks whether lawyers have achieved appropriate
outcomes with their clients. There are certain legal cases that

yield outcomes (like winning a trial, amount of a fine, or length of a sentence) that are analogous to mortality and morbidity for physicians. Like medicine, however, there is also a large number of cases (Rosenthal, 1984) where good outcomes are more difficult to define and alternative end-point measures are needed (for example, cases involving mergers or custody settlements). Even with good measures, the complexity of the problem influences the outcomes, so methods of adjusting for case difficulty are needed. Moreover, a single lawyer is rarely the sole cause for any particular result, so other factors need to be taken into account.

Until appropriate outcomes are defined, a legitimate focus is the process of providing legal consultation. Borrowing ideas from medical assessment, Vogt, Silverman, White, and Scanlon (1984) report on a study where attorneys were asked to provide samples of their work and discuss the results in interviews with peer reviewers. Because this design is impractical with large numbers of examinees, perhaps a formal case review process could be substituted. Abstracted cases could be reviewed by a panel of experts, or trained reviewers, and an assessment of competence made. Of course, before this process can be evaluated, the dimensions of competence in providing legal services need to be defined. For example, the skills of building rapport with clients, providing advice and consultation, preparing the appropriate documents in an accurate and timely manner, and negotiating in a skillful style that may avoid a court appearance (DeCotiis and Steele, 1984). Rosenthal (1984) outlined activities in an alternative way, reminiscent of discussions in medicine: information gathering, information sifting, strategy formation, strategy implementation, and strategy review.

One major problem in using process-related outcomes measures in law is the confidential nature of the client-attorney relationship. Privileges granted to attorneys to enable them to protect the confidentiality of their clients would likely not be extended to third parties, such as those engaged in the assessment and evaluation of professional competence (Rosenthal,

1984). The preeminence of this feature makes it difficult either
to directly observe interactions between attorneys and clients
or to review records that have not been suitably blinded, a time-
consuming and expensive venture. The importance of confidentiality suggests that methods for conducting outcomes
assessment in law need special attention.

Extensions of Outcomes Assessment to Computer Science. Just as with
other professions, this part of the recertification program is
difficult to develop; it asks whether computer scientists have
achieved appropriate outcomes with their clients. Some professionals do work in settings or create products where the results
of their work could produce measures similar to mortality and
morbidity indices for physicians. Evaluation could focus on the
"product" and how it was assessed in terms of being useful,
adaptable, documented, and correct, or whether it could be
integrated into future needs. Beyond medicine and law, however, there are a large number of cases where good outcomes
are difficult to define and thus different kinds of end-point
measures are needed. Even with good measures, problems vary
in difficulty and importance and this influences the outcomes,
so methods of adjusting for case mix are again needed. Until
such measures are developed, it is probably necessary to examine the process of providing expert services, rather than focus
on outcomes.

The process dimensions for evaluation might be adapted
from those outlined for law or medicine. Certainly, there are
elements of building rapport with clients, providing advice and
consultation, and preparing the appropriate documents in an
accurate and timely manner. Job analysis of this diverse profession would help explicate other important dimensions. Perhaps like medicine, process questions could be framed in terms
of data gathering (defining what products are being developed), hypotheses generation (outlining possible strategies),
hypotheses development and revision (gathering data about
each proposed strategy), and selection (choosing a strategy to
guide product development). The challenge lies in developing

fair and comparable evaluation processes that are appropriate for the diverse profession. An exploration of a process analogous to chart review might be a good starting point.

Component 2: Assessment of Potential to Practice

The first component of recertification, assessment of outcomes, provides assurances to the public and the profession that an individual produces reasonable results given what he or she deals with routinely in practice. Beyond these typical issues, there are important aspects of competence that are less frequently encountered. In most fields, there are also new developments that influence the nature of practice. Relicensure and recertification must attest to ability in these areas as well. Consequently, the second component of a relicensure and recertification program is an assessment of potential to practice.

Justification for the Assessment of Potential to Practice

There are three reasons to assess the potential to practice. First, in the conduct of a profession, there are situations or problems that arise infrequently but have considerable importance in terms of outcomes and where appropriate action by a practitioner has a significant impact. It is relatively easy to envision a medical condition that is rare, but where appropriate recognition or treatment of the problem would avoid mortality or reduce morbidity. Since they occur infrequently, these conditions will not be reflected in a typical assessment of outcomes and must be captured in some other fashion to ensure competence in high-stakes situations.

Second, the knowledge and practice of most professions are transformed over the career of an individual. Recent advances in the treatment of heart disease and recent changes in the criminal code and tax laws are examples. These rapid and extensive changes have significant impact on the quality of the services delivered by a professional and make it imperative to engage in the process of lifelong learning or continuing scholarship. Moreover, these changes are unlikely to be reflected immediately in practice outcomes, and, consequently, there must be a mechanism for ensuring that the practitioner is keeping up and has the potential to employ new information where appropriate (Panel on the General Professional Education of the Physician, 1984).

Third, holding a license or certificate implies competence in a relatively broad domain. For example, admittance to the bar permits a lawyer to practice most any aspect of the law, and a medical license permits a physician to provide virtually any kind of medical or surgical treatment. Since most practitioners tend to specialize in an area, an assessment of outcomes alone is insufficient to ensure competence in the broader field. Consequently, relicensure and recertification must attest to potential in these areas.

Methods of Evaluation

As noted above, the goal of this component of recertification is to ensure that the practitioner is able to respond appropriately to those cases or situations that are important, new, or infrequently encountered. This goal can be achieved by an evaluation system with two complementary facets. The first facet should support and encourage a process of ongoing or continuous learning. That is, a well-designed relicensure or recertification process should encourage the practitioner to learn, or relearn, how to handle as many of the cases or situations as possible that he or she might encounter in practice. Naturally, this learning process should use the best methods currently available in the discipline. The second facet should warrant that the practitioner has met certain minimum standards, thereby protecting the public. A reasonable way to achieve these two ends is to develop and administer a two-part examination. The first part should provide the examinee diagnostic information that is linked in some obvious way to formal and informal continuing education. The second part should provide a summative decision about the potential to practice.

Diagnostic Tests. The purpose of diagnostic testing is to stimulate continuous improvement. Results of this type of testing can inform practitioners of their potential to deal with relatively rare occurrences and can assess their cognizance of recent advances in their field. Tests that fulfill this purpose possess three characteristics: (1) the questions are relevant to the practice of the profession even if the topic is new or emerging, (2) the method of testing samples content in a broad and efficient fashion, and (3) feedback on performance is specific and linked in an obvious way to education. In order for the diagnostic testing to be credible to practitioners, it is crucial that it be relevant to the practice of the profession. For physicians, the questions should focus on aspects of medicine that are relevant to the diagnosis and treatment of patients. For a computer programmer, they should focus on aspects of the discipline that are relevant to particular hardware, software, or systems decisions. Consequently, the majority of questions should be posed in the context of a problem or situation that the professional faces routinely (the program for the computer programmer, the patient for the physician, and the client for the lawyer). Although knowledge-based questions do measure aspects of competence (Norcini and others, 1984), use of case-based scenarios that describe real-life situations helps ensure that the knowledge tested is consistent with actual practice. Moreover, diagnostic testing supports the practitioner in more easily generalizing and incorporating recent advances into day-to-day behavior. This focus on relevance is enhanced by including practitioners in the test-writing process and by ensuring that they can attest the relevance of the final product.

There is a large body of literature indicating that the performance of professionals is situation or case specific; performance in one situation does not predict performance in another (for example, Elstein, Shulman, and Sprafka, 1978). For example, knowing how well an attorney advises a client on a particular child custody case says little about how well he or she will advise another client on a slightly different case. As a result of this specificity, broad sampling of situations is required to produce a stable or reproducible estimate of performance in any single content area. Moreover, to accomplish the purposes of diagnostic testing, several content areas need to be tested. Given the busy schedules of most practitioners, the method of testing must be able to sample broadly in a reasonable amount of time.

The intent of diagnostic testing is to provide the kind of information that a practitioner can use to direct his or her future educational endeavors (Escovitz and Davis, 1990). To be useful, a pattern of strengths and weakness must emerge from the test. Feedback for areas of weakness must be at a level that is sufficiently detailed to help examinees gain a good understanding of where their knowledge is deficient. For instance, it would not be very useful to tell a lawyer that he or she has a knowledge deficiency in the area of Pennsylvania state law; the domain is too broad and the time to learn it all is too short. It would be more useful to indicate a deficiency in particular aspects of the Pennsylvania penal code.

Although provision of education per se is not the responsibility of licensing or certifying bodies, it would be helpful if there was some obvious link between the feedback and education. This would close the education-evaluation loop and promote efficient, effective, and continuous improvement. Law is relatively advanced in its ability to provide continuing education that is tailored to the practitioner's interest (Brooks, 1991). However, the quality of the education is uneven from one jurisdiction to another (Frye, 1990), with some states giving credit for activities such as in-house training, luncheon and dinner speeches, or writing (Brooks, 1991) and others requiring education in ethics or professional conduct. For the diagnostic summary, it would be useful to apply the MCLE requirements nationally and tie them specifically to assessment devices. Computer science and medicine also have reasonably well developed systems of continuing education that could be linked with diagnostic testing.

Methods of Diagnostic Testing. By far, the largest body of work on different methods of assessing professional competence is in medicine, and very few of the testing methods studied have all the characteristics of a good diagnostic test. However, within medicine there are several methods that meet the need for placing test material in the context of a relevant clinical situation that simulates the physician-patient interaction, and many of these methods could be adapted for use in other professions. From lowest to highest fidelity, options range from patient-based multiple-choice questions that assess higher-order aspects of competence (Norcini and others, 1984), through oral examinations (Lloyd, 1983), to standardized patients where an actor or actress simulates a patient with a particular medical problem (Barrows, Williams, and Moy, 1987; Stillman, Rutala, Stillman, and Sabers, 1982). Between these extremes is a long menu of written, computer-based, and video simulations as well as models, heart sound machines, and the like (for example, Webster, 1984; Shea and others, 1992b; Norcini and Swanson, 1989). Similar methods from law include the writing of briefs and moot court.

While the high-fidelity simulations are most appealing, they have other characteristics that make them less than ideal candidates for use in diagnostic testing. The closer a method of evaluation comes to faithfully reproducing reality, the longer it takes to administer each case or time. As previously stated, it is essential that a diagnostic test be able to sample broadly and efficiently. Unfortunately, many of the written, computer-based, and patient-based simulations require at least four hours of testing time to produce a reproducible score in a single content area (Swanson, Norcini, and Grosso, 1987); this is so long as to render them unacceptable for use in diagnostic testing.

Given present testing limitations, situation-based multiple-choice questions provide the best alternative. Although they lack the face validity of some other measures, they permit very broad sampling of content in a reasonably short amount of testing time. Moreover, the feedback can be very specific and linked to prior education. It should be mentioned, however, that if multiple-choice questions are used for such a purpose, they should stress higher-order cognitive skills. It is crucial to avoid an overreliance on items that require the simple recall of knowledge; such items have, unfortunately, characterized the use of this format.

Gaps Between Ideal and Available Methods. Over the next decade, research efforts should be directed at improving the high-fidelity simulations and implementing them in disciplines other than medicine. Specifically, work can be directed at making the more realistic item formats efficient, improving the case generation process, and developing strategies for sharing the logistics and costs of these evaluation methods.

Two lines of work might hold promise for making the formats more efficient. First, focused simulations that emphasize a single objective might produce better results. For example, it may be better to ask a computer programmer to write a small crucial portion of a program rather than the whole thing. It is important, however, to avoid shortening the cases so much that it affects their validity. Second, and more important, tests developed within the classical test theory framework are inefficient. All examinees receive the same questions even though their abilities vary widely. Consequently, most of the examinee's time is spent responding to items that are either too easy or too hard. Recent work in psychometrics has produced more sophisticated and more demanding models for tests (for example, Hambleton and Swaminathan, 1985). If the test data from simulations are found to fit these models, adaptive testing should be impossible. In this form of testing, items are chosen based on the examinee's responses to previous questions. This permits precise measurement in approximately half the amount of testing time (Wainer, 1990).

Development of items or case materials for many of the diagnostic evaluation methods is expensive and time-consuming. Test material is often created de novo by individuals, reviewed by committees, field-tested, and reviewed again. Work on more efficient methods of item generation with multiple-choice questions has begun (Roid and Haladyna, 1982; LaDuca, Staples, Templeton, and Holzman, 1986; Shea and others, 1992a), but such methods receive far too little attention. Further, these new item-writing techniques need to be generalized to the situation or case-based formats where the development of test material is more complex.

Finally, considerable resources are required to use the high-fidelity simulations. Depending on the method chosen, testing centers are needed as well as computer facilities or special types of human resources (for example, standardized patients). Over the next decade, development of more efficient delivery systems will help defray the large costs (Marshall, this volume). In the meantime, the development of national consortia that share the costs might be helpful. Local versions of this concept are already productive (Stillman and others, 1986).

Summative Tests in Medicine. The purpose of summative testing is to ensure that the practitioner has met certain minimum standards, thus protecting the public. As with diagnostic assessment, it is just as important that the summative evaluation be credible to practitioners. Consequently, the test questions should focus on aspects of the profession that are relevant to practice, and they should be posed in the context of a situation that the practitioner might face (for example, a particular patient or a particular case). In addition to their other advantages, realistic scenarios support the examinee in making appropriate generalizations to and from practice. Again, development of relevant materials is more likely if practitioners are included in the test-writing process, or if they are surveyed about the relevance of the material before it is administered.

Summative examinations differ from diagnostic examinations in at least three important ways. First, given the need to protect the public by ensuring that the candidate has at least a minimal level of knowledge, a summative test must be administered in a secure environment. With today's technology, that typically means a proctored examination with confidential test material, although computer-administered tests should be feasible in the near future. Second, the purpose of summative examination feedback is to convey a sense of overall performance rather than performance to identify areas of particular strength or weakness, the item formats used for summative tests do not need to be quite as efficient as the formats used for diagnostic tests.

Methods of Summative Testing. Many of the testing methods previously mentioned would be suitable as summative measures of cognitive ability. As with diagnostic examinations, the need for relevant test material presented in a practice-appropriate setting gives an edge to the simulation methods, as opposed to techniques that ask for simple recall of knowledge. Once again, the options range from situation-based multiple-choice questions that assess higher-order aspects of competence to standardized patients and oral examinations, with a host of measures between these extremes.

While the high-fidelity simulations are most appealing, as stated above they are more expensive to develop and administer. Moreover, simulations are less reliable per unit of testing time and, if used, the tests are relatively long. Moreover, the measurement characteristics of some of the newer simulations (for example, simulated patients) have not been thoroughly explored, and therefore the methods are not yet ready for use in high-stakes testing situations. Despite these limitations, some of the high-fidelity simulations are currently feasible and add credibility to the process, thus enhancing examinee acceptance.

Situation-based multiple-choice questions still have the advantages of efficiency and cost-effectiveness. Moreover, there is considerable experience with their use in summative evaluation. In a recent study of a recertification process in medicine, multiple-choice questions were found to yield the same results as the more realistic, but expensive, oral examination formats (Munger and Reinhart, 1987). Consequently, the board involved in that study decided to offer candidates a choice in formats until more definitive work is completed.

Gaps Between Ideal and Available Methods. Medicine has considerable experience in producing summative examinations of the kind appropriate for recertification. Similarly, computer scientists have an initial certifying examination that could provide a mechanism for summative evaluation for recertification. Their examination contains a core section, after which candidates select from a menu of modules. This same modular examination could be used for recertification. The core section would verify that practitioners remain knowledgeable in the broad domain. The self-selected sections would recognize the diversity of the field and the fact that practitioners specialize

within it. Given that this field is relatively fluid, constant attention to appropriate content and blueprint development may
play a more central role in this field than in others.

In contrast to medicine and computer science, there has
been little discussion about a formal, secure examination that
would be given to all attorneys as a summative evaluation.
However, there is recognition that the amount of material with
which one should be acquainted is rapidly growing (Frye,
1990), as is the tendency for attorneys to specialize (Kaufman,
1984). Thus, it appears that the rationale for developing a
secure, summative evaluation exists in law just as it does in
medicine and computer science.

Over the next decade, at least two kinds of research
would be useful for all professions. First, it would be helpful if
various technological advances could be brought to bear on the
problem of examination security. The ability to administer a
summative examination in more convenient and less forebod-
ing ways would have a positive effect on examinees' acceptance
of the process. Second, many of the newer simulations, such as
standardized patients in medicine, require considerable work
before they are ready for use in a high-stakes testing situation.
Issues of standardization, bias, validity, and the like are yet to be
fully addressed.

Component 3: Assessment of Professional Qualities

The first component of the recertification process warrants that
the practitioner produces reasonable results given the cases
that he or she encounters routinely. The second component
attests that the practitioner has the potential to handle important, new, and infrequently encountered conditions. These two
components speak to technical skills, but the practice of any
profession goes far beyond these aspects of competence. Therefore, the third component of recertification provides an assessment of the nontechnical facets of competence. Specifically, it
reassures the profession and the public that (1) the practitioner's behavior is moral and ethical, (2) the practitioner is
not impaired, and (3) the practitioner has reasonable relation-

ships with clients or patients (Norcini and Dawson-Saunders, forthcoming).

Justification for the Assessment of Professional Qualities

There are several reasons to assess professional qualities. First, the relationship between a practitioner and his or her clients is one of unequal authority by virtue of the special knowledge possessed by the professional. This makes the client vulnerable to the less than scrupulous practitioner. Unprincipled behavior would not necessarily be evident in an assessment of outcomes or the potential to practice. Since relicensure or recertification is the pathway to continuing practice, it must attest to the moral and ethical standing of the professional.

Similarly, there are various kinds of impairments that might not be apparent in assessments of outcomes or potential. For instance, substance abuse or psychological problems could affect the practitioner's judgment in certain instances but might not be associated with a dramatic increase in the number or type of bad outcomes. Such impairment is also unlikely to be evident in a cognitive examination. Consequently, this component of relicensure and recertification must attest that the practitioner is not impaired.

While the first two reasons for the assessment of professional competence concentrate on absolute qualifications for practice, the third focusses on a less precise but equally important aspect of competence. A major piece of professional practice is the interpersonal relationship between the practitioner and the client. At all times, the client deserves to be treated with integrity, compassion, and respect. This aspect of competence is probably not captured completely in an assessment of outcomes.

Methods of Evaluation

To achieve the goals of the third component of a recertification process, information is needed from a variety of sources, including credentialing authorities (where applicable), colleagues, and clients. The purpose of credentialing information is to establish the moral and ethical characteristics of the practitioner, and to determine whether problematic impairment exists. The data can come from several sources. First, information regarding disciplinary actions by licensing bodies or state bars should be reviewed prior to final relicensure and recertification decisions. For medicine, this information has recently been assembled in a national data base that permits the tracking of unscrupulous physicians across state boundaries. However, it should be noted that the numbers of professionals actually found to be negligent in law (Rosenthal, 1984) and medicine are small. Second, data from local credentialing bodies, such as law firms or hospitals, should be reviewed. Third, because there are legitimate reasons why such information would not be available (for example, a physician does not have hospital privileges, a lawyer or computer scientist works by himself or herself), alternative forms of evaluation could be utilized. For example, statements about the practitioner's moral and ethical standing could be sought from responsible parties in the local community.

Collection of data from colleagues and clients provides a slightly different orientation to assessment of professional behavior. Rather than legal or moral issues, such data can assess the interpersonal relationship between the practitioner and client. Currently, the most practical method for gathering such information is via rating forms. Recent assessment work in medicine used the ratings of patients to gauge their satisfaction with the interpersonal aspects of care provided by their physicians (Swanson, Webster, and Norcini, 1989). Ratings from thirty to fifty patients were required to obtain a stable estimate of the behavior of an individual physician. Butterfield and Pearsol (1988) found similar results in summarizing nurses' ratings of the physicians with whom they worked. Ramsey and colleagues have shown that ratings of professional qualities obtained from physician colleagues identified by the practitioner yielded reasonable results with ten to twenty ratings (Carline, Wenrich, and Ramsey, 1989; Ramsey and others, 1990), though these were slightly more optimistic than the ratings by patients or nurses. Overall, much work remains to refine the efforts to efficiently obtain reliable information about physician-patient interaction.

Perhaps more than any other profession, law has spelled out expectations for acceptable behavior (Gillers and Simon, 1991). The *ABA Model Rules of Professional Conduct* and *ABA Model Code of Professional Responsibility* have been adopted, though sometimes altered, by most states. Some of the rules address very specific behaviors such as maintaining confidentiality or marketing legal services, but many focus on softer issues such as treating clients with integrity and respect.

One rule requires each lawyer to maintain the integrity of the profession by reporting unethical or inappropriate behavior by peers. Thus, if the legal profession should decide to systematically monitor professional conduct as part of the privilege of ongoing practice, the profession could borrow from medicine and obtain ratings by peers and clients.

Computer science may be a bit different because the number of client contacts in a given period of time is probably smaller than experienced by the practicing physician or attorney. For example, a physician might see dozens of patients a week, or an attorney might counsel as many a month. However, many computer specialists work for just one employer or organization over a relatively long period of time. Thus, there is a need to utilize methods of evaluation that are not dependent on numerous evaluations from different sources. If the profession decides to systematically monitor professional conduct as part of the privilege of ongoing practice, it could also borrow from medicine and obtain ratings by peers where the number of clients are too few.

Gaps Between Ideal and Available Methods. There are certainly gaps between the actual and ideal in the methods for collecting accurate information about the ethical standing, impairment, or interpersonal relationships of practitioners. Formal disciplinary action and withdrawal of privileges are relatively rare events. The credentialing process needs to be tightened and standards need to be raised.

Likewise, ratings of individual practitioners from various

sources are imperfect. Law, medicine, and other professions are built on intricate networks of peer relationships that provide support, recognition, and financial rewards. The use of fellow professionals to gather negative information about a practitioner has obvious flaws. Likewise, the use of allied professionals (for example, nurses for physicians or legal aides for lawyers) as a source of information tends to bring out interprofessional jealousies and problems of perspective. Finally, while clients or patients may be ideal sources of information, it is important to recognize that aspects of the outcome over which the professional has no control may be more influential than the performance of the professional. Considerable work is required to encourage the professions to police themselves more vigorously and to develop alternate sources of information about these important aspects of competence.

Conclusion

The assessment procedures and processes used in recertification and relicensure programs should provide a complete picture of the competence of the practitioner, and they should have three goals. First, some aspect of the evaluation should warrant the competence of the individual in actual practice. The first component of a relicensure or recertification program would ideally achieve this goal through an assessment of the outcomes of professional activity. Since outcomes methodology is not yet ready for implementation, process-related outcomes measures provide an interim solution.

Second, the evaluation should warrant that the practitioner can respond appropriately to a range of problems that he or she does not routinely see in practice. This is especially important in professions in which there is a rapid expansion in information. There are two facets to achieving this goal. First, a relicensure or recertification process should encourage the practitioner to learn, or relearn, how to handle as many of these cases or situations as possible; it should set in motion a process of continuous improvement. Second, the process needs to warrant that the practitioner has met certain minimal standards, thus protecting the public. To achieve these two ends, a two-part examination is necessary. The first part should provide the examinee diagnostic information that is tied in some obvious way to continuing education. Patient-based multiple-choice questions are the best alternative currently available; additional work needs to be done with more focused simulations of clinical situations and adaptive testing. The second part should provide a summative decision about the potential to practice. There are many reasonable alternatives for assessing this aspect of competence.

Third, in acknowledging that the practice of a profession requires much more than achievement of reasonable outcomes and adequate potential, recertification and relicensure should ensure the interpersonal and moral characteristics of the practitioner. This goal can be achieved by a credentials review and by peer and client ratings of performance. Considerable work remains on establishing reasonable measures of this important aspect of competence.

PART TWO

Meeting New Requirements
Through
Professional Education

These next five chapters pull together the challenges posed in Part One and suggest how professional curricula might respond to them.

In Chapter Five, Sally Hixon Cavanaugh sets the stage with a wide-ranging critique of where and how professional curricula fall short of the new requirements. She urges several fundamental changes to help resolve the "education-practice discontinuity," including more practice-oriented learning, a larger role for program evaluation in curriculum improvement, and an educational research agenda that is more multidisciplinary in focus and more naturalistic in method.

In Chapter Six, Robert A. Armour and Barbara S. Fuhrmann propose a new definition for liberal education, one that has major implications for how we think about the skills and perspectives needed in today's society. Armour and Fuhrmann argue that liberal learning, far from being the sole concern of undergraduate education, is the underpinning of effective professional education as well, and they describe how liberal learning goals can be adapted for, and assessed in, specific professional curricula.

105

In Chapter Seven, David T. Ozar takes on professional ethics, long a part of the formal credo of every profession but often relegated to a peripheral role in professional schools. He describes the nature of professional obligation, debunks some common misconceptions about professional ethics education, and then sets forth sensible goals and educational strategies. Ethics can be taught, Ozar argues, and learned.

In Chapter Eight, Charles E. Wales, Anne H. Nardi, and Robert A. Stager consider the difficult task of teaching problem solving, long a mainstay of the professional's art. Their chapter is specific and practical and thus complements Ilene B. Harris's discussion of the need for greater attention to reflective practice in Chapter Two and Sally Hixon Cavanaugh's call for more practice-oriented learning in Chapter Five.

In Chapter Nine, Robert Rippey describes what professional education in universities could learn from professional education in corporations. Corporate settings, often highly suspect to the academic community, nonetheless offer intriguing models of education that are worth considering, and, as Rippey points out, these models are often based more on established principles of teaching and learning than are the models found in academe.

CHAPTER 5

Connecting Education
and Practice

Sally Hixon Cavanaugh

Current criticism of professional education's performance in preparing graduates for professional practice environments is wide-ranging (Brown, 1988; Carter, 1983; Dinham and Stritter, 1986; Edwards, 1988; Grabowski, 1983; Halpern, 1982; Porter and McKibbin, 1988; Tomain and Solimine, 1990; Watson, Meyer, and Wotman, 1987). The criticism is long-standing as well. The poor relationship between course grades and occupational success was reported more than fifteen years ago by Jencks and Riesman (1977); a review of twenty-seven published articles also found no relationship between academic grades and subsequent professional performance for business, education, and medicine graduates (Wingard and Williamson, 1973).

More recently, Dahlgren and Pramling (1985) described mismatches between education program content and the nature of professional demands in first-year practice as perceived by graduates in medicine, business administration, and engineering. In this study, physicians uniformly expressed the need to reorganize knowledge acquired in medical school, shifting from a subdiscipline orientation to an emphasis on more common clinical problems. Engineers and business administrators complained of being underutilized because their jobs called for application of only a small portion of the knowledge and skills learned in school; these professionals further claimed that the theories espoused by their teachers were too simplistic to be useful in dealing with the ambiguities of real-life problems.

Considered collectively, this evidence points to a discontinuity between the education to which aspiring professionals are typically exposed and the nature of work demands encountered in contemporary professional practice. I should acknowledge that the discontinuity is fostered, at least in part, by forces outside the control of professional education. For example, McGuire (this volume) describes how consumerism and demand for greater professional accountability are changing the nature of professional practice. Add to those two factors the proliferation of new knowledge and technological change (see Marshall, this volume) and it is easy to understand the shock felt by many new graduates entering practice.

But the discontinuity is also fostered by professional education's failure to be responsive to the different nature of nonacademic, service-oriented practice environments. Unintentional neglect is bad enough; what is more disturbing is Dinham and Stritter's (1986) comprehensive review of professional education practices, where they found cause to write that "a correspondence between education and practice may or *may not be* the intent of professional education faculties" (p. 953, emphasis added). How can this be if professional education is supposed to produce knowledgeable graduates prepared for entry into contemporary professional practice?

Freidson's (1986) work is helpful in addressing this question. He describes a central characteristic of the organization of professional occupations as the differentiation of members into teachers-researchers, practitioners, and administrators, each with different roles, perspectives, and priorities. While practitioners must effectively be *users* of technical knowledge, teachers-researchers are better characterized as *pursuers* of knowledge. Teachers-researchers, therefore, emphasize knowledge as discrete packages of scientific and technical information. Aspiring professionals become indoctrinated to

these perspectives and priorities in university-based or affiliated academic settings, following which they enter practice in
primarily nonacademic, service-oriented work settings where
they are immersed in the differing roles, perspectives, and
priorities of practitioners and administrators. The academic
context of professional education interferes with the achievement of educational relevance to practice.

My premise is that academic program environments are
incongruent with service-oriented professional work settings,
and that there are three related reasons for this: (1) Professional education faculty and students are pervasively influenced by an academic culture that values and rewards scientific
knowledge and research more highly than applied professional
service skill. (2) The discipline-specific organizational structure of academic institutions serves these scientific knowledge
and research priorities but creates barriers to curriculum integration. (3) The effects of poor curriculum integration are
frequently made worse by an inadequate evaluation methodology that is unable to identify shortcomings of either the individual student or the education program, and thus to direct
student remediation and program improvement efforts. In this
chapter, I discuss some of the organizational and operational
forces prevalent in the academic setting that contribute to the
education-practice discontinuity, and then I present recommendations aimed at resolving this discontinuity.

Roots of the Education-Practice Discontinuity

The forces that keep education and practice apart have a long
history, and they will be difficult to reverse. Three of the most
fundamental forces are the academic culture, the dominance
of research as a valued faculty activity, and the traditional
organization of professional curricula.

Influences of the Academic Culture on Professional Education

Professional education is profoundly influenced by the culture
of academic institutions because the education programs are

situated within the larger bureaucracy of higher education. The culture of this system holds the pursuit and generation of new knowledge according to the rules, norms, procedures, and traditions of the scientific method as the overarching goal. The omnipotent status of scientific knowledge is reflected in the reward and advancement mechanisms for faculty, which place nearly exclusive emphasis on research and publication productivity at the expense of teaching expertise, instructional effectiveness, and other contributions to curriculum effectiveness.

One effect of this emphasis on research and publication is the acquisition of specialized knowledge, to which I have already alluded. A related effect is its implicit influence in role modeling. The importance of educators as role models is well recognized; typically, long before professional education programs link students with practitioners, the students have been markedly influenced by professionals pursuing *academic* careers.

This is not to say that the research activities of professionals who pursue academic careers are unimportant; rather, the challenge to professional education is to improve the integration of academic scholarship with an educational process suitable to preparing professionals for contemporary, service-oriented, dynamic, and demanding practice environments. I believe, as do Lynton and Elman (1987), that academic professionals are ideally suited to help the professions adapt to the demands of proliferating data, information, knowledge, and technology in modern society. But this type of assistance will require higher education to adopt a broader operational definition of scholarship.

Influences of Research Priorities on Professional Education

A scholar may be described as a person with great learning in a particular subject who is skilled in academic work; scholarship may be described as the methods and achievements characteristic of scholars and academic work. Certainly, discipline-oriented scientific inquiry is a worthy scholarly activity, but so too effective teaching ability and contributions to professional practice should be highly valued as worthy scholarly achievements of faculty. Overall, the reward and advancement system for faculty should incorporate a less restricted operational definition of scholarship and be better balanced so that both the research and teaching-learning missions of higher education are valued more equitably.

In a special report published by The Carnegie Foundation for the Advancement of Teaching, Boyer (1990, p. xii) states that "the most important obligation now confronting the nation's colleges and universities is to break out of the tired old teaching versus research debate and define, in more creative ways, what it means to be a scholar." He argues that to define and measure faculty scholarship in terms of research publications is much too restrictive and proposes instead a much broader definition, discussed in detail by Rice and Richlin (this volume).

Lynton and Elman (1987) similarly call for higher education to adopt a more utilitarian perspective on scholarship in order to meet the knowledge needs of modern society. These authors advise that it would be useful for faculty to engage in more "applied scholarship," both in their teaching and other professional activities, "because the nature and importance of knowledge in modern society are changing both quantitatively and qualitatively" (p. 1). They argue that faculty involvement in aggregating, interpreting, and disseminating data and information for external knowledge applications, should be valued equitably with original discipline-based research.

In evaluating business management schools, Porter and McKibbin (1988) cited the need for a better internal-external balance with regard to faculty scholarship activities, but they note that this is difficult within higher education because external areas "do not clearly belong to any single discipline" (p. 318). Indeed, the fragmentation of faculties into distinct disciplines is common in higher education, a feature of what Jencks and Riesman (1977) refer to as the monolithic status system in American universities wherein the higher education system is based on the model of the large, research university. Lynton and Elman (1987) explain that during the post–World War II growth in higher education, newer institutions strived to gain academic respectability by adopting the traditional academic department structure and research goals of established institutions. But they warn that this approach does not accommodate the ways in which disciplines need to relate to one another and does not acknowledge the variety of ways in which scientific knowledge must be applied to the needs of contemporary society.

But higher education's academic discipline structure, and its focus on research and publication as tickets to faculty advancement, are deeply ingrained. Despite the growing recognition that closer ties are needed among teachers-researchers, practitioners, and administrators in order to address the increasingly complex and dynamic nature of professional practice, it is unlikely that the fundamental structure of higher education will be revamped in any major way. A more feasible course is to broaden the system of priorities and rewards for faculty. For example, Lynton and Elman (1987) propose that institutions establish two streams of funding, one of which would support projects that are problem oriented and cut across disciplinary lines. As long as this second stream is not ad hoc, second-class, or the resource base solely for non–tenure track faculty, it would help make legitimate scholarly activities that are not discipline specific and would foster curriculum integration.

Barriers to Curriculum Integration in Professional Education

Because most professional education curricula are organized by discipline, they are presented as loose aggregates of discipline-specific components. Students in these programs typically progress through a series of courses; each course addresses a specialized body of scientific knowledge, and each is taught as if the students were preparing to become specialists in that area. Given this arrangement, the dominant instructional approach is for faculty to profess on the scientific knowledge and research considered most important to their particular disciplines, reflecting the influence of their own preparation for, and pursuit of, careers in academia. For example, the faculty member responsible for providing a course in sociology teaches students as if they were preparing to become sociologists.

Clearly, the approach of designing a professional education curriculum by drawing on faculty members from different academic departments and asking them to provide the content pieces has major problems. Whereas most students will practice in problem-oriented environments, addressing situations that cannot be neatly packaged by subject area, they study in discipline-oriented environments (Carter, 1983). Brown's (1988) profile of the typical medical school curriculum reflects how the academic culture creates barriers to curriculum integration, and it generalizes well to the model employed in many other professional education programs: the curriculum is composed of segments of specialized knowledge, each segment is commonly taught by specialists, and assessment focuses primarily on knowledge acquisition. Wurman (1989, p. 150) claims that the "extraordinary emphasis on short-term memory at the expense of long-term understanding" is pervasive throughout our educational system.

Perhaps in recognition of the inherently poor relationship of this type of learning to practice, the designers of professional education curricula have traditionally incorporated experiential learning (practica, clinical education, field experiences, apprenticeships, and so on) to bridge the gap between knowledge and application to professional practice settings. These experiences are also intended to develop technical skills, and to provide encounters in which the student "assimilates the rich fabric of socialization, interpersonal skills, moral reasoning, and attitudes distinguishing the profession's members" (Dinham and Stritter, 1986, p. 955). These are truly lofty goals and ask much from educational experiences that are segmentally provided toward the end of the program or occur only intermittently throughout. Additionally, it is widely recognized that training sites used for this purpose tend to have inherent limitations: they do not represent typical professional practice environments well, and student experiences are uneven or skewed (Brown, 1988; Gallagher and Searle, 1989, LaFrance, 1987).

Summary

Academic institutions create a culture in which the aims of education programs are placed secondary to the goals and position of the institution within the academic community. Bloom (1988) characterizes this arrangement as a dominance of structure over ideology and describes the problem as one in which "the protection of territorial domains supercedes the achievement of educational goals as the driving force of the institution" (p. 301). The organization of academic departments by discipline, coupled with institutional adherence to a narrow definition of scholarship, influences faculty roles and priorities, which in turn influence the teaching and learning process in professional education programs. In sum, higher education's organization by academic discipline serves to facilitate research productivity, but it does not lend itself well to the development of flexible integrated learning that students need to function effectively in complex and dynamic professional practice environments.

Toward Resolving the Education-Practice Discontinuity

The problems of an academic culture that is unresponsive to practice needs, and a discipline-specific organizational structure that blocks curriculum integration, call for solutions at many levels. One fundamental solution is to reevaluate faculty roles and priorities and to define scholarship more broadly. Another fundamental solution is to change the teaching and learning practices in professional education. Curriculum change is the common thread in the following five recommendations.

Recommendation 1: Professional Education Must Help Students Develop an Effective System for Learning That Will Facilitate Their Transition from Education into Practice

We should not assume that professional education students possess sufficient learning skills at the time of entrance to the program. These students have demonstrated an academic ability, but their learning has been directed toward advancement to still higher levels of formal education. Within this traditional design, academic achievement is a central concern, and, indeed, much of the standardized testing used to make advancement decisions is intended to predict future academic achievement. But professional education is responsible for preparing aspiring professionals for a lifetime of practice, commonly without further formal academic training. Professional education must therefore develop students' understanding of, and mechanisms for, self-directed, lifelong learning.

The point is that formal academic and continuing professional education programs merely represent two tangible ways in which professionals pursue learning. Considerably more learning takes place on a daily basis, through reading and discussions with colleagues, as well as by experience in everyday practice. The challenge is thus to render these latter forms of learning effective because the issues and problems faced in professional practice arise in unique and varied forms, entail considerable uncertainty, and are rarely amenable to solution by deterministic application of standardized knowledge (see Bennett and Fox, this volume).

Therefore, the acquisition of technical knowledge through formal academic training is better viewed as necessary but wholly insufficient in the development and maintenance of professional expertise. While knowledge acquisition is an important component of the continuum intended to link professional education and practice, student development of effective mechanisms for self-directed, lifelong learning is key to the cohesiveness of the continuum. This cohesiveness should be the ultimate goal of all involved in professional education, because learning is a necessary part of practice throughout professional life.

*Recommendation 2: Professional Education Must Integrate
Problem-Solving Experiences with Knowledge Acquisition in
Order to Emphasize the Continuous Need to Utilize and
Apply Knowledge in Practice*

It is customary for professional education programs to supplement traditional didactic instruction and experiential learning with problem- or case-based methods, or with one or more of a wide variety of simulation techniques (for example, role-playing exercises, responsive laboratory models that can be manipulated, and written or computerized professional practice simulations). These methods and techniques generally allow for greater instructional control and standardization than is possible in experiential learning environments but at the same time attempt to provide lifelike problems for students to solve. The often-stated aim of these instructional methodologies is to develop professional problem-solving ability.

Although the information-processing theory of problem solving offers great insight into cognitive structures and processes involved in human problem solving (Simon and Newell, 1971), there is no method for teaching this ability per se, and, indeed, there is controversy as to whether problem-solving ability can even be taught. Only a very few gross characteristics of the human information-processing system are invariant across tasks and problem solvers (Simon and Newell, 1971), but experience with the type of problems to be solved is known to be important in successful problem-solving behavior. For example, the positive effects of contextual experience with the types of professional problems to be solved have been demonstrated in the problem-solving abilities of physicians and medical students (Elstein, Shulman, and Sprafka, 1978), law students (Alderman, Evans, and Wilder, 1981; Nathanson, 1989), and clinical psychologists (Hammond, Hursch, and Todd, 1964). Thus, any sustained instructional efforts must use a wide range of problem contexts and emphasize those most likely to be encountered in day-to-day professional practice.

Developments in cognitive psychology, coupled with recent computer and videodisk technologies may soon offer new instructional approaches to training novices in problem-solving methods. The Cognition and Technology Group at Vanderbilt (1990) has reported on the formative development of "anchored instruction," which incorporates these technologies in simulated apprenticeship-type training to "help students develop the confidence, skills and knowledge necessary to solve problems and become independent thinkers and learners" (p. 2). The approach is consonant with the concept of situated cognition (Brown, Collins, and Duguid, 1989), emphasizing apprenticeship training that focuses on everyday cognition and authentic tasks with the aim of creating effective, contextual learning experiences.

It is noteworthy that the discussion of situated cognition and anchored instruction includes reference to Whitehead's (1929) description of the "inert knowledge" problem, which is defined as "knowledge that can usually be recalled when people are explicitly asked to do so, but is not used spontaneously in problem solving even though it is relevant" (Cognition and Technology Group at Vanderbilt, 1990, p. 2). In essence, this problem typifies what we seek to overcome in preparing professionals for practice. Anchored instruction is designed to activate inert knowledge by guiding students in the discovery of knowledge useful in solving a variety of problems. As contrasted with case-based instruction, in which each case is intended to represent a larger problem domain, anchored instruction is a sustained exploration of complex problems; and by exploring the same problem setting from multiple perspectives, students experience how knowledge and information are used to identify and solve problems.

However, it is worth a note of caution that simply incorporating new technology or making incremental curriculum additions in the form of one or two "capstone" courses provided late in the professional preparation of students will not go very far in resolving the education-practice discontinuity. If methods such as problem-based or case-based learning, anchored instruction, or other simulation-based techniques are implemented only cosmetically in the curriculum, they will not succeed in diminishing the contextual divergence between education and practice. So long as curriculum structure and instructional approaches remain fragmented by a disciplinary emphasis, academically oriented knowledge acquisition (rather than practitioner-oriented knowledge utilization) will win out as the predominantly reinforced student behavior.

Wales, Nardi, and Stager (this volume) discuss the importance of having students recognize knowledge as a means, rather than the end, in learning. These authors provide an excellent discussion of the seminal ideas of Dewey ([1910] 1933) and Schön (1983, 1987), and they present a related process model that can be incorporated into a teaching strategy aimed at developing critical thinking and problem-solving skills.

Recommendation 3: Professional Education Should Embrace a Pluralism in Research Paradigms and Seek to Integrate Research Activities with Professional Education and Practice Concerns

Dinham and Stritter (1986) have delineated a three-dimensional "practical research agenda" that demonstrates the need for professional education research to address the relationship between learning experiences and the professional practice characteristics to be developed. Multidisciplinary professional education research may consequently facilitate a broader conception of scholarship given its orientation toward real-world professional practice. Because applied research in complex and multifaceted settings is fraught with problems that may be more intellectually challenging than are addressed in traditional forms of scholarship, such research deserves academic parity.

However, the real world is "messy," and a difficult problem is "how to bring to bear high-level, scholarly research on issues not rooted in traditional disciplinary fields and hence not particularly amenable to vigorous and well-accepted methodological approaches" (Porter and McKibbin, 1988, p. 318). For example, the traditional research approach (the empirical or positivist paradigm) has its origins in the natural sciences and emphasizes experimental control in conjunction with empirical measurement in order to seek causal explanations; this framework often requires the research to be reductionist or fragmentary in nature. Keeves (1988, p. 5) argues that a rigid scientific approach to education research is incomplete and inadequate due to the complex nature of education problems in which "many variables are necessary to describe antecedent forces, mediating conditions, and the products or outcomes of the educational process." He describes an alternative paradigm developed from the humanities that emphasizes holistic and qualitative information in order to provide understanding and interpretation rather than causal explanation.

Keeves (1988) also argues that although there are methodological distinctions between scientific and humanistic approaches to research, the two approaches can be applied in a complementary manner to accomplish pragmatic, problem-oriented education research; when jointly applied in well-designed research programs, causal explanation may be achieved pursuant to (or in tandem with) a developing understanding and interpretation of education phenomena. Ultimately, theory construction will require experimental procedures, but investigations conducted according to alternative paradigms should not be undervalued as they may provide results highly useful in the short run by enhancing our understanding of the education process. Indeed, Eisner (1992, pp. 29–30) has expressed well the need for an open acceptance of pluralism in research paradigms: "It wasn't very long ago when the idea of using narrative to account for the way in which the educational world turned was regarded as essentially outside the world of knowledge. . . . Yet today, narrative and other forms of qualitative inquiry are regarded as legitimate, indeed most appropriate, ways to address particular kinds of problems and issues. . . . My point here is that the unexamined acceptance of conventional methods is the surest way to generate conventional research."

Recommendation 4: Professional Education Should Study and Utilize Program Evaluation Methodology in Order to Monitor and Improve Educational Effectiveness and Relevance to Practice

It may be that the exclusive method of choice is not research at all. Dinham and Stritter (1986) noted that many of the studies included in their review could be classified as evaluations due to their limited generalizability. Nevertheless, these evaluations tended to emulate the traditional research process and, therefore, to provide a fragmented, snapshot view of the education process under at least somewhat contrived conditions. The integration of naturalistic inquiry methods may help to alleviate some of these shortcomings, but an evaluation process of high utility for assessing program effectiveness and directing improvements needs to be broader in scope and longer in duration and to address the many complexities of the education process.

The emerging field of education program evaluation has much to offer professional education. So-called systematic evaluation (Stufflebeam and Shinkfield, 1985) views an education program as a system of interrelated components designed to produce a designated output (such as a graduate professional well prepared to function in complex practice environments). Moreover, a system approach to program evaluation is very different from one-shot evaluations of an instructional method, assessment technique, or the like. For example, Stufflebeam's classic context-input-process-product (CIPP) model takes a systems view of education and human services that is oriented toward providing ongoing evaluation as a tool for continuous program improvement (Stufflebeam and Shinkfield, 1985). The Evaluation Training Consortium Project at Western Michigan University offers an improvement-oriented program evaluation model based on stages of training within an education program; the results of this project describe different kinds of evaluation activities that are appropriate to assess the effectiveness of each stage and the integration of training functions (Brinkerhoff, Brethower, Hluchyj, and Nowakowski, 1983).

Stufflebeam and Shinkfield (1985) also suggest that evaluation studies should be planned with regard for how findings might be useful in promoting the understanding of phenomena and thereby contribute (or lead) to research activities, as well as to assessments and improvements of program quality. Shadish, Cook, and Leviton (1991) point out that "evaluations often provide partial probes of theoretical ideas" (p. 9), and that although program evaluation may be considered a practice-driven field, it "has moved toward greater theoretical breadth and sophistication over the last two decades" (p. 20). They present a cogent review of the more enduring theories of program evaluation, noting that evaluation "is just one part of a complex, interdependent, nonlinear set of problem-solving activities" (p. 21) and that the kinds of evaluation questions addressed, as well as the types of methods used, are influenced by the evaluation theory chosen. Program evaluation has emerged as a distinct field of scholarly inquiry, promoting continuing scholarly efforts to foster our understanding of, as well as to refine, evaluation theory and practice. Professional education provides fertile ground for such pursuits.

It is important to stress that effective program evaluation is not the independent effort of an individual; just as research endeavors are strengthened by teamwork and collaboration (in part due to the intellectual and logistical demands of systematic inquiry), so too are well-designed and well-conducted program evaluations. A participatory methodology from the field of curriculum studies has been gaining attention for its usefulness in addressing problems of curriculum integration in professional education. Deliberative curriculum inquiry engages a group of individuals in rational deliberation in the spirit of Schön's reflective practice model—in this case, the practice of curriculum evaluation. The group is purposely diverse so that multiple perspectives are incorporated, including perspectives of learners and teachers, as well as those pertaining to subject matter and the context of education and practice. Harris (this volume) discusses deliberative curriculum inquiry at length, revealing its utility as a nonempirical approach to the study of curriculum and its potential for facilitating curriculum integration. In brief, the power of deliberative curriculum inquiry derives from the skillfulness and diversity of the participant group and the nature of the deliberation process, which is designed to educate participants, generate alternative solutions, and build consensus concerning a course of action. Indeed, the process is integrative and holds promise for overcoming barriers to curriculum integration in professional education.

Group-based methods such as deliberative curriculum inquiry, and others with the similar characteristic of bringing together carefully selected individuals who represent a diversity of perspectives (such as nominal and focus groups), should be highly useful for program evaluation efforts aimed at better integration of education and practice. Program evaluation endeavors operationalized in this manner are also appealing for their congruence with the concepts of total quality management and continuous quality improvement, which have been utilized in business and industry for some time and are now increasingly being applied in the service-oriented professional practice sector. These methods characteristically emphasize systematic, rational analysis focused on interrelated process issues and involve multidisciplinary groups in participant-oriented problem solving aimed at building teamwork and improving quality.

Recommendation 5: Professional Education Should Use Assessment Primarily to Diagnose Student and Practitioner Learning Needs

Frederiksen (1984) describes how testing has become an integral part of accountability in education and traces the onset of this development to 1965 when the Elementary and Secondary Education Act was passed, requiring federally funded programs to incorporate evaluation. Indeed, the early methodology in program evaluation focused on the congruence between learning outcomes and behavioral objectives, rendering testing nearly synonymous with the notion of program evaluation. Although this narrow view of program evaluation is no longer held, testing still greatly influences the teaching and learning that take place both in professional school and in practice. Frederiksen (1984) terms the influences of testing on teaching and learning "the real test bias" and summarizes the situation as follows: "Thus, tests tend to increase the time and effort spent in learning and teaching what the tests measure and (to the extent that amount of time and effort is fixed) decrease efforts to learn and teach skills not measured by the test. A possible consequence is that the abilities that are most easily and economically tested become the ones that are most taught" (p. 193).

Clearly, testing can be seen to affect teaching and learning and to be intricately entwined with accountability. In professional education, faculty hold students accountable for learning the use of tests, educational programs are in turn held accountable for student learning as demonstrated on licensure and certification tests, and, concomitantly, practitioners are held accountable to demonstrate their capacity for professional practice by these same standardized tests. (McGaghie, this volume, underscores the pervasive role of testing in professional competence evaluation.) Because testing is explicitly linked to teaching, learning, and accountability, the need to achieve a passing standard of performance (either in the form of a singular test score or as derived from a combination of test scores) makes each test situation a high-stakes hurdle that overshadows the utility of testing as an effective learning experience.

But this is not to say that testing per se is inherently negative; rather, it is predominantly the manner in which assessment is operationalized, test outcomes reported, and decisions rendered on the basis of test outcomes that interferes with potential learning. Clearly, there is an overreliance on tests of lower-level cognitive abilities in the professions; multiple-choice examinations are the single, most widely utilized form of assessment. My purpose here is not to debate the potential psychometric and logistical advantages of this test format, nor to deny that demonstrated mastery of a technical knowledge base is a necessary component of the repertoire of professional ability. However, it is clear that multiple-choice tests are inherently limited to the assessment of well-defined tasks and problems, focus on knowledge acquisition nearly exclusively, and, in general, bear a minimal relationship to performance in professional practice. Consequently, the widespread use of multiple-choice tests in professional education and external professional evaluation imparts the wrong emphasis to students and practitioners—a premium is placed on demonstrated knowledge acquisition at the expense of higher-order cognitive abilities and affective skills required for analyzing and solving problems in complex professional situations. Furthermore, of course, this testing fails to be a functional learning experience.

There is a proper role for multiple-choice tests in student and practitioner evaluation, however. For example, in the formative development of knowledge structures, such as when students must master factual information that is novel to them (for example, terminology, definitions, and procedural rules), well-constructed multiple-choice tests may be the method of choice, though the potential to identify learning deficiencies from the tests must be realized. Too often the test results are merely relayed in the form of single scores with little or no insight provided as to areas of deficiency. For example, because faculty wish to preserve the security of items for later use, typically students either are not provided with copies of the test for their own review or else are permitted such a review but only by special arrangement, which is often inconvenient to manage for both student and teacher.

In order to emphasize the role of testing as a learning experience and to allow for the potential to recognize errors, a guided review of each test following scoring should be part of the instructional process. Even if test questions cannot be released, the test can be reviewed in class. A fruitful way to do this is to organize the guided review by items of similar content, paying particular attention to the content that gave students the most difficulty. If the test in fact addressed important knowledge, there is implicit learning value in this exercise: it can reinforce important facts and concepts for those who answered correctly, solidify information for those who may have successfully guessed correct answers, and remediate learning deficiencies for the remaining others. Moreover, the faculty member may gain useful insights into learning difficulties pertaining to course content and be better able to tailor instruction. Overall, the importance of timely and sufficient test performance feedback in facilitating learning cannot be overstated.

Multiple-choice tests may also be appropriate as *one* component of licensure and certification testing. In the optimal case, the test would be released to the candidate with his or her score report, an answer key, and a delineation of questions answered incorrectly. Even if standardized multiple-choice test booklets cannot be released, greater attention needs to be paid to providing feedback that reveals deficiencies as specifically as possible. This may be done in the form of subscores by carefully defined and delineated content areas; either additionally or as an alternative, a brief description of the content addressed by each incorrectly answered question can be provided.

Most important, however, there must be much less reliance on multiple-choice tests and more emphasis on assessments that have a high fidelity to professional practice situations, and that are therefore perceived by students and practitioners as useful in providing feedback for improvement of their professional practice (assuming that meaningful feedback is provided). There has been increasing movement in this direction, both in professional education and certification. Norcini and Shea (this volume) and McGaghie (this volume) describe some of these efforts and further elucidate issues and concerns related to this recommendation.

Professional education should take the lead in making education and evaluation a continuous loop. Testing should be reconfigured as an integral part of the learning process, with students provided timely and useful feedback. In concert with the aim to develop lifelong learning skills, students in professional education should be helped to maximize the use of assessment information for perceptive self-evaluation. Through faculty involvement in licensure and certification activities, a reorientation of standardized testing to facilitate learning should also be pursued. Moreover, if professionals, as students, experience the value of testing as a learning tool, they may grow to expect (even demand) continuing evaluations of competence. Perhaps then, with efforts to more directly link licensure, certification, and recertification assessments to practice, professional competence evaluation could effectively contribute to the lifelong learning of professionals.

CHAPTER 6

Confirming the Centrality
of Liberal Learning

Robert A. Armour
Barbara S. Fuhrmann

The requirement that students complement their professional major with liberal education differentiates a college or university from institutes designed to train students in specific professional programs. The intent to develop liberally educated graduates, rather than competent technicians, is what makes a university a university.

For too long, educators in the professions have focused narrowly on the development of their students' professional knowledge, skills, and attitudes and have left the fulfillment of the broader aims of education to others. In one sense, this focus is entirely appropriate since professional programs are usually filled with required courses; and, of course, universities hire others to teach general education. Professional educators quickly acknowledge the importance of liberal education, and in fact, most accreditation agencies of professional programs require a substantial liberal core. Most often, however, professional faculty do not understand the importance of liberal education beyond the insistence that their students be able to think, compute, and write. Lunchtime conversation among professional educators is often filled with complaints about the

126

failure of the English department to teach basic writing skills or of the history department to teach anything that a person can use in the professions.

This widely accepted division between general education requirements and professional requirements does not leave the student with much of an understanding of how general and professional education come together. Our position is that the concept of *liberal learning* provides the common denominator between general and professional education. Liberal learning is not the territory of one group of faculty but rather the responsibility of all who teach. Too often, the concept of liberal learning appears to professional educators as fuzzy, intangible, and mysterious. (To liberal arts educators, it too often seems like just another day's work, but that topic is another chapter in another book.) The purpose of this chapter is to define the concept of liberal learning in essential terms and to invite professional educators to think seriously about their responsibility for liberal education. If we reduce liberal learning to its essence and demystify it, professional educators will understand that they already play a significant role in the liberal education of their majors. With effort and an understanding of the problem, they can then greatly improve the broader education that their students receive.

Liberal learning is a complex and even contradictory process. To reduce the process to its core essence is to risk overlooking essential features of the concept at its fringes. For this reason, we invite professional educators to sift with us through some of the thinking about liberal education in order to reach a consensus in definition. We discuss as well some common misconceptions of liberal learning.

In simple terms, our point of view is that liberal learning fosters thinking skills in students, provides them with an intellectual and social context for that thought, helps them develop and question values, and provides them with the skills to communicate the results of the thought process. We develop these four essential components of liberal learning later in the chapter and suggest ways that professional educators might enhance their value to students in professional programs.

The Essence of Liberal Learning

In our view, the essence of liberal learning encompasses that which develops in students sound thought processes, a context of experiences in which to think, values, and the ability to communicate.

What Liberal Learning Is Not

Before looking at what liberal learning is, it is important that we eliminate some confusion by showing what it is not. Too often conventional concepts of liberal education are both simplistic and convenient. Here we discuss three common misconceptions about liberal learning.

First, liberal education is sometimes equated with *general education*. General education is the collection of courses, typically from the arts and sciences, from which students must choose one-third to one-half of all of their courses, whereas liberal learning provides a broader framework for thought that frees students from limitations on their thinking. General education clearly contributes to liberal learning but it is not the entirety of it. In addition, the mere exposure to general education courses is no guarantee that a student will achieve any sense of liberation in thought.

General education requirements represent the areas of study with which any well-educated person should be familiar. In many colleges and universities today, the courses are categorized by academic discipline, and students are required to take a specific number of courses from each grouping, such as literature, history, foreign languages, and mathematics. Frequently, the lists present a smorgasbord of possibilities; in 1991, students at one large university could choose from a list specifically naming 272 courses, and many other unnamed courses (any sociology course, for example). If the advising and the student's course selection are not good, these general education experiences may be disconnected and have little to do with liberal learning as we are here defining it. The needs for general education—and, by extension in some people's minds, for liberal education—are defined in terms of *coverage* and *breadth.* There is, according to the theory, a need for coverage of specific topics necessary for a student to be considered educated or to follow advanced study. One must know the periodic table, basic algebra, and the principles of economics before being able to master higher science, statistics, and the fundamentals of management. One must take physics before becoming an engineer and biology before becoming a nurse. One must cover basic knowledge before going on to higher education. And one must have breadth. A lawyer must know something of history, political science, psychology, ethics, sociology, economics, and communications (especially speaking and writing). His or her practice could well go in the direction of the environment, which would call for an understanding of science, or of corporate mergers, which would call for an understanding of finance, pension funds, and health plans. A professional must have a breadth of education in order to muster an array of knowledge on behalf of her or his specific professional skills. Liberal learning acknowledges the value of coverage and breadth, but they are not the defining factors of liberal learning.

Second, liberal learning is sometimes confused with the *liberal arts.* The liberal arts, for the sake of simplicity, may be considered the academic disciplines that develop general intellectual ability and that deal in a general way with culture. Most often the liberal arts are thought of as English (or literature), history, art history, languages, philosophy, and religion. They are seen in contrast to other disciplinary groupings such as the physical and the social sciences. Liberal learning makes use of all of these disciplines but goes far beyond the confines of any one grouping. It is not defined by or confined to particular disciplines. As A. Bartlett Giamatti, former president of Yale University (and former baseball commissioner), put it, "To study the liberal arts or the humanities is not necessarily to acquire a liberal education unless one studies these and allied subjects in a spirit that, as [John Henry] Newman has it, seeks no immediate sequel, that is independent of a profession's advantage" (1988, pp. 120–121).

Third, liberal learning is not *religion.* Caroline Bird (1975,

p. 10) caught the essence of this problem when she observed
that the way some discuss the liberal arts makes them sound like
"a religion in every sense of the word. When people talk about
them, their language becomes elevated, metaphorical, extrava-
gant, theoretical, and reverent." What is true for the liberal arts
is no less true of the broader concept of liberal learning. Liberal
learning has been seen by some critics of higher education as
the messianic antidote to creeping vocationalism, to the disar-
ray of most academic programs, to the rejection of traditionally
revered texts and interpretations, to lowered standards for both
culture and education. Listen, for example, to the language of
philosopher Brand Blanshard (1973, p. 43): "Does anything of
[the classical period] remain? Yes, the Greek spirit remains.
The thought of Plato remains, the art of Sophocles, the logic
and ethics of Aristotle. Literature, it has been said, is the
immortal part of history. No doubt there were hardheaded
practical men in Athens who stopped before the door of Plato's
academy and asked what was the use of it all. They and their
names have vanished; the little Academy became a thousand
academies among nations unborn. There is a moral, I think, in
this history. It is the usefulness, the transcendent usefulness, of
useless things."

We must be careful not to promise too much for liberal
learning. It is the heart of an educated person's education, but
it is not by itself going to save the world from the sweep of
vocationalism, from the disunity of curricula, from lowered
standards, or from war, pestilence, and hunger. Liberal learning will not save the world from what threatens it, but it will
enable humans to have at least a decent chance to bring
change. It will, if diligently pursued and properly understood,
enable us to understand and analyze our professions, our
society, and our lives.

What Liberal Learning Is

The characteristics of general education, the liberal arts, and
liberal learning as religion are tangential to the fullest meaning
of liberal learning. Nevertheless, those characteristics help us
understand our term more exactly. So too do numerous schol-

ars who have tried to explain the impact of liberal studies on students. Blanshard (1973) works energetically to prove that liberal learning is useful. He argues that liberal studies are useful in three ways: "First, they are useful *directly* because they satisfy some of the deepest wants in our nature. Secondly, they are useful *indirectly* through enabling us to borrow the best insights and standards of others. Thirdly, if taken seriously, they may permeate with their influence all our thought and feeling and action" (p. 31). Here he is on to something. It is likely true that liberal learning touches something deep within us, something that is difficult to describe or define. Blanshard mentions several of these needs: the hunger to know, the search for truth, the joy of beauty, the satisfaction of friendship. His general points are useful: liberal studies do reach something deep within us and do expose us to the best that the world has to offer (the debate over what is the best is even itself part of liberal learning, though Blanshard never acknowledges this point). The major problem with his thinking from our point of view is that he sees liberal studies and professional education as opposites, as distinctly different activities. We hold that liberal learning is as much a part of professional education as it is of general studies.

Bratchell and Heald (1966) initiate a more satisfactory approach in their book, *The Aims and Organization of Liberal Studies.* They use the meaning of the word *liberal* to propose a process: "To be liberal is to be free and open-minded, given to reflection and free inquiry. . . . It follows that a liberal education is one that leads to the formation of habits of free inquiry, of reflection, of an unprejudiced search for truth in her many guises" (p. 1). Liberal learning, then, is the study that fosters openness and reflection in the search for truth. They see liberal study as more grounded in this real world than in some idealized world. They see liberal learning as influential in the internalization of society and in the need to deal with social concerns. They encourage an interdisciplinary approach to education and the development of habits of thought that carry through a lifetime. They argue that the needs of vocation and the needs of liberal learning need not be seen as conflicting.

Frederick Stirton Weaver (1991), in his book *Liberal Education,* is concerned with students' critical and individual thinking and sees liberal learning in more intellectual terms than exhibited by earlier thinkers. He sees undergraduate education as fostering habits of mind—mental discipline— that carry over into majors and professions, as well as into everyday life. He believes that knowledge should be "socially constructed, dependent on interpretation, and requiring a context of values to give it meaning" (pp. 53–54). Students should learn that knowledge is complex, multifaceted, and open to interpretation. He proposes a critical inquiry curriculum in which students in both general education and the majors develop and hone critical abilities through training. He does not deny the importance of the coverage-breadth argument, but he takes the concept of liberal learning beyond that debate. General education and professional preparation courses can both train students to develop their abilities in critical inquiry.

Weaver observes that one important effect of liberal learning is enhanced participation in the democratic process. Since the time of Thomas Jefferson and other eighteenth-century thinkers, observers have argued that one advantage of improving one's thinking is the outgrowth of clearer decisions about our national agenda and about the people who are elected to set it. The principle has been demonstrated in our time by such diverse authors as A. Whitney Griswold (1962), former president of Yale, in *Liberal Education and the Democratic Ideal* and Allan Bloom (1987) in *The Closing of the American Mind.* If liberal learning can train people to think clearly, exhibit mental discipline, and work within clearly developed value systems, then it is an article of faith that they will be better citizens and professionals and will lead richer lives.

The dichotomous view of liberal and professional learning held by some critics, such as John Stuart Mill, who advocated the teaching of liberal and professional studies in different sorts of institutions (Bratchell and Heald, 1966), does not hold up when this broader view of liberal learning is understood. As a result of the thinking of scholars such as A. Bartlett Giamatti,

David Riesman, and the participants in the Professional Preparation Network (a project that is discussed later), our contemporary view of the relation between liberal and professional studies is less diverse. General education and professional education are seen as different studies, but liberal learning runs through both of them. Riesman (1986, p. 39) claims that he sees "no inherent distinction between a liberating education in the traditional arts and sciences and a liberating education in such professional fields as engineering, management, or applied art and music." The liberating professor, regardless of discipline, teaches the student more than simply how to do the work of the field. In an address to Yale freshmen, Giamatti (1988, pp. 109–110) eloquently touched on the essence of liberal learning:

> I believe a liberal education is an education in the root meaning of *liberal—liber,* "free"—the liberty of the mind free to explore itself, to draw itself out, to connect with other minds and spirits in the quest for truth. Its goal is to train the whole person to be at once intellectually discerning and humanly flexible, tough-minded and openhearted; to be responsive to the new and responsible for values that make us civilized. It is to teach us to meet what is new and different with reasoned judgment and humanity. A liberal education is an education for freedom, the freedom to assert the liberty of the mind to make itself new for the other minds it cherishes.

We might well ask what a person needs to be free from. The answer is that we must be free from personal rigidity and prejudices that prohibit the quest for truth. And we must be intellectually free from political, religious, and social pressures that attempt to restrict or shape our thinking. Giamatti severely attacks the Moral Majority, the right-wing threat to our intellectual liberties in the 1980s, for its attempts to prescribe what is good for the rest of us out of its sense of what is morally correct. It is entertaining to speculate on what Giamatti would have had to say about the "politically correct" movement of the early 1990s. The major themes of Giamatti's description of liberal studies—the uninhibited quest for truth, the combination of intellectual toughness and human sensitivity, and the ability to confront, even encourage, the new—are central to our view of liberal learning.

The Goals of Liberal Learning

If we look at these past and contemporary critics of education for common threads in their thoughts, we see that the essence of their views of liberal learning concerns the thought process, a context of experiences in which to develop thought and values. From this essence, three primary goals of liberal learning emerge, to which we add a fourth, communication. This latter goal is not much discussed by the scholars mentioned here but is clearly taken for granted by them.

The foremost goal of liberal learning is to teach students to develop and hone critical thinking skills. The quest for truth begins here. Higher-level thinking involves at least the ability to reason without being overpowered by personal biases and experiences, the ability to marshal evidence from outside sources, and the ability to evaluate others' opinions and appreciate the best of them. In order for thinking to be most effective, we must have a variety of experiences to which we can react and address our thoughts. The general education goals of coverage and breadth are of value here insofar as they provide a context for thought. The more we read, the more we see and hear, the more we experience, the larger the context for our thinking and the greater the opportunity for fresh, imaginative, and persuasive thought.

A second goal of liberal learning, then, is to establish the kind of context in which thinking is most valuable. In the best of academic programs, the student-thinker gains valuable exposure to literature, history, social sciences, physical sciences, art, culture in general, and so on. In the worst of situations, this exposure is merely an exercise in choosing courses from general education menus or an exercise in the trivial pursuit of lists of what an educated person is supposed to know, such as the materials proposed by Hirsch (1987). Contrary to this limited vision, there is no one intellectual context that sets the stage for academic thinking. Each person's context is idiosyncratic, which is, of course, one of the factors that makes going to college or working in one an enriching experience. Each person in a classroom can approach a problem from her or his own experiences and set it in a personal context. The resultant variations of analysis, interpretation, and synthesis will stretch and challenge all who participate. But in order for that to happen, there must be some more general context of inquiry. This is not to say that any more general context will do, but if students develop their idiosyncratic contexts within the best available from outside themselves, critical thinking should result.

Thought is not thought without standards with which to measure and evaluate new ideas and experiences. So the third goal of liberal learning is to develop values in students that are appropriate to educated people. It would be foolish to assume that students come to higher education without values, but it is probably safe to assume that few young students have value systems that are fully tried and set. The collegiate experience exposes students to new values and therefore provides a testing ground for all values, both old and new. College study should challenge values, tempt with exciting and appealing values that were taboo in students' earlier lives, teach the importance of personal responsibility for one's values, and demonstrate that values—through the actions that follow from them—have consequences.

Value formation is one of the more controversial features of education. What values get fostered? Whose values? What standards are used to judge them? The answers to these questions vary from age to age and place to place. Some general values, such as those articulated here in regard to critical thinking, are broadly acknowledged and accepted. Others, such as opposition to racism and sexism and support for internationalism, are more recent in their coinage but no less firmly fixed in the value systems of higher education. And still others, such as the fundamentalism of conservative religious institutions and the radicalism of a few colleges and universities, by no means find common acceptance. Even across similar institutions, the differences in values can be great, as in the debate among highly regarded English departments over the issue of the traditional canon versus minority and feminist voices.

The controversies help to focus the role of values in liberal learning. Within the confines of liberal studies, there are some values on which we can generally agree. Few would attempt to codify these values, but most would agree that higher education values the quest for truth, freedom of expression, service to others, a desire for excellence, and so on. Central to an understanding of values, however, is the value that views values as important to the thought process, essential to the development of our society, and always subject to challenge. We value values, but we know that the intellectual process continuously questions, pushes, deconstructs, and reconstructs them. In no place in society does this process occur with better protection of all involved than in institutions of higher education. And nowhere in higher education does it occur with greater frequency or greater inclusiveness than in educational environments devoted to liberal learning. Since liberal learning is not tied to the standards of a particular profession and is by definition multidisciplinary, it is a natural testing ground for ideas. Since liberal learning is not limited or controlled by any professional code (accreditation standards, for example), liberal learners have the freedom to follow wherever the paths of clear and imaginative thinking lead them. This freedom of thought, however, is not a luxury that society can suspend whenever it becomes suspicious of the current directions of learning. Rather, it is a societal necessity that must be protected at all costs.

Finally, we add communication to the goals of liberal learning. The sharpest thinking and the clearest values are of no use if an individual is incapable of communicating them to others. Communication is as fundamental to education as teamwork is to a sports team. Nowhere in education do the skills of reading, writing, speaking, and listening get more attention than in liberal learning. The ability to communicate is essential in both general and professional education.

Students mastering the principles of liberal learning exhibit habits of mind that make intellectual activity a joy and an opportunity for both personal and societal enrichment. The intellectual life of Leonardo da Vinci serves as a model of enlightened use of liberal learning. Levenson (1991, p. 9) described Leonardo's use of learning as follows: "Whether drawing the human face, recording the results of his dissections, or studying plant and animal life, Leonardo always concentrated on the unity underlying nature's diversity. Probing beneath surface appearances, he aimed at uncovering the fundamental laws governing the physical world. By mastering nature's first causes, he believed, man could use them to remake the world." However men and women wish to remake the world—whether through art, medicine, social work, journalism, engineering, or any other profession—the ability to perceive unity amid diversity, to look beneath appearances, and to recognize fundamental laws serves as a foundation for all other learning.

The Professions Look at Liberal Learning

Professional organizations strongly acknowledge the importance of liberal learning for those entering the professions. Their concept of liberal learning may, at times, be limited to the coverage-breadth argument or to a fairly narrow view of general education. There are, however, signs that some professional training programs are looking at the broader picture of liberal learning. In this section, we analyze pronouncements on liberal studies from a variety of professional organizations.

We begin not with professional organizations but with reports from national education advocacy groups that have set the stage for professional reconsideration of the value of liberal studies. In the mid-1980s, several organizations that speak either for prominent education institutions or for the federal government issued reports that were highly critical of American higher education in an effort to bring its deficiencies to the forefront of the national agenda. In all of the reports, high on the lists of obligatory changes was the need to pay more attention to liberal learning.

In 1984, the National Institute of Education issued its report, *Involvement in Learning: Realizing the Potential of American Higher Education*. Among its proposals for improving the state of higher education is the following: "Liberal education requirements should be expanded and reinvigorated to ensure that (1) curricular content is directly addressed not only to subject matter but also to the development of capacities of analysis, problem solving, communication, and synthesis, and (2) students and faculty integrate knowledge from various disciplines" (1984, p. 43). The report recognizes the importance of liberal learning as preparation for professional work: "The best preparation for the future is not narrow training for a specific job, but rather an education that will enable students to adapt to a changing world" (p. 43). It encourages skills in thinking and communication, and knowledge of an intellectual context. And it emphasizes the importance of a student being able to integrate and synthesize what is learned from a variety of disciplines.

A few months later, the Association of American Colleges published *Integrity in the College Curriculum: A Report to the Academic Community* (1985), with Frederick Rudolph as primary author. He and his colleagues blasted the current condition of higher education. They propose as partial remedy additional emphasis on critical analysis, abstract logical thinking, historical consciousness, understanding of mathematical data, as well as international and multicultural experiences. Rudolph and his colleagues also believe that men and women "must make real choices, assume responsibility for their decisions, be comfortable with their own behavior and know why" (p. 20).

Hacker (1985), in a review of these reports, raises the question of how a curriculum can develop skills in thinking and analysis. Who should teach it and where? Hacker points out that many faculty claim to be developing these skills in their students now, but the question remains about how well students can perform them.

Given the nature of his former position as head of the National Endowment for the Humanities, it is no surprise that William J. Bennett (1984) supports increased attention to liberal learning in *To Reclaim a Legacy*. He clearly wants the role of the humanities—admittedly, only one part of liberal learning—enhanced. He decries reduced requirements in history and foreign languages and blames faculty and administrators for abdicating their responsibility to our intellectual legacy. This work, along with the other two reports cited, focused national attention on the type of liberal learning available to most students. Professional organizations responded by revisiting their accreditation standards.

To analyze the intent and the practice of liberal education goals and expectations within professional programs, we examined the literature, including accreditation standards, in six professions. We found that the professions do, indeed, value liberal learning, and they express that value in often eloquent language. However, when it comes to practice, the professions succumb to the breadth and coverage approach of requiring distribution credits in traditional general education courses, with little or no attempt to integrate disparate experiences into a whole that ensures liberal learning outcomes. This is not to single out and criticize education in these professions, for the same criticism can just as appropriately be leveled against the traditional disciplines, which also rely on distribution requirements to meet their liberal learning goals. Only very infrequently did we find a concerted effort to develop liberal learning in an integrative fashion either outside or within the major or profession. (Those instances found in the literature are discussed at the end of this chapter.) And whether or not students achieve the goals that are assumed to develop from broad exposure to general education courses is almost never assessed, at least not in any meaningful way.

To illustrate the gap between rhetoric and practice, we note that educators in these professions affirm the goals of liberal learning in their programs but then assume that these goals can be achieved by mere exposure to general education courses. We argue that this assumption is wrong.

In the field of architecture, we found a theoretical explanation for liberal education requirements in the professional program. As stated in the literature from a major university architecture program, the liberal learning goals are to develop problem-solving skills and new ways of thinking, a set of professional values, and skills in self-criticism. Although the rhetoric pays special attention to thinking and cultural values, the assumption is that these skills can be developed within the professional curriculum and through six credits in English, six in mathematics, six in humanities or fine arts, eight in natural sciences, and six in social sciences. That professional preparation is assumed to contribute to the development of these skills is evidenced by the fact that only 20 percent of the students' curriculum is in the area of general education.

In business, the accreditation standards recognize that changes in society are challenging business people. Among the changes are an emerging global economy, conflicting values, changing technology, and demographic diversity. To prepare students to enter useful professional and societal lives, the business curriculum combines the study of business with general education (distribution credits) comprising at least 50 percent of the undergraduate program. Capacities to be developed include written and oral competence; critical thinking; appreciation for the arts, literature, history, and science; and an understanding of technology, value systems, and the international environment. Again it is assumed that these abilities can be developed through student selection of distribution requirements in general education.

Accreditation standards in education demand both breadth and integration; in fact, many states now require that all prospective teachers major in a traditional academic discipline rather than in professional education. In all events, faculty in professional programs are required to work with faculty who teach general education courses in planning and evaluating the general education curriculum. In principle at least, general education constitutes a well-planned sequence of courses and experiences that includes theoretical and practical knowledge gained from study in communications, mathematics, science, history, philosophy, literature, and fine arts. Never-theless, in practice, students are expected to select courses that provide an intellectual foundation in liberal arts and general education, and no inherently integrating experiences are identified.

In an eloquent statement of the "essential knowledge" in the preparation of engineers, Francis J. Cashin (1989, p. 6), former president of the Accreditation Board for Engineering and Technology (ABET), acknowledged the importance of liberal learning for engineers:

> We all recognize the need to educate our new engineers in the finest tradition of a well versed person. The need to learn about other cultures, languages and customs is now essential to the practice of engineering. The seeds to this global awareness are planted in college education.
>
> From Philosophy, we engineers must obtain the working tools of logic and reasoning. We need such essential elements in our education, together with principles of accounting, the concepts of management and the basic theories of economics. Engineers are by their nature managers and team players in dealing with the productive industries of the world but should be exposed to the latest techniques used in practice. Of utmost impor-tance is the need to understand the values of pro-fessionalism and ethics because of the engineer's profound effect on human society and the envi-ronment. This also requires an understanding of the principles of Roman and English law.

ABET accreditation standards support this attitude. They stress the liberal learning goals of (1) a capability to delineate and solve societal problems that are susceptible to engineering treatment, (2) a sensitivity to socially related technological issues, (3) an understanding of the ethical nature of the profes-sion, (4) an appreciation of responsibility to health and safety, and (5) an attitude that supports lifelong learning. Although the standards demand an integrated educational experience, curriculum requirements are limited to one year (thirty-two semester credit hours) in mathematics and physical sciences and one-half year (sixteen credit hours) in humanities and social sciences. The standards also demand written and oral communication skills, and they acknowledge that these skills are not developed only in English courses. There is, however, virtually no direction offered in the standards for how the various outcomes should be attained or assessed.

Like education, journalism and mass communications standards demand balance between professional and general education courses in arriving at professional and liberal outcomes. Over one-half of the curriculum must be taken in the liberal arts and sciences. Again, however, although integration is considered essential, there is no attempt to articulate how such integration might occur and no attempt to assess liberal outcomes; instead, distribution requirements are assumed to support the development of necessary liberal learning abilities.

Finally, of the six professional areas surveyed in this review, standards in pharmacy have the least to say about the role of liberal education. For the baccalaureate in pharmacy, the standards call for a curriculum that provides the student with a basic core of professional knowledge and skills as well as a sound general education base. General education is defined as behavioral, social, and humanistic areas of knowledge, and thirty semester credit hours are required. The pharmacy curriculum assumes no responsibility for the development of liberal outcomes, and, beyond the thirty credit hours, there are no requirements for liberal education.

Taken as a group, these professional programs show a traditional and routine use of the liberal arts. Most of them have generally assumed that some general education is good for students, the way that mothers assume that chicken soup is good for children with colds. The commitment to liberal learning outcomes seems genuine in all of these programs as educators and accreditors for professional programs readily admit that liberal learning adds important ingredients to their curricula. Sometimes the vision of what can be added is limited (ethics, critical thinking, mathematics, and writing); other times the vision is more expansive.

Based on this examination of literature from professional programs, we are concerned about whether students' journeys through what is supposed to be a liberalizing education can be made without a road map. Too often selections from the general education menu are made for reasons that have little to do with where the student is going ("the course fits my schedule," "I like this professor," "that course demands too much writing," and so on). We propose that faculty in professional programs work with their colleagues in the liberal arts to prescribe liberal learning experiences, in both general education and professional courses and experiences, that would best equip students for the future. Such learning would aid students' thought processes by assisting them with the integration of ideas, by providing the broadest possible context for ideas, and by presenting conflicts that result from competing values systems.

Such cooperation can best be developed in an atmosphere that avoids the them versus us syndrome. Faculty in one discipline cannot be permitted to assume that liberal learning is done over there in another discipline, whether English or political science or philosophy. And faculty in the liberal arts cannot be permitted to assume that only they have insights into broad, philosophical subjects. All must remember that liberal learning is best developed within the context of professional education.

In planning students' liberal learning, faculty from both the professional programs and the liberal arts can best serve students by focusing on the four basic elements or goals of liberal studies identified earlier: thinking, context, values, and communication.

Integrating Liberal and Professional Learning

The goals of liberal and professional education can best be achieved when faculty from both areas cooperate. Neither group can, or should, give up the prerogatives—or the essential ways of looking at knowledge—that come with discipline. But each group should look for ways to further the education process by advancing liberal learning beyond the disciplines.

The Professional Preparation Network, directed by Joan Stark and Malcolm Lowther of the University of Michigan and supported by the Fund for the Improvement of Postsecondary Education, brought liberal arts faculty together with faculty from undergraduate professional programs to seek common ground. Stark and Lowther's (1988) report, *Strengthening the Ties That Bind: Integrating Undergraduate Liberal and Professional Study*, is a blueprint for this cooperation. The project identified ten areas of overlap between liberal and professional education and encouraged faculty from both camps to work together to develop these competencies in students. Stated in different terms from those used in this chapter, the following outcomes define liberal learning: communication competence, critical thinking, contextual competence, aesthetic sensibility, professional identity, professional ethics, adaptive competence, leadership capacity, scholarly concern for improvement, and motivation for continued learning. The report defines these outcomes in detail and suggests methods whereby they can be achieved across disciplinary lines. The theoretical and research basis for this project is presented in Stark, Lowther, and Hagerty's (1986) book, *Responsive Professional Education: Balancing Outcomes and Opportunities*.

In a volume that we edited in the New Directions for Teaching and Learning series, *Integrating Liberal Learning and Professional Education* (Armour and Fuhrmann, 1989), faculty and administrators from a variety of institutions described their experiences at uniting liberal and professional studies. The undergraduate professional programs covered included architecture, business, education, engineering, journalism, nursing, pharmacy, and social work. Chapters on these disciplines describe ways that professional faculty and liberal arts faculty have collaborated to try to achieve the ten consensus outcomes of the Professional Preparation Project.

Another project with similar goals was conducted at Syracuse University, under the leadership of Peter Marsh. This project invited faculty from across the campus to discuss ways of breaking down barriers between liberal and professional education. The project had four components: "(1) collaborative enquiry among faculty from a variety of departments and colleges; (2) various forms of communication—visual as well as spoken and written; (3) the identification of some concepts or themes of interest that run through all fields of learning; and (4) the creation of undergraduate courses" (Marsh, 1988b, p. 5). Results of their project are described in Marsh (1988a).

At Virginia Commonwealth University, a general education reform project resulted in the articulation of eight outcomes for general education (competence in communications and mathematics; scientific literacy; understanding of the social environment, values systems, and cultural diversity; appreciation of the historical dimensions of humanity; and the habit of self-exploration). These outcomes apply across all baccalaureate programs, but because there is no universitywide core curriculum, each of the twelve schools in the university is charged with the responsibility for further defining them as they apply to its programs, for addressing them in its professional curriculum and in required general education courses, and for assessing its students' attainment in them in ways that are most meaningful to its programs' goals.

These efforts demonstrate that the goals of liberal learning can be achieved through a variety of means. The ultimate question for educators in the professions is, "How can we ensure that graduates of our programs have developed the skills and attitudes of liberally educated persons as well as the professional knowledge and skills essential to professional practice?" The answer, we propose, lies in close examination of where and how students develop the skills of higher-order thinking, establishing contexts of inquiry, formulating values, and communicating. One reason that we have reduced liberal learning to these four key components is that this small number of goals makes it easier for faculty to study their program requirements to determine how, where, and how well these liberal attributes are developed. A model for such examination

includes the following: (1) *defining* each of the attributes as
appropriate to the particular program; (2) *identifying* where in
the curriculum requirements these attributes are addressed;
(3) *assessing* students' attainment of them, not only in specific
courses but also in terms of the total program; and (4) *using* the
assessment information obtained to revise curriculum and
pedagogy.

For example, all professions value practitioners who have
developed sound communication skills, both written and oral,
and all realize that English and speech faculty can contribute
to, but cannot define, these skills as they apply in a particular
profession. The professional faculty must therefore further
define the communication skills that are essential to the practice of their respective professions. Nurses may need relatively
greater individual counseling skills than do engineers, who
need relatively greater ability to communicate complex ideas in
writing. Only the faculty in a profession can define the liberal
learning skills and knowledge essential to professional practice.
Once the liberal outcomes, in this case, communication skills,
are clearly articulated, the next step is for the faculty in the
profession to identify where in the curricula—the professional
curriculum and the general education curriculum—these communication skills are developed. This step requires collaboration among all those who teach within the program as well as
with the faculty in the liberal arts who teach courses in which
the identified communication skills might also be developed. It
will not be unusual, we think, for faculty to discover that their
implicit communication goals for students are never explicitly
addressed in any required experiences. Such a discovery indicates a need for curriculum reform, even without taking the
next step of assessing students' attainment of the identified
communication skills.

Once specific communication skills are defined, and
once it is clear where in the overall curriculum they are developed, the faculty should turn attention to assessing students'
attainment of the skills throughout the program. The work of
the assessment movement will provide assistance here. Assessment of student goal attainment will identify the strengths and

weaknesses of the program as a whole in developing the necessary skills, with revision of curriculum and pedagogy following from clear identification of programmatic needs.

The assessment movement, which has continued to develop strength and influence over the past decade, has contributed greatly to our understanding of how change occurs. Most significant, practitioners have learned that the very process of discussion of goals for students leads to reform of curriculum and pedagogy. This reform will undoubtedly follow when faculty in the professions clearly define their students' professional needs for competence in thinking, context, values formation, and communication. Of these four goals, communication skills may provide the easiest place to begin. Further definition of student outcomes related to higher-order thinking, context, and values may be more difficult to address, but the very process of articulation will likely stimulate improvement in our willingness as educators to assume responsibility for fostering them in our students.

Our review of practice to date has revealed that faculty in the professions must assume responsibility for more than narrow technical education knowledge and skills. The place to begin is with discussions about liberal learning. The concept of higher-order thinking, the context for professional practice, the development of a critically evaluated system of values, and the skill to communicate within the profession offer a starting point for those discussions.

CHAPTER 7

Building Awareness of
Ethical Standards
and Conduct

David T. Ozar

In the eyes of many professionals, the professions are in deep trouble and the reason is ethics. An increasingly cynical public sees isolated acts of unprofessional conduct vividly portrayed in the media and wonders if such acts are the norm rather than the exception. The public learns of professionals struggling with ethical uncertainties born of new technologies, new legal situations, or other unprecedented circumstances and wonders if the professions really do understand, ethically, what they are doing.

Never mind that the vast majority of professionals conscientiously conform to the ethical standards of their professions. Never mind the myriad daily judgments in which professionals in numerous professions correctly identify the ethically appropriate path and follow it. Perhaps these are just accidents, blind habits formed in another era and ill-suited to changing times and new patterns of culture and social circumstance.

The public wants stronger assurances, say the critics, that professions and professionals really do understand the norms of conduct that apply to them and understand these norms deeply enough that they can articulate them clearly and apply them creatively to new social and cultural circumstances.

Perhaps the claim that the professions are in deep trouble is overstated, and perhaps it is not. But the cynical public is certainly a reality. Even though most of them, the studies say, still believe that the professionals who serve them personally conduct themselves ethically most of the time, still the public sees too much evidence of uncertainty and nonconformity through the media to go unaffected. It is also true that the times are changing. The social and cultural circumstances of professional practice seem to be changing rapidly. So the professions must demonstrate the depth of their understanding of their role in order to retain what is essential in the midst of change.

Unfortunately, most professionals, as individuals, are inarticulate about their profession's ethical standards; and, except for the general, almost homiletic directives that make up most published codes of ethics and public relations statements from the professions, most professions, as collective voices of their members, are inarticulate as well. Nor is there any tradition in the professions of detailed discussion of the processes of reflection and judgment by which conscientious professionals move from facing alternative courses of action, about which difficult ethical judgments are needed, to making those judgments and then explaining them clearly, in terms that connect with the particular understandings of their respective professions, how they work, what it is they do, and of the institution of professions in general.

This inarticulateness is the reason why the assurances that the public seeks are so hard to provide. The public seeks assurance that ethical conduct by professionals is the rule, not the exception, that it rests on a firm foundation of understanding and commitment. But professions and professionals that cannot articulate thoughtful descriptions of the ethical content of their professional obligations or of the reasoning processes by which they determine what is required of them in response to particular sets of circumstances cannot provide such assurance, and even their sincere protestations of commitment ring hollow.

Professional ethics education is thus critical to the process of forming and inducting new professionals and to the process of continuing education for professionals already in practice. The goal is not principally to eliminate that small fraction of each profession's membership who act outside its ethical norms, though sound ethics education may well have impact in this way. It is rather to assist those who are conscientiously trying to deal more effectively with unusually complex judgments of professional right and wrong, and to help all members of the professions understand and explain more clearly to the larger community the practices of their professions. It is through ethics education, and perhaps through this means alone in these rapidly changing times, that professions and professionals will be able reestablish the public's confidence that they will properly use their special knowledge, skills, and power.

But if the professions are to educate their students and their experienced practitioners much more intensely and much more self-consciously than in the past, how should these educational efforts be designed? The answer to this question has two parts, one practical and the other more theoretical.

The practical part asks questions such as, Which goals should be pursued by those who teach professional ethics? Which characteristics should learners of professional ethics come to possess as a result of the teaching of professional ethics, characteristics that they would otherwise lack or at which they would be less proficient? How can teachers of ethics determine if learners are acquiring these characteristics? In other words, What are the desired outcomes of the teaching of professional ethics and what are the valid indicators of the effectiveness of the learning? Answers to these questions constitute the first part of this chapter.

The theoretical part asks what we mean by professional ethics in the first place. Without a clear definition of terms, those who propose to teach professional ethics could reasonably be asked if they actually know what they are doing. A detailed overview of the topics relevant to this question and a typology of professional obligations are provided in the second and third parts of this chapter.

Finally, I briefly survey the resources that are needed for

effective professional ethics education. Given limitations on space, no attempt is made to survey currently used techniques, materials, and the like. Instead, the aim is simply to try to identify the kinds of questions that teachers of professional ethics and those who administer such programs will need to ask if they are to succeed in their efforts.

Goals of Professional Ethics Education

The best way to introduce a discussion of the proper goals of professional ethics education is to examine the two most common objections to the whole enterprise. The most common objection to formal programs of instruction in professional ethics is the claim that adult students are essentially fully formed in matters of conduct, so that only powerful personal experiences or else very rigorous forms of indoctrination that would be ethically problematic in their own right could significantly alter conduct.

Oddly, this objection has considerable currency among professional school faculty in many professions. The reason this is odd is that most professional school faculty also energetically support the idea that the formation of the school's students into professionals, and not only by way of the transmission of knowledge and technical skills, is one of the school's and the faculty's most important goals. Obviously, this goal makes no sense if such formation were impossible.

This contradiction aside, the proposed objection is more importantly controverted by the lived experience of everyone of adult years. For it is simply not true that one's moral or ethical views and habits are so completely formed and solidified as to be unchangeable by the time one is an adult. We have all had to face new issues in our lives for which the rules, values, virtues, and so on that we brought to the situation did not fully prepare us; and in one way or another we *learned* what we needed in order to address these issues. Regardless of whether we came away from the situation believing that we addressed the new issues well or badly—and the fact that we could reflect on the experience in such a way actually proves the point—we learned to address them.

Moreover, most of us, as mature and experienced adults, have also experienced another form of moral or ethical learning as adults. We have encountered individuals whose lives have embodied traits that we were moved to admire, and perhaps to imitate, even to the point of changing ourselves, habituating ourselves to be more like those persons in those particular respects. The process of learning new values, which most often is prompted by encounters with the new values embodied in whole human beings, does not stop when a person turns twenty-one, forty-one, or even sixty-one years of age.

So this objection to professional ethics education is surely false. Of course, as in all learning, new moral learning must find a place with what was learned before. So a positive lesson for teachers of professional ethics to which this objection may be pointing is that since professionals and students in the professions are adults, they should be treated as adults, that is, as persons with considerable human experience already, with views about human conduct and excellence, and with views about professions, professionalism, and their profession of choice, all of which should be taken as important starting points for the learning and teaching process at hand.

This lesson is particularly important for teachers in professional schools, since most professional schools tend to treat their students as if they were adolescents. Of course, most professional school students are preadults when they first arrive in the sense that they are almost completely unschooled in the specific knowledge and skills that constitute the profession's technical competence and enable it to serve its clients. But these facts about their grasp of the profession's technical competence do not necessarily imply anything about their capacity for ethical reflection or for making adult judgments and choices in many areas of their lives. Since they actually are adults by age, those who teach professional students may significantly inhibit the learning process if they treat them like preadults.

A second objection concedes that ethical learning is possible for professional students but holds that formal instruction is both unnecessary and ineffective. By this view, formal instructional programs are unnecessary because the ethical learning that is needed is principally effected through a process of role modeling by other, often senior, members of the profession and imitation of their example by the learners. It is, in fact, this very process that was cited earlier as an example of moral learning by adults.

Here, the objection makes a correct point but draws an incorrect conclusion. It certainly is true that a learner's grasp of the general norms of conduct of a profession derives from observation of the relevant values, principles, and virtues as these are embodied in whole human beings, from admiration and imitation of what has been observed, and then from gradual habituation of these traits as part of the learner's own professional character. But this fact does not prove that the modeling-imitating-habituating process is invariably either correct or complete, much less that there is no value to formal instruction in ethics.

In fact, far more dependable learning by way of modeling-imitating-habituating will occur if the learner admires and imitates *reflectively*, conscious of what he or she is observing and absorbing. For it simply is not the case that every characteristic of every member of the profession that a learner might imitate is worthy of imitation. The process by which role models are chosen when the process remains principally nonreflective is a kind of psychological and emotional lottery. Even the good qualities that are learned by this means will not constitute a *whole* professional, moral personality. From these considerations, we can now identify one important goal of professional ethics education.

Goal 1: Enhance the Modeling-Imitating-Habituating Process That Is Part of All Professional Formation

How can a learner demonstrate that such learning has taken place? Appropriate measures of this learning can be found in students' descriptions of relevant experiences and judgments: heightened student awareness that the process is going on in them and the use by the students of sophisticated conceptual tools (for example, knowledge about the content of the profession's obligations) to make the process more discriminating and more reflective.

The other half of the second objection is that formal instructional programs in professional ethics are ineffective. That is, they cannot contribute to ethical learning. Most often this objection is supported only by assertions, usually based on a misunderstanding of how professional ethics education proceeds when it is well done. Thus, the most common argument offered in support of the objection is of the form, "You can't tell me that simply telling people how to act is going to make them act any differently."

But formal instruction in professional ethics does not attempt, as one of its immediate goals, to change behavior. Instead, it works to compensate for the deficits that seem most correlated with inappropriate behavior. One thoughtful identification of these deficits is by the educational psychologist James Rest. He identifies four such deficits and proposes, therefore, four goals for ethics education in order to correct them: (1) inadequate awareness that moral or ethical matters are at stake in a situation, (2) inadequate ability to reason effectively about such matters, (3) insufficient motivation to perform what moral reasoning identifies as the ethically correct action, and (4) insufficient understanding of how to implement the ethically correct action in a particular situation (Rest, 1982, 1983). It is the first, second, and fourth of these deficits that ethics education can address most directly. The topic of motivation will be addressed at the close of this chapter.

Before discussing the next three goals for professional ethics education, which derive from Rest's account of deficits, it is worth noting that there is a sizable body of empirical research on moral learning, and a growing literature specifically on learning in professional ethics by professional students (Bebeau, 1991). In the important areas of (1) moral learning and moral sensitivity or awareness and (2) moral judgment or reasoning skills, there is solid empirical evidence that properly constructed professional school learning experiences, that is, proper formal professional ethics instruction, can effect significant gains by professional students in both areas.

Of course, the key to the effectiveness of formal instruction in professional ethics is doing it the right way. The critic is correct in thinking that professional ethics instruction that consists of "telling people how to act" is ineffective. But the critic is incorrect in thinking that this is what is being proposed in any carefully constructed program in professional ethics education. Moreover, in addition to the evidence of effective learning in professional ethics that has been formally confirmed by behavioral scientists, there is a tremendous amount of anecdotal evidence from ethics teachers in many professions, and in institutions of higher education of many other sorts, to the same effect. This is not only evidence in the form of teachers observing changes in students' awareness and reasoning skills over the course of an instructional program but also evidence in the form of the students' own reports of the effects of such programs on their awareness and their reasoning skills. Here, then, are five other goals for professional ethics education.

Goal 2: Heighten Students' Awareness of Ethical Issues in Professional Practice

Appropriate outcomes measures—expressed in the students' ability to describe relevant concerns—are increased sensitivity to the rights, duties, and aspects of human well-being that are at stake in examples of professional practice; increased sensitivity to the commitments of professionals and to the various aspects of trust in the professionals' clients that are correlated with these commitments; and increased awareness of the points of view of each participant in examples of professional practice situations.

Goal 3: Strengthen Students' Moral Reasoning Skills, Particularly in the Application of Norms of the Profession to Practice Situations and in Judgments of Whether Norms of the Profession Are Appropriate and Sufficient

Appropriate outcomes measures are advances in the qualities of good professional ethical reasoning as expressed, for example, in students' oral and written analyses of case studies: (1)

The sample of reasoning is clear, internally consistent, and complete, that is, no significant steps are missing. (2) The sample is inclusive of all professional norms relevant to the issues raised. (3) The sample is attentive to competing views of the profession or of specific elements of the profession's norms when these are in dispute. And (4) the sample determines which of several competing courses of action (or policy) ought to be undertaken on the basis of the reasons given (or, if necessary, explains why such a determination cannot be offered).

Goal 4: A Basic Understanding of the Nature of a Profession and the General Character of Professional Obligations and an Understanding of the Content of Norms of the Profession

Achievement of this goal of professional ethics education is actually presupposed by the three goals already mentioned. Each of them presumes that students understand the nature of professions, the general character of professional obligation, and the content of the norms (including any published codes of ethical conduct) of the particular profession that the student is preparing to join. That is, in order to achieve the first three goals with any measure of sophistication, the student should not only appreciate the importance of the various practical and theoretical questions outlined earlier in this chapter but also be able to offer intelligent answers to each of them. Appropriate outcomes measures would be accurate descriptions of these matters in oral assignments, essays, or other assignments.

Goal 5: Enhance the Students' Ability to Implement Careful Ethical Judgments and to Formulate Appropriate Strategies for Addressing Barriers to Such Implementation

This fifth goal, when achieved, ensures that learners can deal with the complexities of life that make it difficult to carry out what their careful moral reflections tell them they ought to do. This is the ability to implement moral judgments and to strategize effectively in order to implement them. In one sense, the reflective and practical skills involved here might already have been accounted for, in a thoughtful decision maker, when the various alternatives available are being identified in preparation for careful moral evaluation.

But whether one pictures this step as coming last, after the moral judgment is complete and needs to be implemented, or first, as part of the process of identifying the courses of action to be judged—or as ongoing during the whole course of moral reflection, as is most realistic—the point is that professional students may be extremely naive about the intermediate steps that members of the profession have to take in order to act in the most professionally ethical manner. Included here are communication skills, to enable the professional to achieve, for example, the most interactive relationship possible with the client, and negotiating skills, to enable the professional to find an ethically appropriate path between conflicting parties or institutions. Whatever the particular skills to be learned, their mastery by the students should be an important goal of professional ethics education. Appropriate outcomes measures are relevant and realistic proposals by the students—expressed, most often, in oral discussions or written essays, or in "clinical rounds" discussions when actual clinical situations are the subject matter—about how to carry out a course of action judged professionally ethically appropriate.

Goal 6: Make Students More Articulate in Discussing the Ethical Dimensions of Professional Practice and More Effective Listeners When Such Matters Are Being Discussed by Others

This last goal is hardly ever discussed in the professional ethics literature even though its achievement materially affects the students' ability to act on the learning achieved under the first four goals, and even though it is important in many other ways in the students' professional lives. Appropriate outcome measures typically include intersubjective tests, that is, a comparison of what the student intended to say and what a listener hears, or between what a student hears and the intended explanation.

Because articulateness in ethical matters is so far from being viewed as an important end product of professional education in our society that it is difficult to imagine professional school programs being adjusted to give it any measure of priority, all conceptions of how instructors would seek evidence of its achievement seem almost whimsical. It can be hoped that this goal will be achieved in at least some small measure in the course of working as effectively as possible for the first five goals. But it is important to note not only the difference of this goal from the first five but also its distinctive importance.

Nature of Professional Obligations

Few professionals, including professional school faculty, have a clear, articulate understanding of the nature and general categories of professional obligations, or of the relations between professional obligations and obligations from other sources, or of any number of other important topics of this sort. These topics are essential foundations for the teaching of professional ethics. They are substantive foundations in that those who teach, and those who learn, ought to know what they mean by the terms professional ethics, profession, and role-based ethics. They are also procedural foundations in that much of what has already been said here about the teaching of professional ethics depends on an understanding both of the nature of the institution of professions and of the general character of role-based obligations.

There is, unfortunately, little literature available to teachers of professional ethics on the nature of the institution of professions, on the nature and bases of professional obligations, or on the principal categories of professional norms of conduct. The moral philosophers and scholars in related disciplines who study ethics have paid little attention to the professions and their role-based obligations. And the sociologists and scholars in related disciplines who study important social institutions rarely bring an adequate grasp of the nature of role-based obligations to their work. Therefore, I provide here an overview of what we currently know about these matters.

There are at least two competing views of the nature or general character of the institution of professions. One of these holds that being a professional entails certain obligations because this is how the institution of professions is actually understood by the people of this society. The opposing view sees professional activity as no different from the activity of any other producer in the marketplace and holds that a person has no particular or special obligations simply because he or she is a professional. Any obligations that such a person would have, other than the general requirement that individuals operating in the marketplace not coerce or defraud one another, are incurred only through specific contractual commitments with other individuals.

Both of these views deserve thoughtful examination in any carefully constructed program of professional ethics education; but the support that can be offered for each of them cannot be explored carefully here. In a similar way, alternative views about the source of the content of a profession's obligations, and about the relationship between a person's professional obligations and his or her obligations from other sources, cannot be carefully examined here. Therefore, because of these limitations on space, a number of important preliminary points about the institution of professions and the nature of professional obligation are set down here in the form of assumptions, to which several other important preliminaries are added.

First, I take it for granted that membership in a profession means that one has undertaken certain obligations. The content of these obligations depends on the specific profession of which one is a member; and the implications of this content for particular actions in a particular situation, as in all such judgments, depend upon the details of the situation at hand. But it is a fundamental characteristic of professions that professions and professionals have distinctive obligations.

Second, although some people hold the view that the content of a given profession's obligations is determined by the members of that profession and no one else, the assumption here is instead that the content of a particular profession's obligations at a given point in time is the product of a dialogue between the professional group and the larger community. This dialogue is admittedly subtle and complex, it is continuous, and it is rarely explicit or formal. But it is nevertheless the source of the contents of each profession's obligations. As a consequence, a professional can never adequately determine his or her professional obligations simply by asking what the members of the profession say or what the profession's organizations say. One must also ask to what the larger community understands the members of that profession to be committed.

This fundamental question about the source of professional obligations deserves careful consideration by professionals learning about their professional obligations. It should be carefully examined and the arguments on both sides carefully evaluated on their merits in any sound program of professional ethics education. But for the purposes of this chapter, the issue will be resolved by the above assumption, namely, that a profession's obligations are not the product of the profession alone but are also the fruit of an ongoing dialogue between the profession and the larger community.

A third issue concerns the place of a person's professional obligations in relation to moral or ethical decision making in general and in relation to the general topic of moral character, personal ethics, or virtue. These topics are much too broad to even summarize here. But the point needs to be raised that a person's other obligations may come in conflict with his or her professional obligations in a particular situation. Is it the case that the professional obligations should always "win"? Are they always the determining factors of what the person ought to do when all things are considered?

In this chapter, I assume, because there are good reasons for maintaining this position, that one's professional obligations are not necessarily absolute. They do not always determine what a person ought to do because other obligations can sometimes outweigh them. As is the case with other role-based obligations, a person can be in a situation in which it is perfectly clear that the professional obligation is to do X, but the person has other obligations to do Y instead, and these latter obligations are more important. Under such circumstances, I assume, a person is not morally or ethically justified but may even be morally or ethically required to conscientiously disobey his or her professional duty (Ozar, 1987). This issue needs to be carefully considered in any sound program of professional ethics education.

Another preliminary point concerns the terms *moral* and *ethical.* For present purposes, an issue is considered a moral or ethical issue when someone's well-being or rights or duties are in question or at stake. In addition, because some people use these two terms with different meanings, although there is no widely or consistently employed distinction between them, it seems best to treat the terms ethical and moral as synonyms here and to use them interchangeably to indicate simply whatever *ought* or *ought not* to be done in light of the rights, duties, or human well-being involved. More complicated distinctions within this large arena of discussion are made explicit here.

It is also important to specifically distinguish moral or ethical issues regarding professional practice from legal issues, and, similarly, to distinguish the teaching of professional ethics from teaching professionals how to be law abiding and how to protect themselves from legal risk.

Questions about what is morally or ethically required or permitted are logically distinct from questions about what is legally required or permitted. While the law may direct a person to do what is morally correct, the law is not a fundamental determinant of what is morally correct, which is why we look to morality to tell us what the law ought to be, rather than vice versa. In practice, of course, determinations of a person's strategies of action must include questions about the law and its impact on one's own life and the lives of others. But the bearing of legal requirements on what is morally or ethically best in a given situation always depends more radically on what morality requires than on what the law requires. If a person determines that the law supports what morality requires, all the better; but if it is determined that the law hinders or runs counter to what is ethical, then this is a sign that the law ought to be changed, or perhaps even that the person ought to disobey the law in order to act morally.

In this chapter, the primary focus is on what professional ethics or professional morality require, not on what the law requires. In practice, in fact, it is ordinarily best to keep the teaching of these two topics separate, not only because it is rare when the same faculty are experts in both (except, of course, for lawyers expert in legal professional ethics) but also to help students incorporate the distinction into their own thinking.

A final preliminary point is to notice that whenever a social rule, such as a norm of a profession, is accepted or adopted by a group of people, such as a professional group and the larger community in dialogue, then three distinct kinds of questions about what ought or ought not to be the case can then be asked. First, what does the social rule, the professional norm, require or forbid? That is, what does it require of the relevant people in a given situation? It is important to notice that this kind of question is about what *is* the case, that is, about what the relevant communities do in fact accept as a professional's obligations in this particular matter.

Second, what, all things considered, ought to be the case or ought to be done by a person? Here, underlying ethical values, moral principles, and so on are used together with obligations deriving from professional and other sorts of commitments to determine what a person ought to do in a particular situation. As has already been noted, I assume here that circumstances could arise in which, once all morally relevant features of the situation are considered, the action that a person ought morally to undertake is different from what he or she is professionally obligated to do. Presumably, such situations are rare (or either the person should get into another profession, the profession's norms are in need of profound change, or both). But the possibility of such a situation needs to be stressed, along with the difference between asking what professional norms require in a situation and asking what one ought to do when all morally relevant considerations have been taken into account.

Third, what ought to be the professional norm for this situation? That is, should X be the relevant social rule for this situation, or should Y, or should there be no rule at all on this matter? What ought to be the norm that the group (in this instance, the professional group and the larger community in dialogue) establishes or accepts for its actions in this matter?

Day-in and day-out, most decisions about how a member of a profession ought or ought not to act and how the profession as a whole ought and ought not to function are determined by the profession's norms *as they are*. It is important to remember, however, that a description of what a profession's norm is in some matter is not the same as a question about what the norm covering that matter *ought* to be or about the standards that should be used to determine what it ought to be. Every human institution is inherently conservative, that is, its task is to keep relatively fixed a pattern of social life that the community has found valuable so that the members of the community can count on mutual conformity. Thus, it can sometimes appear that asking questions of the third kind is inappropriate and disloyal to one's profession. But a profession could not possibly have the norms that it does have if questions of the third kind had not been asked at least once before; and it is important that they be asked regularly and often.

Professional students sometimes find it difficult, and even frightening, to ask questions of the third kind. They are making great sacrifices to become members of the profession as (they think) it is. Questions that imply that it should, perhaps, be different from what it is can be quite unsettling. Therefore, our education must help them see that questions of the first kind, which they ordinarily know they must learn to ask and answer if they are to practice well, depend on asking and answering questions of the third kind.

A determination of what a profession's norms are, that is, answers to questions of the first kind about a particular profession, is often a much more subtle enterprise than it might seem. Some professions have published codes of conduct, but such codes rarely cover more than the most obvious principles and categories of conduct that individual members and the group as a whole have to deal with in the daily life of the profession. So codes are necessarily very limited in the guidance offered. Consequently, asking questions of the first kind and learning how to answer them in daily practice is one of the most important skills of every practicing professional. One useful way to facilitate the development of this skill is to identify the chief categories of the norms of professions.

Seven Categories of Professional Obligations

The seven categories of professional obligations described in this section have been culled from studies of numerous professional groups. They constitute a set of patterns of norms that can be found in almost every group that is called a profession.

One way to think about these categories is to see them as a set of questions about the norms that every profession actually employs. One would expect, then, that every profession can provide careful answers to each of these seven sets of questions. Unfortunately, many professions are not articulate about the content of their professional norms. It would not be surprising if a great many experienced professionals had great difficulty in articulating answers to these sets of questions. Yet, if a profession or a professional does not know how to answer these questions, if a profession or a professional does not know what the norms of that profession require in each of these seven areas, then in essence they do not know what they are doing in their professional lives.

Chief Type of Client

Every profession has a chief type of client. This is the set of persons whose well-being the profession and its members are chiefly committed to serving. For some professions, the identification of the chief client seems quite easy. Surely, we might say, the chief client of the physician and the nurse, for example, is the patient. But who is the chief client of a lawyer? Is it simply the party whose case the lawyer represents or pleads or to whom the lawyer gives advice? Lawyers are told, however, and announce in their self-descriptions and codes of conduct, that they have obligations to the whole justice system, and therefore that there are things they may not ethically do, as professionals, even if doing them would advance the interests of the parties whom they represent or advise. So it appears that the answer to the question about the chief client of the legal profession is complex, involving both the people that lawyers represent or advise and the whole justice system, and perhaps the whole larger community whom that system serves.

Once this sort of complexity about the chief client is noticed, even what appear to be simple cases prove much more complex. The physician and the nurse must attend not only to the patient before them, for example, but also to those in the waiting room or to the other patients in the hospital unit, and so on. In fact, they have obligations to all of the patients in the hospital or other institution where they work, or to all of their patients of record if they are in private practice. They also have significant obligations to the public as a whole; for example, their obligation to practice with caution so as not to spread infection from their patients to either themselves or others.

It turns out that the question about who is a profession's chief client is rarely as simple as it first appears, and it often does not appear simple even at the start. Who, to take another example studied in Ozar (1990), is the chief client of the engineer? Is it the engineer's business client, the party who will pay the engineer's fee? Or if the engineer is employed, is it the engineer's employer? Or is the engineer's chief client possibly the people who will use the fruits of the engineer's practice, the bridge or the building, for example? Or is it those whose environment will be affected by what the engineer produces?

In any case, this is one of the first questions that we must ask if we wish to understand a particular profession's obligations, or the obligations of anyone who plays a distinctive social role (Ozar, Kelly, and Begue, 1988, 1989). It must also, therefore, be one of the first questions that we must address when we are educating the members of a profession about their professional obligations.

Central Values of the Profession

Every profession is focused only on certain aspects of the well-being of its clients. The professions' rhetoric to the contrary, no professional group is expected by the larger community to be expert in their clients' entire well-being. No profession is committed to securing for its clients everything that is of value for them. Rather, a certain central value or set of values is the focus of each profession's expertise, and it is the job and obligation of that profession to work to secure those values for its clients.

In addition, most professions are committed to pursuing more than one central value at a time for clients. One reason is that, whatever other values are central for a given profession, the value of the clients' autonomy is ordinarily a central value as well. In any case, assuming there is more than one central value for a given profession, the question can then be asked whether these values are all equal in rank, or whether the members of the profession are committed to choosing them in some ranked order when they cannot all be realized at once.

A good case can be made, for example, that the central values that the dental profession is committed to pursuing for its patients are, in this order, (1) life and general health, (2) oral health, understood as appropriate and pain-free oral functioning, (3) autonomy, that is, the patients' control, if able, over what happens to their bodies, (4) preferred patterns of practice by the dentist, (5) aesthetic considerations, and (6) efficiency in the use of resources (Ozar, Schiedermayer, and Siegler, 1988).

For every profession, then, the following questions need to be asked and answered: What are its central values? What specific aspects of human well-being must each member of this profession secure for clients? If there is more than one central value, we also have to ask if they are of equal importance or if some of these values take precedence over others when they cannot all be simultaneously achieved. That is, do they form some sort of hierarchy?

Ideal Relationship Between Professional and Client

The point of the relationship between a professional and a client is to bring about certain values for the client, values that cannot be achieved for the client without the expertise of the professional. Achievement of these values requires both the professional and the client to make a number of judgments and choices about the professional's interventions. The question that this third category of professional obligation addresses concerns the proper roles of the professional and the client as they make these judgments and choices.

At least four general models of the professional-client relationship can be distinguished: (1) *commercial*, in which only the minimal morality of the marketplace governs, that is, neither party has any obligations beyond a general prohibition of coercion and fraud unless and until individuals freely contract together to be obligated toward each other in specific ways; (2) *guild*, in which the emphasis is on the professional's expertise and the client's lack of it, so that the active member in all judgments and choices about professional services for the client is necessarily the professional alone; (3) *agent*, in which the expertise of the professional is simply placed at the service of the values and goals of the client without interference by any competing goals or values, for example, values to which the profession is committed from the start; and (4) *interactive*, in which both parties have unique and irreplacable contributions to make in the decision-making process, with the professional offering expertise to help meet the client's needs, as well as a commitment to the profession's central values, and the client bringing his or her own values and priorities and the value of self-determination, the ideal being that the two parties choose together how the professional shall benefit the client.

A crucial element of the content of any profession's obligations, then, worked out in the ongoing dialogue between the professional group and the larger community, is a description of the ideal professional-client relationship for that profession. The ideal that is most often discussed today, at least when the client is a fully functioning adult, is some variant of the interactive model (Ozar, 1984). But however the ideal relationship is described in regard to fully functioning adults, the profession must also have an understanding of how its members are to interact with clients who are not capable of full participation in decision making about the professional's interventions, for example, children, the developmentally disabled, and persons whose capacity to participate is diminished by fear, illness, or other conditions. So to meet this professional obligation, a profession must not only describe the ideal relationship that is realizable in the best of circumstances but also have a set of standards to apply in suboptimal situations as well.

Relative Priority of the Client's Well-Being

Most sociologists who study professions mention commitment to service or commitment to the public as one of the characteristic features of a profession. Similarly, in most professions' self-descriptions, in their codes of ethics and the like, the client's best interest or service to the public is given a prominent place. But these expressions admit of many different interpretations with significantly different implications for actual practice.

Consider, for example, what could be called a minimalist interpretation of this general norm. On this interpretation, a professional would have only an obligation to consider the well-being of the client as *among the professional's most important concerns,* without the client's well-being having any further or more specific priority over any other concerns of the professional. This is rightly called a minimalist interpretation because if any less consideration than stated were given, we could not really say that the client's well-being had any priority for the professional at all.

On the other hand, on a maximalist interpretation, the professional's commitment to the priority of the client's well-being could be understood to mean that the professional has an obligation to place the well-being of the client *ahead of every other consideration,* both the professional's own interests and all other obligations or concerns that the professional might have regarding any other individual or group.

It is doubtful that either of these extremes in interpretation accurately represents what the larger community wants or understands in this matter. Professional obligation requires, for every profession, that members accept certain sacrifices of other interests in the interest of their clients. But even if only to ensure a continuous supply of professionals to meet its needs in the future, the larger community certainly does not understand the commitment of the professional to be absolute or to entail, in all circumstances, the utmost of sacrifices for the sake of the client.

Thus, the well-being of the client is to be given some priority, but not absolute priority. But, then, how much priority is it to be given? There is no single correct answer to this question that applies for every professional group. Instead, each professional group has, as part of the content of its obligations worked out over time in dialogue with the larger community, an obligation to accept certain kinds of sacrifices, certain degrees of risk of loss in certain matters, and so on. The risk may be of infection, if facing it is necessary for the sake of one's clients, as for health professionals, or the risk of financial loss, or the risk of social loss or criticism, and so on. In any case, professional ethics education should raise and discuss this issue, and try to identify the kinds and degrees of risk that are part of the professional obligations that the students eventually will be undertaking when they enter their respective professions.

Competence

All professionals are obligated both to acquire and to maintain the expertise needed to undertake their professional tasks, and all are obligated to undertake only those tasks that are within their competence.

Competence is probably the most obvious category of professional obligation. It is also the easiest to describe in a general way. For if a professional fails to apply his or her expertise, or fails to obtain the expertise for undertaking some task, these failures directly contradict both the point of being an expert and the very foundation of the larger community's award of decision-making power to the professional in the first place.

But the determination of what counts as sufficient or minimally adequate competence of a member of a given profession, both in general and in relation to specific kinds of tasks, is a complex problem. In practice, almost of necessity the working out of detailed judgments about requisite expertise is left to the members of the expert group, the profession. But, for the sake of public scrutiny, the larger community usually requires explanations to be given regarding the general structure of the reasoning involved and, especially, the inevitable trade-offs of values involved in determining minimal competence, which is unavoidably a risk-benefit judgment about the relative availability of expert assistance.

Ideal Relationships Among Coprofessionals

Each profession also has norms, usually implicit and unexamined, concerning the proper relationship among members of the same profession in various matters and also between members of different professions when they are dealing with the same clients.

Some of these relationships are dictated by a professional's obligation of competence, that is, the requirement that a professional not practice beyond his or her competence. This obligation clearly requires a professional to seek assistance from other, usually more specialized professionals when a particular matter requires expertise that the first professional does not possess. But other aspects of coprofessional relationships, which are not matters of practicing within one's competence, are also governed by professional norms.

It would facilitate the practice of most professionals, especially in a world in which increasingly more work is becoming specialized and thus assigned to exclusive expert groups, if the accepted standards of interaction among professionals were more clearly grasped by them and their clients alike. So this is another topic for careful consideration, though one rarely addressed carefully, in professional ethics education programs.

Relationship Between the Profession and the Larger Community

In addition to relationships of professionals and their clients and of professionals with one another, the activities of every profession also involve relationships between the profession as a group or its individual members and persons who are neither coprofessionals nor clients. These relationships may involve the larger community as a whole, various significant subgroups of it, or specific individuals. Obviously, a wide range of diverse relationships are included under this umbrella, and which among them are of the greatest importance in a given situation depends on the particular profession under discussion and the details of the situation.

Several important examples of a profession's and its members' obligations to the larger community are easy to state. It is incumbent on a profession that is permitted to be self-regulating by the larger community, for example, to carry out this task of self-regulation conscientiously. This oversight includes provision and monitoring of educational programs and institutions in which new members of the profession learn and receive their formation as professionals, and monitoring of the collective activities of members of the profession in their various professional organizations, to make sure that these organizations act in ways consistent with the other professional obligations of the members. It also includes such measures as are necessary to monitor and correct incompetent or other professionally inappropriate practice by individual members of the group.

The profession as a group and its individual members are also the principal educators of the community regarding elements of the profession's expertise that the lay community needs to know in order to function effectively in everyday life. Thus, for example, the health professions have obligations regarding public education in matters of ordinary health care and hygiene; and the engineering and scientific professions have obligations regarding knowledge of safety practices that the lay community needs to know in daily life.

A more subtle kind of obligation has to do with the content of key values that have become part of the public culture, and that play crucial roles in people's private lives and especially in public policy, but whose content is significantly influenced by the members of a profession or of a group of professions. For example, the health professions are educationally more responsible than any other group for the public's understanding of what it means to be healthy; and the engineering professions have a powerful formative influence on the culturally dominant notions of safety and physical risk. This is an area of professional obligation to the larger community that has received little attention, but it has continuing significance (Ozar, 1985).

These seven categories have already proved useful in my research and in others' research on a number of professions. But there are probably other, equally useful ways of dividing the general topic of professional obligations. The point here is not to accord privileged status to the typology above but rather to offer one useful example of the kinds of conceptual tools that can be useful in both studying and teaching professional ethics. By using conceptual tools such as the seven categories and the general and the specific questions about a profession that they suggest, professional ethics educators can ask lucid questions and thus work for a clearer understanding of the standards of professional practice in whatever profession they are addressing. In addition, by employing a common set of categories, whether these seven or others, teachers and students of professional ethics, and the practicing members of the professions, can make more effective comparisons among professions and thus facilitate a kind of learning that is rare today, learning from other professions about one's own.

Means of Professional Ethics Education

A common either/or misconception about ethics education holds that either the teacher is an expert in what people ought to do and so teaches by telling the students what people ought to do, or else the teacher has nothing to offer the students, except perhaps to be a skilled leader of discussions. Since most people doubt that there are ethics experts, in the sense of people who routinely have correct answers to questions about how other people ought and ought not to act, if the claims in this either/or misconception are believed, it follows that those who teach professional ethics need only be good discussion leaders. It also follows, in many people's minds, that professional ethics education is merely an exercise in chatting together, that there is no substance to it.

In practice, few of those who are asked to teach professional ethics in professional schools are trained in the study of ethics or its teaching. Even if they believe that there are correct answers to many professional ethics questions, they may seriously doubt that they know all of these answers; and even if they believe that they know many of them, they may doubt that it is their task to simply give these answers to students. But if the either/or misconception is simply accepted without challenge, it may appear that there is little for them to do other than lead good discussions without any clear focus on correct answers. That is, if they are not simply to indoctrinate—which, even if it were the right course, seems unlikely to be effective—then what they are to do is not at all clear.

In this chapter, I presume that there are no experts, in the usual sense, in ethics or morality. Objectivity (the move away from subjectivity) in ethical judgments is increasingly achieved as one's ethical judgments are grounded in an ever broader base of human experience—both one's own personal experience and the experience of other humans shared in dialogue. (Such objectivity, in fact, closely parallels the objectivity of the natural sciences.) Since experience that is relevant to the discussion of ethical issues is not exclusive to any particular individual or group, it follows that all humans can learn from each other on these matters. Since there are no special experts on ethical matters, every person who reflects carefully on his or her own experience has expertise to share with others. This is why discussion is such an important tool in ethics education.

But this fact does not mean that all the ethics teacher can or should do is lead a good discussion. Nor does it mean that there is no such thing as relevant expertise for teaching professional ethics. What has to happen first, however, is rejection of the either/or misconception. The appropriate starting point for discussions of the best means to ethics education is not this misconception but rather the *goals* of professional ethics education. Each goal identifies a set of resources with which the ethics teacher can facilitate its achievement; and some of the best means of employing those resources become obvious as soon as the resources are identified.

For example, when the goal is to enhance students' awareness of the process of their own professionalization or their awareness of the rights, duties, and well-being involved in professional practice, it follows that it is not simply open-ended discussion that is needed but discussion guided by questions about these matters. Moreover, the teacher's own comments can model the desired awareness, that is, awareness of the teacher's own moral learning, in the past and at present, and awareness of the morally significant features of practice situations. In the teacher's comments, and in other students' comments, the students can see what it is like for a professional to be aware of these matters.

Similarly, when the goal is to enhance students' skills at sound moral reasoning and judgment, it is not simply any old comments that will do in the discussion of a practice situation. Rather, comments are needed that point to an ethical judgment, specifically, a judgment for which reasons can be given, counterreasons can be weighed and rebutted, and so on. In the same way, in students' written essays, the qualities of sound moral reasoning can be used as evaluation tools in order to provide the students with detailed feedback on the quality of this sample of their ethical reasoning.

As a third example, when the goal is understanding of the nature of professions and of the general character of professional obligations and the particular profession's answers to the questions prompted by the seven categories of professional obligations—or whatever other construct is used to explicate these matters—then the teacher can offer alternative accounts of these matters, and the reasons given in support of them, as a basis for the students' discussions.

Each of the six goals identified earlier points to resources that can make a teacher's achievement of the goal more likely. None of these resources consists of the teacher being an "expert" at giving correct answers to other people's ethical questions. But every one of them involves expertise, both specialized knowledge and particular teaching skills. In fact, one of the principal consequences of the either/or conception criticized here is that it turns attention away from the real forms of expertise that are needed for the most effective teaching of professional ethics.

Most articulate professionals of good will could model for students a sensitivity to the rights, duties, and well-being at stake in a given professional situation. But a sophisticated understanding of the qualities of sound moral reasoning and judgment, and, especially, an enhanced sensitivity to their presence in a given sample of student reflections, are rare abilities. They are ordinarily found only in those who have formally studied ethical issues, whether in a school of philosophy or theology or through the law (although those familiar with the law must exercise special caution that they do not confuse ethical and legal matters in their ethics teaching), by intensive self-education, or in some other way. Consequently, the effective achievement of the third goal of professional ethics education—the strengthening of students' moral reasoning skills—requires educational expertise that is not common in professional school faculty.

Many professional schools turn, therefore, to persons formally trained in ethics, and preferably also experienced in ethics teaching, to assist them in this regard. It is important to remember, however, that the effective achievement of the fourth and fifth goals, and, to some extent, of the first as well, requires extensive understanding not only of the institution of professions and professional obligations in general but also of the particular profession in question and the accepted content of each category of professional obligation as it functions in this profession's practice. The willingness of the ethicist to develop specific expertise about this profession is therefore an essential prerequisite for effective ethics teaching by a trained ethicist in the professional setting. The same considerations are also good reasons to work toward an effective team-teaching approach, by the ethicist and a member of the professional faculty together, if the two parties are willing to make the commitments of time and effort necessary for effective collaboration.

Finally, even experienced teachers with the best of personal resources need time with the students, and time for the students to reflect, read, write, discuss, and reflect further, if they are to produce the desired results. Even more serious than the lack of faculty with optimal resources for teaching professional ethics is the lack of time available for professional ethics education in most professional schools.

Although there is a loud hue and cry in contemporary society for increased professionalism among professionals, a concern that is often echoed within the professions, nevertheless the amount of time that professional schools are willing to devote to professional ethics education is minute in comparison with the importance of the goals and the extent and complexity of the means needed to achieve them. Any professional school that devotes more than 3 percent of its curriculum time to the teaching of professional ethics is, by contemporary standards, giving unusually great emphasis to this subject. The average commitment of curriculum time to professional ethics is far less than this amount.

But professional ethics education, as a formal component of the professional school program, has inherent limitations that must be recognized. It can, with appropriate faculty resources and enough time, effect a high level of understanding of professional ethics among the students. But it cannot directly address one other essential element of the moral life: motivation.

To be sure, ethics educators can materially affect students' motivation to acquire the understanding and the reasoning skills needed to be ethical professionals. They do this by modeling such understanding and such skills. And ethics educators who are also members of the profession into which the students are entering, or who are effective in modeling what a good professional is in their own professions, can, by their modeling, materially affect the students' motivation to be good professionals and good members of the profession.

But, obviously, the modeling of a good professional life, in general and especially in the students' chosen profession, cannot be left only to the ethics educators. It is the task of every member of the professional school faculty to be conscious of their role as models of professional life to the students. Therefore, just as making the modeling-imitating-habituating process self-conscious and discriminating among the students is a goal of ethics educators, it should also be one of their chief goals to make this process self-conscious and discriminating among the faculty.

The whole faculty, in other words, are ethics educators when it comes to the motivational component of professional life. So too, ultimately, are all members of the profession. But this means, if the school's educational program is well considered and coherent, that the whole faculty must consciously attend to this function. They should be asking themselves both what they want to be modeling to the students and what they are in fact modeling, not only in their individual professional lives but also in their lives within the institution of the professional school, including the institutional characteristics of the school that they allow to continue, for such institutional characteristics shape both the faculty and the students.

There is, then, a final task for the ethics educator, besides the acquisition and maintenance of the resources noted above and the complex political task of getting more time for formal ethics education in the professional school curriculum. The final task is to call on all members of the professional school faculty to pay attention to their role as teachers of professional motivation and to examine the process collectively in order to explicitly identify what its goals ought to be, and to determine not just how the members of the faculty ought to act in order to achieve these goals but also how they can help one another through mutual observation, correction, and support.

Like the goal of helping students become articulate about professional ethical matters, this final proposal may seem almost whimsical when compared with what is ordinarily done, or even possible, in today's professional schools. But if we do not articulate the ideal, we will remain blind to how far short of it we fall. In our efforts to send out the best-formed young professionals that we can, we need to attend as effectively as we can not only to their understanding of their professional obligations but also to their motivation to perform them.

CHAPTER 8

Emphasizing Critical Thinking and Problem Solving

Charles E. Wales
Anne H. Nardi
Robert A. Stager

Human beings have always recognized that the ability to think makes people valuable. That ability was passed from one generation to another over thousands of years by an artisan apprenticeship system that functioned within and across families and societies. That workable pattern did not change in a significant way until about two hundred years ago when "formal" schools and colleges were established and teachers introduced students to a wider variety of intellectual ideas than ever before presented.

Teachers in these early schools had two goals: to help their students develop a broad view of the world and to teach them to think their way through complex intellectual problems. Those educators could not have anticipated that a time would come when teaching students how to think would all but disappear from the academy. That time arrived with the onset of the industrial revolution, a time when the ideas, discoveries, inventions, developments, research, and writing of thinking graduates were not only welcome but helped to propel change at a revolutionary rate that no one could have anticipated.

One result of this revolution was a better life for more

people. Another result, which occurred over time, was an exponential increase in knowledge, an explosion that overwhelmed educators and pushed the thinking that produced it from course after course at all levels of education. In just a few generations, the thinking curriculum became the knowledge curriculum that we have today. Educators no longer had time to teach individual students how to think because they were too busy teaching still more of them about the great thoughts of other people.

Basics of Teaching Thinking

The explosion of knowledge is not out of control. Many of the educators who recognize this see the teaching of thinking as the key to the future. One of the important supports for that change in direction is a National Research Council (NRC) report on *Education and Learning to Think* (Resnick, 1987a). The NRC committee was searching for a set of general, higher-order "thinking skills that would produce improved ability to learn across many traditional disciplines" (pp. 15–16). The report defined "higher order" as thinking that is complex, requires judgment, involves multiple solutions, conflicting criteria, uncertainty, and self-regulation and effort that result in structure and meaning (p. 3). These elements are found in each of the models of thinking presented in this chapter.

The NRC reports describes some of the obstacles that must be overcome. One of the obstacles to an effective program is faculty who decide that the best way to teach thinking is through lessons on creativity, critical thinking, logic, ethics, or a combination thereof. These are all component skills that students should learn to use as they think their way through the process of decision making, and the skills should be taught, but not in separate courses. The NRC report explains the point in this way: "Isolated instruction in thinking skills, no matter how elegant the training provided, is unlikely to produce broadly used thinking ability" (Resnick, 1987a, p. 48). In fact, programs that appear to teach thinking actually address skills found in aptitude tests or specific "IQ-like tasks that may not generalize.

Direct assessment of transfer is needed" (p. 29) but has not been done. There is, for example, no empirical evidence to support the idea that teaching critical thinking or informal logic helps students in their own thinking (p. 39). The fact that students can demonstrate competence with component skills does not necessarily tell us anything about their ability to use those skills at an appropriate point in the larger process that they serve. Thus, skills such as brainstorming, synectics, and lateral thinking should be taught and practiced as part of the complete thinking process.

Another problem that must be addressed is faculty who see thinking as just another subject that they must somehow fit into the curriculum. That is the approach described in a 1991 report from the Association of American Colleges (1991). The two-volume report, *Liberal Learning and the Arts and Sciences Major,* "urges departments to structure the major so students can build on their knowledge, tying it all together in a final 'capstone' course or other senior-year experience" (Mooney, 1991, p. A1). If we can judge by what has happened in disciplines that have already tried that approach, we can conclude that it is necessary, but not sufficient. Some engineering programs, for example, have included a capstone course in their curricula for twenty or more years. The engineering accreditation agency now requires a minimum of sixteen semester credits of "design" spread throughout the curriculum. The most effective programs distribute these credits over a sequence of major courses. That, in fact, is exactly what the NRC report recommends: "Prudent educational practice should seek to embed efforts to teach cognitive skills into one or another—preferably all—of the traditional school disciplines" at all levels of education (Resnick, 1987a, p. 35).

Faculty who plan to teach thinking may also find William Perry's (1970) ideas about the way students think to be relevant. Perry's data show that some, but certainly not all, college students evolve from dualists, who believe that all problems have answers that are right or wrong or true or false, to relativists, who recognize that most problems have good, better, and best answers. Relativists also recognize that the choice of the best answer lies in the eye of the beholder and not in the solution.

Students who have not yet moved beyond the dualist level treat thinking exercises as games played by the faculty, who know but will not reveal the correct answers. Other students resist the whole idea of thinking exercises simply because the approach is different. There is almost nothing to memorize, and problems are likely to involve material from a variety of courses or disciplines. These students have been conditioned to believe that education entails something else. For these reasons, thinking is probably best taught by professional faculty who take it seriously. These faculty should heed the advice given in the NRC report. Students must learn that "they have the ability, the permission, and even the obligation to think" (Resnick, 1987a, p. 41). Teachers must provide a clear, explicit model of the way that a professional thinks through a problem. Students must practice using that model in social settings where they interact with other students and deal with different values and viewpoints.

One of the major conclusions in the NRC report is that thinking skills can be learned, and "if we can find effective ways to teach them, we can imagine an important increase in educational efficiency" (Resnick, 1987a, p. 16). The words "educational efficiency" sound good, but they must be defined. Many of those who have taught thinking for some time would define efficiency as a long-term gain in the number of important concepts that are remembered well enough to be useful. Without a tie to thinking, many of the facts, concepts, and principles that are memorized for a test are quickly forgotten or remembered in a way that is not useful.

Over the years, many educators have argued that knowledge is a means not an end, and that thinking must be taught. We do not have the space here to do justice to all of these educators or even the whole body of work of any one or two educators. Harris (this volume) provides a comprehensive presentation of ideas central to what we have described as the process approach. Her commentary also provides a conceptual structure to link contemporary cognitive research on expert-novice distinctions with the breadth of issues related to the world of practice and the education of the practitioner as well as in-depth coverage of the influential work of Donald Schön.

Both John Dewey and Donald Schön identified important components of the thinking process associated with the professional. In this chapter, we focus on the ideas presented in a single work by John Dewey and in two books by Donald Schön. The Dewey work that we have chosen is *How We Think* ([1910] 1933). Following in the philosophical tradition of Dewey, Schön, in *The Reflective Practitioner* (1983) and *Educating the Reflective Practitioner* (1987), has articulated the concept of reflective practice and its applicability to the often ill defined problems of practice.

We selected these two educators because they wrote in times that are worlds apart, but they share a vision of what should be. Both are champions of the idea that thinking *must* be taught. For both, thinking involves a process. And for both, there is value in teaching students how experienced professionals approach intellectual problems with a strategy that Dewey called *reflective thinking* and that Schön calls *reflection-in-action*.

John Dewey

In *How We Think,* John Dewey ([1910] 1933) accurately described the difference between the thinking of a teenager and that of an adult. Typically, teenagers react to a problem with the first solution that comes to mind. In contrast, even if adults do not fully understand the thinking process, they have learned that they make better decisions if they delay action long enough to think. Dewey, however, wanted more than that. He wanted students to learn how an educated adult or, better still, how a professional thinks. Those who fully understand the thinking process delay action long enough to understand the situation as fully as possible, to consider the end that they hope to achieve, to generate and weigh as many options as they can, and to plan before they take action. Dewey wanted to help students learn to use both the process that includes these steps and the reflective thinking that is characteristic of a professional.

For Dewey, thinking was not just daydreaming but rather an orderly chain of ideas. Thinking was not just mental pictures, but thoughts that had a controlling purpose and end ([1910] 1933, p. 8). And thinking was not just accepting the beliefs of an authority, but beliefs based on evidence supported by personal mental activity. Dewey wanted students to learn to "discriminate between beliefs that rest upon tested evidence and those that do not" (p. 97). That, he believed, was "the central factor in all reflective or distinctly intellectual thinking" (p. 11).

To help teachers understand the logic of the thinking process, Dewey provided several examples and an explanation of their common factors. One of those examples involves a problem familiar to most of us: how to get somewhere on time.

Dewey found himself in downtown Manhattan at 16th Street when a clock caught his eye. It was 12:20 in the afternoon. At that moment, Dewey realized he had a 1:00 P.M. appointment in uptown Manhattan at 124th Street. He remembered that it took an hour to come down by surface car, so returning that way would not do. He thought of a subway express. That would do if a station was nearby. But was there one? What about the elevated? That would not be as fast, but a station might be closer. He also remembered that the subway express went closer to where he had to be. He made his choice, the subway express, and arrived on time (Dewey, [1910] 1933, p. 92). Let us consider how Dewey related these events to the thinking process that he defined.

Dewey's Process

Dewey described the concepts presented here as the set of indispensable traits, essential functions, and phases of the process that thinking people should use.

Prereflective

"The origin of thinking is some perplexity, confusion, or doubt" ([1910] 1933, p. 15). Dewey realized that time was short if he wanted to make his appointment.

"When a situation arises containing a difficulty or perplexity" (p. 102), the person may decide to avoid it and do something else, fantasize a solution, or face it. Dewey decided to face his problem.

"The moment he begins to reflect, he begins of necessity to observe in order to take stock of conditions" (p. 102). This step may involve direct observation or recollection of what was seen or is known. In the case of his appointment problem, Dewey asked and answered questions such as, "What time is it?" "Where am I?" "Where must I be at one o'clock?" "How long do I have to get there?"

"In this way he gets as clear and distinct a recognition as possible of the nature of the situation" (p. 102). Dewey defined the facts of the appointment problem.

Phase 1

Along with the facts come suggestions for a solution. Dewey considered various alternatives: surface car, subway express, and elevated train.

Phase 2

Next, there is "an intellectualization of the difficulty or perplexity that has been felt (directly experienced) into a problem to be solved, a question for which the answer must be sought" (p. 107). The problem, in Dewey's case, was that he did not have time to return the way he came.

"There is not at first a situation and a problem, much less just a problem and no situation." "Problem and solution stand out *completely* at the same time" (p. 108). Dewey had "an engagement to keep at a time that is near and a place that is distant" (p. 109).

Phase 3

"The facts or data set the problem before us, and insight into the problem corrects, modifies, expands the suggestion that originally occurred" (p. 109). That and other suggestions are evaluated, mentally, and the hypothesis most likely to solve the problem is selected. That choice guides the steps that follow, for example, Dewey's decision to take the subway express.

Phase 4

Next comes "the mental elaboration of the idea" (p. 107) that was selected. The "conditions are deliberately arranged in accord with the requirements of an idea or hypothesis to see whether the results theoretically indicated by the idea actually occur" (p. 114). How well this job is done "depends not only upon the prior experience and special education of the individual . . . and the state of culture and science of the age and place" (p. 111). For the appointment problem, Dewey does not share with us the details of his mental elaboration.

Phase 5

Finally, we test "the hypothesis by overt or imaginative action." The elaborated idea is tested "by action to see whether the consequences that are anticipated in thought occur in fact" (p. 97). Dewey acted on his hypothesis and reached his destination by one o'clock.

Schön's Process

Seventy-three years after Dewey's book was originally published, Donald Schön wrote *The Reflective Practitioner* (1983). As mentioned earlier, the ideas that Schön and Dewey present in their books have a great deal in common. Dewey, for example, was concerned with teaching both reflective thinking and the process of thinking. Schön is concerned with teaching a parallel process of thinking and reflection-in-action. Both agree that schools focus on a convergent knowledge base and not on the divergent thinking required to function as a thinking professional. Schön argues that today's professional schools are, in effect, nothing more than schools of natural science (p. 46). That focus does not prepare students for the unique role that they will and must play as professional decision makers.

Schön believes that one of the reasons that professional schools do not teach thinking is their failure to define an appropriate process for the instruction. In the absence of that insight, teachers may assign problems, such as case studies, that require students to think, they may expect students to think, and they may ask them to think, but they do not teach students how to think. To change this situation, Schön set out to see if he could find a generic thinking process that applies across what appear to be quite different professions (1983, pp. 77–78). "I propose that by attending to the practitioner's reflection-in-action . . . it is possible to discover a fundamental structure of professional inquiry which underlies the many varieties of design or therapy advocated by the contending schools of practice" (p. 130).

The Architect

Schön's first example of the thinking process takes place in a design studio where a student, Petra, has begun a project under the guidance of a master architect, Quist. Petra's assignment is to design an elementary school that meets a set of given specifications on a peculiar site (1983, pp. 79–80). Schön's explanation of Quist's and Petra's work parallels in many ways the thinking process that Dewey defined, but there is one difference. Because the problem is assigned, the work starts with the goal. That difference is also present in professional work in law and medicine where at least the general nature of the goal is known before the situation is defined. That goal is, of course, stated much more explicitly after the situation has been defined.

Quist's Decision Making

Petra's problem is clear, she must deal with an assigned project. The goal is to design an elementary school.

Step 1: Problem Setting. Schön, like Dewey, understands that problem solving must begin with "problem setting, the process by which we define the decision to be made, the ends to be achieved, the means which may be chosen" (p. 40). Schön put it this way: "When we set the problem, we select what we will treat as the 'things' of the situation, we set the boundaries of our attention to it, and we impose upon it a coherence which allows us to say what is wrong and in what directions the situation needs to be changed. Problem setting is a process in which, interactively, we name the things to which we will attend and frame the context in which we will attend to them" (p. 40).

The relevant characteristics of the situation were supplied by Quist, who gave Petra a set of design specifications and elevations of the site. Petra quickly asked and answered a variety of questions. She knows who is involved, what has happened so far, what types of space are required, when the plans must be completed, and where the school is to be located. She may not know why the school is going to be built on that site, but she quickly discovers that she has a twofold problem: to complete an assigned project and to put it on a site that has unique contours. Her goal is to design an elementary school that fits the contoured site.

Step 2: Frame and Plan. Petra worked for several weeks before Quist reviewed her work. She had "taken the contours of the land seriously" and tried the experiment of butting the buildings into the slope. This is how Schön described the meeting: "Petra presents her preliminary sketches and describes the problems she encountered. Quist then focuses on one of these problems. He reframes it in his own terms and proceeds to demonstrate the working out of a design solution" (p. 82).

Step 3: Reframe and Plan. Quist covered Petra's design with a sheet of tracing paper and began to sketch a new idea. Schön described Quist's move in this way: "When he finds himself stuck in a problematic situation which he cannot readily convert to a manageable problem, he may construct a new way of setting the problem—a new frame which . . . he tries to impose on the situation" (p. 63).

"The main problem, in Quist's view, is not that of fitting the shape of the building to the slope, the site is too 'screwy' for that. Instead, coherence must be given to the site in the form of a geometry—a 'discipline'—which can be imposed upon it" (p. 85).

Schön argues that successful practitioners use framing to find a new idea or hypothesis that may be used to achieve their goal. In a typical situation where a student and a professional are working together, the teacher reacts to the student's less than insightful framing of the situation, reframes it, and "suggests a new direction for reshaping the situation" (p. 131). Quist does exactly that; he pursues his new hypothesis or frame by sketching one part of the school after another. This is not the sophisticated detailed plan that will come later; it is a preliminary plan, an experiment designed to test the new idea. If the experiment does not seem likely to achieve the goal, Quist or Petra will have to reframe and generate another hypothesis.

The practice of reframing a situation to generate a new hypothesis and reflection-in-action are the two major themes in Schön (1983). He ties these two themes together in a single sentence: "When someone reflects-in-action, he becomes a researcher in the practice context" (p. 68). Schön goes to great lengths in his book to explain how the practitioner's hypothesis is similar to, and yet different from, that of a researcher. Both generate a logical, deductively valid argument that includes the idea for a hypothesis, the idea for an experiment that provides a test of that hypothesis, and a prediction that the goal will be achieved. Then, both the researcher and the practitioner prepare a detailed plan for the experiment selected. If that plan is accepted, it serves as the basis for action, for the physical test of the hypothesis that follows.

Although the pattern of the thinking process is the same for the researcher and the practitioner, there are some significant differences. The researcher's problem is to determine the answer to a why question. The researcher does not know the cause of the situation and wants to discover it. The goal is to explain why the situation exists. To achieve that goal, the researcher usually generates two or more hypotheses and tests each one with at least one experiment to see if the logically deducted prediction is true. Schön explained but, unlike Dewey, did not model the work of researchers.

Both Dewey and Schön described the thinking of the practitioner who is not satisfied with the consequences of the situation. The practitioner's goal is to change those consequences, to transform the situation from what it is to what it should be. The practitioner uses the same deductive logic as the researcher to generate a hypothesis, experiment, and prediction. However, the practitioner does not just test the hypothesis through the experiment but instead attempts to use the experiment to make the hypothesis come true. If it does, the practitioner may stop, satisfied that the goal has been achieved. Dewey illustrates this process in his appointment example. He did not have to shift his frame and try another hypothesis because the first idea achieved his goal.

If, on the other hand, the prediction does not come true, if the results of the action do not satisfy the criteria, the musts and wants that have been specified, the practitioner must reframe the situation, generate a new hypothesis, and try again to make it come true. That is what Quist did with Petra's project. Schön put it this way: "The practitioner makes his hypothesis come true. . . . The action by which he tests his hypothesis is also a move by which he tries to effect a desired change in the situation, and a probe by which he explores it, and considers the resulting changes not as a defect of experimental method but as the essence of its success" (p. 151).

Wales, Nardi, and Stager's Process

The fact that the ideas proposed by Dewey and Schön have not been widely adopted by educators can be explained in a variety of ways. One of the reasons is surely the ever-present pressure to cover still more concepts and subjects in the curriculum at all levels. Since we now know infinitely more than we did eighty years ago, that pressure is even worse today than it was in Dewey's time. Another reason might be that neither Dewey nor Schön devised a unique method of presentation that would help educators teach the process. Just telling teachers to talk about problems in class is not solid enough advice for most. And a third reason may be that the almost parallel processes of thinking proposed by Dewey and Schön are not, given what we know today, as clearly defined as they might be.

Today, it seems clear that those who hope to teach thinking need at least two tools: a carefully defined model of the process and an explicit method of presentation. Both Dewey and Schön provide reasonably good models of the way people think or should think when they deal with intellectual problems. However, after twenty-two years of helping students learn how to think and helping faculty learn how to teach thinking in a wide range of disciplines, we (Wales, Nardi, and Stager, 1986) realized that Dewey's five phases should be arranged in the slightly different way shown in Exhibit 8.1. The end result of the reflective thinking used in each of these phases is a decision. Thus, we describe a process of five decision-making operations.

As everyone knows, the list in Exhibit 8.1 does not necessarily represent the order in which thinking actually takes place. We do know that some sort of internal or external stimulus starts the process, but what happens next is not predictable. For a typical teenager, it may be action based on whatever idea came to mind. For an adult, it may be an unconscious evaluation of the situation based on what has been or is being sensed at that moment, coupled with thoughts about both the goal and possible solutions. One of those ideas may actually be mentally tested all the way through a preliminary plan. But, in the end, successful decision makers know that they must bring order from all this chaos.

Why must there be order? Because each of the five decisions in the list of decision-making operations depends on those above it. Intelligent action is based on a well thought out plan; that plan is created around an idea that was selected from

Exhibit 8.1. The Process of Decision Making.

Stimulus

Define the who, what, when, where, why, and how of the situation.

Identify the problem and state the goal.

Generate strategy ideas.

Prepare a detailed plan for the strategy selected.

Take action and evaluate the results.

the two or more that were generated earlier; those ideas are developed in response to the problem that was identified and the goal that one expects to achieve; and each of those decisions depends on the situation in which people find themselves. Thus, in Exhibit 8.1, the five phases or operations are arranged in the order in which the decisions must finally occur.

The human mind may leap and dodge or thrust and parry through the process, but in the end it demands order. An understanding of that pattern is critical to the development of a professional. Students must be encouraged and taught to use their minds to freely generate questions, problems, goals, ideas, plans, and actions. They must also learn to use reflective thinking in each operation where there is an analysis to identify the problem involved, a generation and synthesis of options, and an evaluation to select the best option. But they must also learn to bring their thoughts back to the list of decision-making operations so what they decide makes sense in terms of the whole process.

The latter is a key point for those who hope to teach thinking. Educators can encourage their students to think freely and reflectively, they can offer lessons on creative or critical thinking, they can model in class, and they can provide opportunities for discussions, but if they do not teach students to bring their thinking back to the five decisions and the process, the students will be no further ahead than they were at the start. It is that unconscious logic that makes competent practitioners and researchers successful.

Teaching the Thinking Process

During our years of teaching thinking to both students and faculty, we learned that people are better prepared to think for themselves if they first learn how to use the decision-making process through carefully guided practice. Schön (1983) described what happens when the teacher and the student are not prepared to reflect on the same wavelength. Petra had surely learned a great deal about the techniques of design in other classes, but it seems clear that she had learned little about how to function as a reflective professional. Quist modeled the professional process with the wisdom and artistry that come with years of experience, but he did not know how to teach that process to Petra. They did not discuss the process, where they were in the process, or what should be taking place. From Schön's point of view, this "approach to instruction consists in demonstrating and advocating a kind of ... reflection-in-action, but it is also an approach of mystery and mastery. He demonstrates his mastery of the material, but he keeps the sources of his performance mysterious" (p. 126). Schön was particularly concerned about this approach because practitioners who were "unaware of their frames" will have no "need to choose among them" (p. 310).

Modeling is one of the few effective ways that educators have to show students how mastery and artistry are combined in a professional performance. Schön emphasized a specific approach to modeling in the concept of the *reflective practicum*. In his example of the architecture practicum, discussed above, as well as in the psychotherapist's supervision of a resident (pp. 76–104), Schön described individualized opportunities for the expert to guide an advanced student in discussing the problems of practice (see Harris, this volume, for a compelling argument for the use of the reflective practicum in case-based instruction and demonstrations).

We have come to the conclusion that modeling is an essential experience for student learning but that it is not sufficient to guarantee student mastery (Wales, Nardi, and Stager, 1986). In working with college freshmen, the ultimate novices, it became obvious that students need explicit instruction to understand the process of decision making before they can use it intelligently. To provide the combination of modeling and practice that is needed, we developed a teaching-learning strategy called Guided Design. Students working in teams of four to six are guided one step at a time through each of the decision-making operations by a set of printed "instruction" and "feedback" pages prepared in advance by the teacher. Each student receives a copy of the instruction, which explains the operation about to be performed and asks the student to complete it. When the students are ready, the teacher checks their ideas and approves of what they have done or suggests some additional ideas to consider. When the teacher is satisfied with the work, each student is given a copy of the printed feedback, which describes what a typical student group might be expected to do. If the feedback is well written and the students in the class have done an appropriate amount of thinking, the two results should be in close agreement. This combination of feedback from members of the group, from the teacher, and from the printed material helps students develop the reflective thinking skills that they need. The printed material also helps ensure that similar skills will be developed in multisection courses taught by different instructors.

Although the Guided Design format works well, its success as a teaching-learning strategy depends on the model of the decision-making process that is presented in its instruction and feedback pages. But before we model that format, we illustrate here with an actual Guided Design exercise what we expect the students to do, how they are likely to respond, and some of the facets of the process that they learn as they think their way through the five decision-making operations outlined in Exhibit 8.1.

The Case of the Icy Bridges

The following situation is presented to you as an example of decision making through the Guided Design process.

The Stimulus. A traffic safety organization wants a fresh view of a problem that they have not been able to solve. A group of students has been hired as part of a task force that has been asked to study the problem of highway bridges that ice over when the road is clear and dry. In order to avoid any compromise of the fresh view, the organization has not provided any advance information. Instead, each student is asked to come to the first meeting of the task force with a set of questions that he or she wants the safety experts to answer.

Define the Situation. The initial problem that the members of the task force must face is that they do not have enough information to proceed. To get that information, students learn that they must reflectively interact with the situation and generate a set of questions based on the generic samples shown in Table 8.1. They must also generate and synthesize the answers (1) using personal experience, knowledge, or observation, (2) using some type of media such as books, films, or computer records, (3) by asking experts, or (4) by performing research experiments. And then they must use personal or professional values to determine if the information that has been obtained is sufficient to define the situation and decide whether or not to proceed.

If the students have learned how to use reflective thinking, they will ask WH-questions that probe each area to an appropriate depth. For example, the first category of questions, pertaining to the actors involved, might generate a dialogue such as the following:

Student: Is the person who has one of these accidents a local driver, a traveler, or a big-rig truck driver?

Safety Expert: I'd have to look up the numbers, but as I remember, there were almost no eighteen-wheel drivers and about equal numbers of local drivers and travelers.

Student: What was the split between male and female drivers?

Safety Expert: More male drivers were involved.

Student: Does that reflect the fact that there are more male drivers?

Table 8.1. Generic WH-Questions That Inform the Decision-Making Process.

Situational Variables	Questions
Actors	Who is involved?
Action	What happened?
Props	What things are involved?
Scene	When did it happen?
	Where did it happen?
Cause	Why did it happen?
Consequences	How serious is the situation?

Safety Expert: Yes, the proportion is almost identical.

Student: Were these drivers young or old?

Safety Expert: Here again the data match the normal distribution of the people who are driving. For the drivers, at least—with the exception of the eighteen-wheel drivers—we do not see a unique pattern.

Even before the meeting takes place, skilled reflective thinkers will prepare a set of probing questions such as those given here.

> *Actors:* Who was involved in these accidents? Was it local people, travelers, or truckers? Was the driver a man or a woman, young or old? Was alcohol or drugs involved? Was the driver accident-prone?
>
> *Action:* What happened in a typical accident? Did the vehicle hit the side of the bridge, another car, slide sideways to dry pavement and roll, or go off the bridge or road? What did the driver do when he or she saw the ice?
>
> *Props:* What type of surface was involved: asphalt, concrete, or other? What type and make of vehicle was involved? How old was the vehicle? What type and brand of tires did it have? How worn were the tires? What was under the bridge: another road, a railroad track, or water? What was the condition of the bridge surface? Was it in good repair or not? Was traffic on the bridge going one way or both ways? Two lanes or four?
>
> *Scene:* When do these accidents happen? What month, day, and hour? Where are these icy bridges located? Is it a localized problem or a general problem?
>
> *Cause:* Why does ice form on the bridge surface when there is none on the roadway? Where does the ice come from? What is the source of the water?
>
> *Consequences:* How frequent, serious, and extensive were these accidents? What were the consequences in terms of deaths, personal injuries, and property damage?

As they ask questions to define the situation, the students on the task force should have at least two objectives. The first is to understand the situation surrounding these accidents as fully as possible. The WH-questions serve that objective. The second is to determine if there is any pattern in these accidents that points toward a solution. If, for example, the only people who had these accidents were driving drunk, the concern of the task force would probably shift from the ice and the bridge to the people or laws. To ensure that they get the in-depth data that they need, members of the task force must be prepared to ask very specific questions such as those given here.

To encourage reflective thinking in a classroom setting, students should be asked to put the who, what, when, where, why, and how words across the top of a chalkboard and to list their questions below. Students should be encouraged to use brainstorming as they skip back and forth with ideas for different categories. They should also understand that most people generate ideas for a solution as soon as they sense a problem. Although these ideas may or may not be useful after the situation is fully understood and the goal has been stated, immediate generation of ideas is still a natural thing to do. The danger for inexperienced decision makers is that they act at that point without considering the other essential parts of the process. These ideas should be recorded so that they can be considered later, but in a complex problem such as icy bridges there is no point in pursuing the ideas further until the goal has been selected.

Identify the Problem and State the Goal. As soon as the experts answer the questions about the actors, action, props, and scene, the students on the task force will realize that there are two problems that remain to be addressed: (1) *Cause:* They do not have an answer for the why question; they do not know why ice forms on a bridge and not on the road. (2) *Consequences:* They do not like the consequences that occur. Although the totals vary from one year to the next, there are years when a significant number of accidents, injuries, and deaths occur.

One of the important concepts students must learn is

that there are only two roles that they can play: researcher or practitioner. The problem that they address must come from the answer to either the why (cause) question or the how (consequences) question, and, at least with a simple problem, the goal that they seek will be the mirror image of the problem (Wales, Nardi, and Stager, 1986).

The researcher is not satisfied with the following answer to the why question: "We don't know why the situation exists." If reflective analysis shows that that unknown is the problem to be addressed, then the mirror image is used to generate and synthesize the goal: to explain why things are the way they are. If a careful evaluation determines that the best goal has been stated, the researcher moves on to the next operation. In the icy bridges problem a researcher's goal is to explain why ice forms on the bridge when there is no ice on the road leading to it.

The practitioner is not satisfied with the following answer to the how question: "The result is or is likely to be quite serious." If reflective analysis shows that that result is the problem, a mirror image goal is generated, synthesized, evaluated, and accepted. A typical goal is to change the consequences in a certain direction by a specific amount. Dewey's problem in the case of his appointment was that he was going to be late; the goal was the mirror image of that: to get to the appointment on time.

Successful decision makers know that the goal they select must be based on a problem that comes from the answer to the why or the how question. If the basis for the goal comes from some other part of the situation, the decision maker is likely to deal with some symptom of the problem, but not the problem itself.

In the case of the icy bridges, the agency asked the task force to focus on the practitioner's role of changing the consequences. The problem for the students is that the consequences are not acceptable. The goal discussion that follows provides a good example of reflective thinking. The first idea was the most obvious, to prevent or eliminate the ice. There was general agreement about that goal until someone said, "Why do we want to get rid of the ice?"

"Why do we want to do that?" is among the best reflective goal evaluation questions. If practitioners can answer that question, they will probably identify a broader and better goal.

"Why do we want to get rid of the ice? So we can reduce or eliminate the accidents it causes." "Why do we want to reduce or eliminate these accidents?" "Because people are hurt or killed." "Then I suggest we select that as our goal: to reduce the number of injuries and deaths on icy bridges."

The practitioner in Schön's architect example reframed Petra's idea when the first one did not work. In the problem of icy bridges, the students reframed their goal before they got into trouble. Would trouble have followed if the students had accepted ice removal as their goal? Perhaps! The members of the group might have found an acceptable solution; but unless they go beyond the ice, they will not know what other, even better solutions they might find. When Dewey made it to his appointment on time, he did not care what might have happened if he had made a different choice. In the icy bridges problem, however, other choices might have a significant effect on the number of accidents, injuries, and deaths, so they must be considered.

Another problem might arise if the students cannot find a way to achieve their goal of preventing or removing the ice. What would they do then, give up or start over by searching for a new goal? By asking and answering the "Why do we want to do that?" question, they avoid these problems. In addition, they should discover that rather than being a goal, ice removal is actually a possible solution for a broader problem. It is one way to reduce the number of people who are hurt or killed.

Reduction of the number of accidents has the same characteristics. It may be viewed as a goal; but when people are the goal, accident reduction is a possible solution. That people goal is important because if the students cannot find any practical or economically viable way to remove the ice or prevent accidents, they may still find ways to protect people. Seat belt laws and air bags are two of those solutions.

The final goal that the students select should describe what must be true when the action is completed and the desired change in consequences is achieved. In this case, the must could be to reduce the number of injuries and deaths. The desired change could be a reduction of 50 percent. Some decision makers prefer to delay the specification of the percentage until after the idea operation is completed. At that point, they will have a much better idea of what is possible and probable so that they can intelligently select a value.

Students must also learn the difference between identifying a problem and stating a goal. All too many decision-making models focus on the problem and ignore the goal. Dewey ([1910] 1933, p. 15), for example, states clearly that "the nature of the problem fixes the end of thought, and the end controls the process of thinking," but his process steps focus on just the problem and not the goal. That is not sufficient. The problem is what we hope to solve. It is defined by the current state of the situation. The goal is what we hope to achieve. It describes the situation that we hope to have in the future. It is the goal, not the problem, that is used to evaluate the results, so both must be stated. In complex problems, it may not be possible to identify the problem or state the best goal until the situation has been defined as fully as possible. And at that point it may take a good deal of reflective thinking to arrive at the best goal, so identification of just the problem will not suffice.

Generate Strategy Ideas. The goal of the students on the task force is to reduce the number of injuries and deaths on icy bridges. The first step toward a solution is to identify potential problems. They can do that if they ask, "What might cause an injury or death in this situation?" Through reflective thinking, the task force should see that injuries and deaths may be caused by a number of components: the ice, the design of the bridge and the roadway near it, the design and condition of the car, the education and skill of the driver, and the speed limit or other laws.

It should be obvious that the students did not need to identify these components before they began generating strategy ideas. In fact, that creative activity began as soon as each person received the assignment. They will discover, however,

that the use of a component analysis to organize their work will
increase both the number and the quality of their ideas. Another way to achieve the same end is to answer the question,
"How can we change the who, what, when, where, or why of the
situation so that we can change the consequences?" The result
might be component and strategy ideas such as presented in
Table 8.2.

The generation of ideas may be enhanced by the use of
brainstorming, where ideas flow freely with no criticism allowed, or of synectics, where one visualizes oneself as a part of
the situation: "I am a car rolling along nicely on dry pavement.
Why am I suddenly skidding? Is there something wrong with
me? With my tires? Or did my driver do something wrong? Oh
no, don't tell me the driver hit the brakes? Hasn't my driver ever
heard of Newton's first law?" The students might also try lateral
thinking, where they deliberately reverse, distort, or exaggerate
ideas: "What would happen if the car had square wheels or
bumpers all around like the cars in an amusement park? Why
don't we put studs on the bridge? Why don't we cool the road
so that it freezes first? Or put bumpers on the bridge so cars can
ricochet through?"

Create a Logical, Deductively Valid Argument. Students should
note that each of the ideas they generate is based on a "cause"
they have consciously or unconsciously recognized. They might
decide, for example, that these accidents are caused by a speed
limit that is too high. Given that "cause-theory," the students
may decide to try the idea of reducing the speed limit. At this
point, we ask them to state their idea in a special way—as a
logical, deductively valid argument.

Table 8.2. Sample Component and Strategy Analysis
for the Icy Bridges Problem.

Ice	Bridge/Road	Car/Tires	Driver/Law
Remove	Insulate	Air bag	Educate
Prevent	Cover	Better design	Seatbelt law
Heat	New surface	New tires	Reduce speed limit
Salt	Signs	Chains or studs	

Theory: High speed is the cause of the accidents.

Hypothesis: If the speed limit is reduced when the weather is bad, then there will be fewer injuries and deaths on icy bridges.

Experiment: Lower the speed limit when the weather is bad.

Prediction: There will be fewer injuries and deaths on icy bridges.

Before the students can evaluate their options, they must select the criteria that they will use to make their decision and debate the cost, potential gain, and technical and political feasibility of each strategy. It is at this point that all of the knowledge that they have gained may be particularly relevant. However, intuition and insight are also important factors when the final selection is made.

As the students discussed the experiment that they might use to test this hypothesis, they surely must have agreed that it would be almost impossible to decide when to reduce the speed limit and that people would soon learn to ignore whatever sign is posted and take their chances with the ice. Since it seemed unlikely that they could find a way to make their hypothesis come true, the students had no choice, they had to reframe the situation and start over with a new hypothesis.

It is noteworthy that Dewey ([1910], 1933, p. 74) was careful to point out that the "logical forms" taught in schools might be an "effective way in which to set forth what has already been concluded, so as to convince others . . . of the soundness of the result." However, Dewey also observed that these logical forms are not helpful in the reflective thinking process used to arrive at an answer. That point of view may surprise people who believe that the scientific method is superior to all other ways of thinking because it is a logical, deductively valid process. In fact, both views are partly true and partly false.

Researchers and practitioners eventually use the same five types of operations when they work through the process of decision making. Four of the five operations are based on inductive, reflective thinking, which is the only way either decision maker can ask and answer questions, decide on a goal, prepare a detailed plan, and take action. The one operation that is different and based partly on deductive logic is the generation of strategy ideas. In that operation, both the researcher and the practitioner should use creative, inductive, reflective thinking to generate as many strategy ideas as they can. The idea selected after a careful evaluation should be framed as a logical, deductively valid argument with ideas for a hypothesis, an experiment, and a prediction.

Practitioner Reframing. The students may next decide that ice forms on the bridge and not on the road because air circulates both over and under the bridge while, at least early in the fall, the road is heated by the earth beneath it. When conditions are favorable, dew may condense on the cold bridge and freeze or frost form there.

Given that "cause-theory," the students may decide to insulate the lower surface of the bridge and state this logical, deductively valid argument:

> *Theory:* Ice forms because bridges cool faster than the road when air circulates beneath them.
>
> *Hypothesis:* If bridges are insulated so that ice does not form there first, then the number of accidents, injuries, and deaths will be reduced.
>
> *Experiment:* Insulate one or more bridges.
>
> *Prediction:* There will be fewer accidents, injuries, and deaths on the insulated bridges.

If this idea is selected, a detailed plan for the insulation experiment, for application to one or more bridges, will be prepared in the next decision-making operation.

Prepare a Detailed Plan. When they prepare their detailed plans, these practitioner-students must once again consider *who* will be involved, *what actions* will take place, *what* type of insulation and support will be used, *when* the work will be done, *where* the bridges will be located, *where* the insulation will be placed, *why* something might go wrong, and *how* serious that might be.

A key part of what practitioners must plan is the way they will evaluate the results of their experiment. At the most basic level, they will record data for the number and severity of ice-related accidents on experimental and control bridges. As they complete these plans, they may realize that they can also do research to verify the cause-theory they selected. They could do this by adding temperature-recording devices to the surface of each bridge to determine if the insulation under the bridge does reduce surface cooling.

If practitioners can simultaneously play the role of researchers, the reverse must also be true. As researchers, the goal of these students might have been to explain why ice forms on the bridge and not on the road. One of their ideas might be the following:

> *Theory:* Air passing below the bridge cools the surface so that ice forms there.
> *Hypothesis:* If the bottom of a bridge is insulated, then the surface will not be as cool.
> *Experiment:* Insulate the bottom of one or more bridges.
> *Prediction:* The bridge surface will not be as cool.

The student-researchers' plan would be based on measuring the surface temperature on insulated and uninsulated bridges. Hopefully, they will realize that they can do the work of a practitioner as well by recording data on the number and severity of accidents on the experimental and control bridges. That combination will be a common pattern in applied research situations.

Take Action and Evaluate the Results. Since the task force was assembled to generate new ideas, its work may be finished. If one or more of these ideas appears to have potential, the traffic safety organization may search for an engineering firm or university research center that is interested in performing a preliminary study. The results of the experiments that are performed will be studied carefully to see if the prediction and, therefore, the hypothesis is valid. Even if the answer is yes, however, the gains must be significant enough to justify the cost. Thus, the final decision is whether to recommend the idea to appropriate highway departments or legislatures.

Teaching with Guided Design

Knowledge about what to teach has been our focus throughout this chapter. It is a key element in the development of students' thinking skills. However, faculty must also know how to present those ideas. Lectures will not suffice because students must practice thinking. Teachers must provide a clear, explicit model of "normally hidden mental activities," students must practice and their work must be evaluated (Resnick, 1987a, p. 40). That practice should take place in social settings where students deal with whole tasks, not just isolated skills (p. 41).

Most faculty already know about some strategies that meet these criteria: case studies, simulations, and problem-based or problem-centered coursework. While these are both useful and worthwhile strategies, they have a flaw. As they are usually taught, these strategies do not provide the explicit guidance that is needed. One way to solve that problem is to begin with Guided Design. This approach to teaching thinking was developed in 1969 at West Virginia University in a college that was concerned about losing too many good freshman students. We were asked to deal with this problem, and we discovered that while these freshmen were very bright and could think, they had never learned to think about the type of intellectual problems encountered in college. We set out to see if we could make a difference by integrating thinking with the subject matter in a two-semester sequence of courses. The data that we reported for freshmen entering during the five years before and the five years after the change show three significant gains (Wales, 1979).

Before the thinking course was introduced, the grade point average (GPA) of these freshmen was below the university average. After the change, the "thinking" students were above that average. The gains made in the freshman year persisted through all four years of college; the graduation GPA of these students was 25 percent higher than the GPA of transfer students who had not participated in the program. And because they made better grades, more students were able to continue in school, and the percentage of students who graduated from the program increased by 32 percent. The NRC report said that teaching thinking at an elementary level should improve student performance. It certainly did here! And if the conclusions given in the report are correct, results like these should apply to other programs as well.

The thinking program at West Virginia University involved as many as fourteen sections of the new course, with about twenty-eight students per class. These sections were taught by both regular faculty and graduate students. To ensure that the same kind of thinking skills were taught by the instructors, who had quite different backgrounds, we developed the Guided Design concept described earlier. Guided Design is a combination of the best features of case studies and programmed instruction based on written instruction-feedback pages. The teacher manages the flow of these pages; the students, who work in a social setting in teams of four to six, earn each feedback page by doing their own thinking. When, for example, they have discussed and agreed on their response in one step, the teacher checks the quality of their work and, if satisfied, hands out the feedback page. The students consider the ideas there, revise their ideas if they see fit, and then move on to an instruction that asks them to consider the next step in the process.

One professional group that appears to have recognized the value of teaching thinking is pharmacists. Here is the reasoning given in an article on the teaching of problem solving to pharmacy students (Jang and Solad, 1990, p. 165): "In the traditional subject-centered approach, teaching and learning are organized according to hierarchies. . . . Since patient's problems are typically not presented in accordance to such hierarchies, the student's ability to marshall information to solve the patient's problem requires substantial rearranging of the student's knowledge base."

Jang and Solad (1990) recommend Guided Design, which

has already been applied in a number of pharmacy schools, and problem-based learning as effective tools to begin the process of teaching thinking. A sample Guided Design module developed for an over-the-counter drug course in the West Virginia University School of Pharmacy (Malanga and others, 1987) is presented in Exhibit 8.2. This example models the instruction-feedback pattern of Guided Design with a client who has an unusual case of sunburn.

Guided Design appears to be one of the best ways to begin the development of process skills. Depending on the level and ability of the students, it quickly gives way to less structured and then unstructured open-ended problems. The difference is that the teacher and the students are now working on the same page in the thinking process, so sophisticated modeling has more meaning.

Since few programs have adopted thinking as a goal, it is usually taught by individuals who recognize its importance. Many of these educators have used Guided Design because it provides a concrete basis for organizing their activity. Pharmacy educators have, in the past few years, been among the most active adopters. Nursing, which has a long history of teaching thinking, has had many adopters. In addition, one nursing textbook (de Tornyay and Thompson, 1987) was revised to add a chapter on Guided Design. Other textbooks that feature this approach have been published in social work (Day, Macy, and Jackson, 1984), theater (Borchardt, 1984), psychology (Miller, 1981), business (Coscarelli and White, 1986), economics (Vogt, Cameron, and Dolan, 1992), general education (D'Amour and Wales, 1979), and engineering (Wales, Stager, and Long, 1984).

Conclusion

Perhaps the best way to summarize our ideas as well as the ideas of Dewey and Schön is to show the parallels among the processes presented in the examples. We have done that in Table 8.3, using the five operations of the decision-making process as the basis. As may be seen in the table, both Dewey's and Schön's ideas can be accommodated in the new model of decision making we have developed.

The approach to teaching professional decision making that we advocate is tightly focused on the use of these five operations. We value the work of Dewey and Schön for the articulation of the principles of practice used by the reflective practitioner. Our research has led us to the conclusion that novices who lack experience in practice need explicit structure to guide and inform them on their way to reflective practice.

By now, the message should be quite clear. If the goal of a program is to graduate students who are prepared to become professionals, faculty must teach their students how to think with what they learn. To do less is to deny what is uniquely human. Those who teach thinking skills will have both the personal and professional satisfaction that comes with more interest and enthusiasm for schooling, better student performance, better grades, and an increase in the number of students who complete their work. The theories, equations, and concepts that students learn now may tell them what *has been* discovered and what *has been* done, but these things do not tell them what *will be* discovered and what *should* be done. And in the end, that is where their future lies.

Exhibit 8.2. Sample Guided Design Module: The Pharmacy.

Instruction 1: Define the Situation

Jane Smith phoned the pharmacy on a Saturday evening. "My husband Tom has just returned from a fishing trip to the Chesapeake Bay," Jane said. "He is really sunburned. What can we do to relieve the discomfort? He never experienced this much of a problem with the sun before." The pharmacist called up Tom Smith's profile on the computer.

Tom Smith   Birth date: 6-5-29   Weight: 165 lbs.
Allergies—none known
3-6-86 Hydrochlorothiazide 50 mg. q.d.—hypertension
9-1-87 Septra—b.i.d.—bacterial prostatitis

Given this data, the pharmacist might speculate about the cause of Tom's unexpected sunburn. *What might be the cause? What questions should the pharmacist ask to help define the situation?* (When your group is ready, ask the instructor for the next page.)

Feedback 1: Define the Situation

The pharmacist might speculate that Tom's unexpected photosensitivity is the result of his long-term hydrochlorothiazide therapy. The short-term

Exhibit 8.2. Sample Guided Design Module: The Pharmacy, Cont'd.

Septra therapy for a bacterial prostatitis probably exacerbated Tom's reaction to ultraviolet light.

These are some of the questions that the pharmacist might ask.

> How long was Tom out in the sun?
> Where is the burn?
> How much area does it cover?
> Does he have a fever, chills, or nausea?
> What is his temperature?
> Is the burn painful?
> Has he been taking his blood pressure medication regularly?
> What has he done so far to relieve his discomfort?
> Is there any evidence of blistering?

Instruction 2: Identify the Problem and State the Goal

Mrs. Smith answered the questions this way: "If you will wait a moment, I'll ask Tom to take his temperature. While he does that, I'll answer your questions. Tom was out on the boat for about four hours this morning. The burn is mostly on his face, especially his lips, which seem a little swollen, and some on his hands. He says it is not painful but his skin feels tight and hot. Oh yes, his temperature is normal and there are no chills or nausea."

Tom came to the phone and said, "I take my blood pressure medicine regularly every morning with orange juice. When I first got home, I washed my face and hands with soap and cool water—the coolness felt good."

Given this information, *what would you identify as the problem?* As the pharmacist, *what is your goal?* (When your group is ready, ask the instructor for the next page.)

Feedback 2: Identify the Problem and State the Goal

The problem is Tom Smith's sunburn. The goal is to give him some relief now and instruction on how to prevent future burns.

Instruction 3: Generate Strategy Ideas

What *options* does the pharmacist have for treating Tom's sunburn? What advice can the pharmacist offer to prevent future problems? What are the major *constraints?* What is the *best choice?* (When your group is ready, ask the instructor for the next page.)

Feedback 3: Generate Strategy Ideas

Tom must be told about the photosensitivity that results from his medications and about ways to deal with it using a sunscreen. To deal with the sunburn, the pharmacist might recommend

> Cool tap water compresses for cooling

Exhibit 8.2. Sample Guided Design Module: The Pharmacy, Cont'd.

Hydrocortisone ointment (1/2%) for the lips to reduce
  inflammation
Emollients for the face and hands, for example, petrolatum or
  w/o emulsions like Nivea or Lubriderm to soothe and prevent
  dryness.

A major constraint is the location of the burn. Aerosol sprays
containing local anaesthetics should not be used around the face. Many
contain alcohol, which is drying to the skin. The sunburned skin *should be
protected with an emollient.*

Instruction 4: Prepare the Plan and Take Action

Turn your choice for Tom's therapy into a detailed plan. What is the
pharmacist likely to tell Tom? *When your plan is complete, take action by role-
playing the telephone call to Tom.* In addition, suggest what new type of data
might be added to your computer profile of each patient. (When your
group is ready, ask the instructor for the next page.)

Feedback 4: Prepare the Plan and Take Action

This is what the pharmacist might say on the phone.
  "Tom, since you don't have a fever, chills, or nausea, I think we can
rule out heat stroke. Cool tap water compresses will take the heat out. I
can deliver some 1/2 percent hydrocortisone ointment to be used on your
lips to reduce inflammation, apply it lightly with clean fingertips three to
four times a day. Also, Lubriderm lotion can be used on face and hands.
This treatment should soothe and protect your skin while it heals. Aerosol
sprays that contain a local anaesthetic should *not* be used on your face."
  "I gather you have never had a severe case of sunburn before." "That's
right," Tom replied. "Well, I think I can tell you why it happened now. You
are taking both hydrochlorothiazide and Septra. Both of these drugs are
likely to increase your photosensitivity to ultraviolet light. Call me
tomorrow if you are not better. And you should come into the pharmacy
the next time you plan to be out in the sun for prolonged periods of time
and we'll find a good sunscreen for you to use."
  Given the nature and seriousness of Tom's problem, the pharmacist
decided to add "hobbies" to the profile of each of his patients.

Table 8.3. Comparison of the Four Examples of Reflective Thinking.

Operations of the Decision-Making Process	Icy Bridges	Appointment	School Design	Sunburn
Stimulus	Task force job	Saw a clock	Assignment	Telephone call
Define the situation	Who has accidents? What happens? What surface material? When: month, day, year?	Where am I? Where must I be? When? How serious?	Given design specifications for the size, number, and type of space	Who has the problem? What happened? What history? What symptoms?
Identify the problem	R: Does not know why ice is there P: People hurt or killed	P: Not enough time	P: A unique contoured site	R: Medicine increases photosensitivity P: He is in pain
State the goal	R: Explain why ice forms P: Reduce injuries and deaths	P: Arrive on time	P: Fit school to contoured site	P: Relieve the pain and prevent reoccurrence
Generate strategy ideas	Remove or prevent ice Insulate bridge Heat the surface Seatbelt law	Elevated train Surface car Express subway	Butt the buildings into the slope	Cool water Ointment Emollients Relieve dryness
Selection	Insulate	Express subway	Butt into hill	All: specific brands

Prepare the detailed plan	Take action	Evaluate the results	Generate new strategy ideas
Try insulation test on ___	Tests conducted in research facilities	Determine if gains justify the costs	Heat the surface
Walk to nearest station	Take trip	Arrived on time	None needed
Prepare drawings for buildings on site	No action	Idea does not work	Reframe: carve the rooms into slope
Explanation of what to do, when	Explain over phone, deliver ointment, and so on	Ask for feedback	Come in for advice Add hobbies to computer

Note: **R** = researcher, **P** = practitioner.

CHAPTER 9

Learning from
Corporate Education Programs

Robert Rippey

Because of the large corporate investment in and commitment to training, much interesting education research and development has been made possible. In this chapter, I identify three problems of professional education and then describe five practices derived from corporate education that I believe could help resolve problems. I do not suggest that all five practices should be engaged in blindly. Nor do I suggest that the three problems of professional education have a single source. I do propose that certain insights gained in the corporate world may be useful in other professional settings as well.

As corporations and other large organizations such as the military have grown, they have developed needs for employees with special skills. Often these skilled employees perform in roles that either resemble or duplicate roles commonly ascribed to professionals. A substantial portion of the underlying knowledge base may indeed be identical to what is learned in a professional school.

However, in the corporate world, some knowledge, which is the result of considerable investment, requires secrecy. Patents are sometimes not as effective in protecting proprietary knowledge as is rapid covert action. A sudden rise in a need for special training may require immediate action and cannot wait for a response from traditional academic centers. There may not be time for approval by academic committees and administrative councils. Furthermore, these skills may be required so rapidly that the time lag between proposal and traditional academic program approval would leave the corporation two to three years from meeting its need. In such instances, which have occurred often in the past, certain organizations assume the responsibility for "growing their own." Rather than rely on traditional academic pathways for general education, followed by a period of professional education, some large organizations have developed fairly comprehensive education programs that include both general and specialized aims. Thus, the military has its own academies and colleges, General Motors and Aetna Insurance have their institutes, and Xerox and Bell Laboratories have their vast array of programs and courses, to cite but a few examples. In most cases, these courses are limited to employees. Proprietary restrictions may be imposed, at times, on the dissemination of the learning acquired. Some of these practices may indeed sound antithetical to the traditional academic pursuit of knowledge on a free and open basis.

Education and training within corporations has become a business of its own because of the need for flexibility and timeliness in training persons to fill special highly skilled roles. Despite the current abundance of intellectually well qualified workers, there is still a shortage of personnel with particular specialized skills. In a Darwinian response to the iron hand of the market for skilled employees, many large corporations have become quite expert in education and training. The magnitude of corporate education is often unrecognized. Ernest Boyer (1985, p. ix) estimates the 1985 budget for corporate education at over $40 billion, "approaching the total annual expenditures of all of America's four year colleges and universities." He further estimates that the number of persons participating in such programs approaches eight million per year. These courses "range from remedial English to the Ph.D. . . . and are developing an academic legitimacy of their own" (p. ix).

Outstanding research on teaching and learning has also emanated from these corporate centers of learning. For example, John S. Brown of the Xerox Research Center has done extensive research on the epistemology of learning. He has emphasized the importance of developing, not simply acquiring, formal concepts if the concepts are to be meaningful in practice (Brown, 1990).

Moreover, the facilities for presenting these education programs may exceed those in the most highly regarded universities. For example, the AT&T Hickory Ridge training facility in Lisle, Illinois, has comfortable, acoustically superior classrooms with unmatched computer facilities and unequaled education support services, adaptable to any conceivable education need. A visit to these corporate facilities is likely to draw invidious comparisons to the conventional professional school lecture hall with its cramped, uncomfortable seats, minuscule folding writing space, and poor visual display and acoustics.

Corporate education among the top two hundred corporations has been developing at a more rapid pace and is more adequately financed than either public or private institutions. Corporate education is beginning to look like the best of professional education—or better, if one's criteria are size, facilities, or effectiveness of curriculum in meeting clearly identified needs.

At the same time, the professions are becoming more highly organized, and many practices resemble those in large corporations. The practice of law is no longer the province of the individual attorney. Frank Lloyd Wright might not today operate out of his home in Oak Park, Illinois. Health care has discovered the competitive advantage of large group practices such as Kaiser Permanente and the Mayo clinics. And large numbers of professionals are being ingested by these corporations. For example, Walsh (1987) has studied the dilemmas faced by corporate physicians. Although, currently, only 0.5 percent of practicing physicians are "company doctors," the number may increase substantially as insurance coverage becomes more costly.

Each year, external pressures on the professions demand

lower costs, greater access by the poor, preservation of the environment, and contributions to the quality of life. At the same time, again using medicine as an example, continued training of specialists, somewhat independently of need, has resulted in a glut of specialists and a shortage of primary care physicians (Association of American Medical Colleges, 1991a). Resources may be unnecessarily squandered on training too many specialists who must increase charges to an increasingly smaller pool of the well insured. The concentration of specialists in large cities reduces the availability of these services to the rural poor. Corporations, on the other hand, seldom waste resources training persons in skills not needed by the corporation.

Unfortunately, professional schools have historically been hostile toward corporate education, as proprietary interests are seen as antithetical to peer scrutiny and validation, and to the free pursuit of knowledge. One could argue, of course, that legitimate peer validation is at least of equal interest to the corporate world as it is to the universities. Nor is the free pursuit of knowledge absent. Admittedly, corporate policy normally places limits on the scope of knowledge production. But given the current pressures for greater access to professional services at lower costs to individuals and governments, and the large number of unmet professional service needs of a large segment of the population, it would be wasteful to ignore solutions to education problems that have been worked out by corporate educators, for fear of sleeping with the enemy.

Three Problems of Professional Education

The idea of calling attention to deficiencies of programs for training professionals is not new. Perhaps the most recent and thoughtful criticism of education for the professions comes from Schön (1987, p. 10), who articulates the consensus or, perhaps, fears of many: "In recent years, there has been a growing perception that researchers, who are supposed to feed the professional schools with useful knowledge, have less and less to say that practitioners find useful."

Schön cites studies from each of the professions that reveal crises of confidence. He condenses the thinking about solutions into three categories. Medicine, management, and engineering seem concerned with difficulties of keeping up with expanding knowledge. Their solutions involve simplification and reorganization. Law and architecture focus on aspects of practice that lack any programs of formal preparation. Their suggestions for improved programs involve the addition of programs in professional ethics and professional-client relationships. Other professions, according to Schön, believe that improvement is best achieved by tightening up standards. Schön, of course, rejects these solutions and recommends an alternative curriculum closely integrated with practice, by encouraging reflection on the act of practice itself. Although Schön's writing is thoughtful, his findings are inconclusive. He concludes that "it remains to be seen whether, through a curriculum designed on a better understanding of conflicting demands, we can achieve, at least at threshold level, conditions essential both to a coherent professional curriculum, and to a reflective practicum" (1987, p. 342).

My position is that three problems in professional education stand in the way of the desired conditions to which Schön refers. These are (1) the lengthy response time to technological and environmental challenges, (2) the dominance of teaching and research over service, and (3) the unnatural separation of training from practice. Cavanaugh (this volume) describes the latter two problems in some detail; I simply note and summarize those two here and focus on the first.

Response Time

As new challenges or technologies arise, the response time of traditional professional education is too long. By the time the research is done, the texts written, the faculty trained, and the curriculum change approved, a problem may reach epidemic proportions. The problem of maldistribution of health care services in rural areas has been known for at least twenty years, but how extensive are programs for recruiting, training, and

maintaining the interests and skills of rural health professionals? In a recent article from my hometown paper ("Local
Doctor Shortage," 1992, p. 1), the following was reported: "Its
a no-win situation. . . . The last three to five years have been
really critical in regards to a shortage of doctors in Macomb. . . .
Doctors have either moved or retired and we haven't hired any
to replace them."

Admittedly, the problem of maldistribution of medical
services is not entirely a matter of education. Nevertheless, the
problem of maldistribution is exacerbated by the separation
between training and the system of delivery. Education solutions such as those originated at Southern Illinois University
Medical School have been effective. For example, a graduate
dental student there from Australia received flying lessons as
part of his curriculum, so that when he went home he could
serve in the Outback. In corporations, there is much less of a
dividing line between the system and the educators. Problems
are solved jointly. They are solved according to specific time
lines. Critical path scheduling is employed by corporations not
only in building submarines but also in reaching corporate
personnel goals.

In another field, architecture, we see similar delays between challenge and response. Design and construction of
appropriate housing for the poor and the homeless does not
take top billing away from our interest in housing for the rich
and famous. It is true that some architects have creatively
responded to the problem of affordable housing, but the
evidence from our slums is that the response has been too little
and too late.

In no way is the time lag solely a problem of professional
schools. But even given a strong public will and the funds to
seriously attack the problem, the professional schools might be
hard-pressed to take timely action.

Unbalanced Priorities

A second problem in traditional academic education for the
professions is the dominance of research and teaching over

service as criteria of excellence for faculties. There are, of course, good reasons for this system of priorities. However, in corporations, priorities are in a different order, with service being a *prerequisite* for corporate existence. Both teaching and research are instrumental in corporate training, but the product and the service are paramount. In corporations, people are not knowingly trained to deliver unneeded services. The relative freedom of academic faculties from demands for service may cause some to be unaware of or insensitive to appropriate distributions of services. Thus, an oversupply of unneeded specialists may be trained in spite of good intentions.

Separation of Education and Practice

The third and perhaps the most serious problem in the design of training programs for the professions is separation of professional educators from the design of efficient systems of practice. A common criticism of professional schools is their insensitivity to practice requirements (see Cavanaugh, this volume); it is even rarer for professional educators to play an active role in the design of professional practice. The boundary between a profession and a professional school needs to be more permeable.

Granted, these three problems of professional education—response time, subordination of service, and separation of educators from the design of practice models—are complex and require complex solutions. But the following ideas, all borrowed from successful corporate education programs, offer useful insights.

Corporate Education Practices

Five processes in particular have been used heavily in corporate education but as yet are not highly visible in professional education: (1) management training, (2) just-in-time training, (3) incorporating the cost of students' time into the cost of instruction, (4) applying demonstrated but ignored principles of learning and instruction, and (5) making continuing education more continuous and more specific to needs for professional services.

Management Training

According to Eurich (1985), corporations spend about equal amounts of their education budgets on management training and technical training. If professionals are to work in groups with more highly differentiated functions, then their activities need to be coordinated within an efficient system. We have learned much in the last thirty years about coordinating the activities of massive resources rapidly. Examples include Operation Desert Storm, the construction of the United Nations building, and the conquest of polio.

The commitment to the design of high-performance systems needs to be shared at all levels of the professions. This commitment must grow from an acknowledged identification of flaws in existing professional delivery systems and their antecedent training programs. Such commitment is particularly important at leadership levels.

Management consultant Clifton Smith (1988, p. 7) has suggested that designers of health care education programs might profit from a closer look at corporate training programs in one of the large corporations that he represents: "Managing people in corporate education may compete with, and may well surpass, the function of managing technical operations if, indeed, the two can be separated. Enormous sums of money and energy are spent on courses like Selection Interviewing, Performance Appraisal, Team Building, Effective Listening, Motivating Employees, Effective Leadership. . . . If corporate education must spend this level of effort on interpersonal relations, one must wonder whether schools and colleges have been so individually oriented that students have not learned to work with others."

Corporations make substantial investments in the development of their leaders, who must be well trained in both management and substance. To what extent do the professions ensure that their leaders have adequate training in both the substantial knowledge of the profession and appropriate high-level management skills? Commendable leadership development programs do exist, such as the American Council on Education Fellows program and Harvard's Institute for Educational Leadership. While these programs are useful for developing generic management skills in higher education, more targeted management training, focusing on ways of mobilizing effort to meet critical practice problems, is needed for leaders in professional schools.

Just-in-Time Training (JITT)

JITT is an idea borrowed from production scheduling. Just-in-time production scheduling relies on carefully planning of the flow of materials so that they arrive from suppliers to the assembly line precisely at the instant they are to be assembled. This results in several savings. There is no need for expensive storage space for housing and protecting inventories. There is no capital investment in inventories. Improved subassemblies can be installed as soon as they arrive on the scene. It is not necessary to use up a supply of outmoded components before state-of-the-art developments can be incorporated.

JITT has been applied in corporate training programs, and although it employs the same underlying principle as just-in-time production scheduling, it has quite a different purpose. People are most highly motivated to learn when they know that they will soon have to apply that learning. Shortening of the time interval between learning and application also reduces forgetting. Contiguity of learning and work has the advantage of relating the most newly developed ideas to work as it is, not as it was and not as it is supposed to be. There is no practical value, for example, in learning how to design three-dimensional architectural models on the computer before the technology is available.

JITT may be absolutely essential where rapid change in technology is taking place and where the need for the technology is obvious. Traditional curriculum development and training methods take too long a time to implement when the stakes are high and time is short. JITT has always taken place in emergency situations in all professions. It is efficient. The opportunity to experience it more often could help individuals develop confidence in their adaptability.

Two questions arise. First, is JITT just another name for timely continuing professional education? Many highly effective continuing education programs do indeed resemble JITT. However, as Bennett and Fox (this volume) point out, many continuing education programs are not the direct result of a clear and present need identified by the profession. Also, the timing of continuing education is generally not a critical concern. JITT is given immediately before it is to be applied, not at the convenience of the student. Examples of JITT in the professions might be the immediate team training of a staff just prior to the installation of a Positron Emission Tomogram (PET) scanner or an esoteric language course given to a missionary en route.

Second, is JITT suitable for undergraduates in the professions? Some of the principles of JITT have already been employed in problem-based learning units in medicine. For example, Barrows (1980) confronts students with the realities of practice by presenting them with simulated cases, asking them to research the cases in the literature, and then having them discuss the cases in small groups until they reach an adequate level of understanding. The big difference between Barrows's approach and traditional professional education lies in the JITT aspect of it. That is, Barrows presents students with cases and *then* they have to learn the basic medical principles necessary to solve the puzzle. However, students using Barrows's instructional units are usually a long way from actual practice. Use of JITT could be a response to concern about compartmentalization in all of those professional curricula where students learn first and are expected to practice later.

JITT, however, is not easy, and it does not mean just-in-time preparation. If a profession desires to conduct JITT, it needs to have the personnel and facilities to rapidly and effectively construct the curriculum. Such a group would consist of a combination of full-time curriculum specialists and educational technologists who work with experts brought in from the field or the laboratory to provide the substance of the curriculum. Such facilities might experience a substantial amount of down time waiting for action. However, the hours of down time would be small compared to the hours saved by the learners.

Incorporating the Value of Student Time

When corporations or the military provide training for their high-level personnel, there is no question that one of the expenses of training is the loss of productive work time. An early attempt to utilize this information in the planning of instruction was done by the Rand Corporation for the U.S. Air Force in a project named Method of Designing Instructional Alternatives (MODIA) (Carpenter-Huffman, 1977). New training programs were designed by instructional technologists who classified behavioral objectives and "learning incidents." Students were also classified, according to salaries, travel expenses, and training needs. A sophisticated computer program, based in part on a synthesis of replicated findings concerning learning, then suggested a number of instructional alternatives, including designs that would be less costly. For example, if the trainees were generals who were highly dispersed geographically, teleconferencing might be less costly than bringing them together. Or a competitive model of instruction, pitting the skills of simulated contenders against one another, might compensate for the geographical isolation of students living north of the distant early warning line.

Demonstrated but Ignored Principles of Learning and Instruction

Both the military and corporate education programs have a substantial repository of information about practices that constitute effective teaching and curriculum construction. The MODIA project is a good example of such a repository. The principles are not usually trade secrets but rather practices that often are not applied outside of the corporate area because of the desire of educators to give the appearance of prudence and frugality. This could be a case of being penny wise and pound foolish. One of the well-supported principles of corporate education, for example, is that the quality of instructional materials and programs must not be strained. Efficient and effective learning is too important for false parsimony. Corporate education programs are generally attractive, carefully written, understandable, timely, carefully evaluated, and coordinated with role expectations for the learner. Content is carefully targeted to the audience and the task at hand (see, for example, AT&T Quality Assurance Center, 1989). Such manuals are frequently revised and readers are given self-addressed evaluation forms to make suggestions for improvement for the next edition. In addition, both the military and the corporate education planners are meticulous in applying the current state of the pedagogical arts.

Another important but often ignored principle of learning is constructivism. The origins of constructivism are unclear, but the principle was probably first observed among physicists who were puzzled by their own tendencies to revert to naive or Aristotelian physical principles when their theories were contradicted by fact. Some of the early research on constructivism was done at the Massachusetts Institute of Technology. Gentner and Stevens (1983) edited a collection of work describing the difficulties in debunking naive concepts of reality. For example, Wiser and Carey (1983) are devoted to the misleading effects of the "natural," but medieval and wrong, conclusion that heat and temperature are one. McClosky (1983) and Clement (1983) deal with conceptions about motion, attributable to Aristotle and Galileo, that clutter the minds of physics students and deter their progress. While these naive concepts were adequate for their day, and adequate in our own day to explain frequent everyday experiences, they require a high tolerance for error and a total disregard for precision.

Constructivism has already influenced the engineering profession and is beginning to make itself felt in medical education. The constructivist approach derives from the established psychological concept of proactive inhibition (Underwood and Schultz, 1960), which states that what one already knows may interfere with new learning. This is especially true if the old learning contradicts the new. Bugelski (1971, p. 197) considers proactive inhibition a much more serious threat to learning new materials than retroactive inhibition, which is when new learning interferes with recall of old learning.

Using the constructivist approach, investigators first attempt to uncover simplistic explanations of complex phenomena that are known to interfere with learning. As H. L. Mencken is alleged to have said, "Every complex phenomenon has a number of simple, easy to understand, wrong explanations." The adverse effects of such simple, strongly held, wrong explanations are identified by studying and questioning the concepts that learners bring to the learning situation. Once the naive initial structures likely to possess learners are understood, instruction can begin by seeing which of these counterproductive ideas are prevalent in the minds of the students. Instruction then proceeds to demonstrate their invalidity. Then, and only then, is the new material presented.

If students believe that the heart is a pump and the vessels pipes, those ideas must be disqualified. If students believe that the earth is flat, that idea must be eliminated before teaching celestial navigation. If the student of psychology believes that people and animals respond in a predictable way to negative reinforcement, they must be disabused of that idea. People will strongly resist and quickly forget material that conflicts with early beliefs based on personal experience.

Constructivist principles have been applied to learning in the health sciences by Spiro, Feltovich, Jacobson, and Coulson (1991), Chi, Glaser, and Farr (1988), and Feltovich, Spiro, and Coulson (forthcoming). The latter authors attack the concept that the heart is a pump pushing a liquid through a set of pipes. They document the frequent use of this misguided concept in medical classrooms as well as the life-threatening consequence of its acceptance by students. In addition, they show the kinds of difficulties that students encounter when they have suffered an overdose of the concept of pumps and pipes.

It is important for all professions to examine carefully their curricula to make certain that they are not perpetuating misconceptions that are counterproductive to new learning. It is for each profession to decide which topics are most important to research for their counterproductivity. Here are a few examples of naive questions: Is the judge an impartial interpreter of the law? Is the teacher a conveyor of the truth to the younger generation? Is the physician a healer?

Continuity and Specificity of Continuing Education

Continuing education is conducted systematically and on a large scale in most corporations and in all professions. Access to continuing education in corporations is often limited to those who, in the judgment of the corporations, will put that education to best use. The continuing education offerings are made with the needs of the corporation taking top priority, not the personal interests of the employee or the needs of the institution presenting the continuing education. When a corporation sees a need for continuing education, it may organize a program internally or contract the task with an external education institution or with private consultants. However, the design of the program is driven by the specifications of the corporation. According to Derr, Jones, and Toomey (1988), personnel can enter corporations with a lower level of training than that characteristic of entry into the professions. However, promotion is determined more by the promise of performers whose abilities are enhanced during practice. The model suggested here for the professions includes early entry, early introduction to meaningful tasks under supervision, and planned continuing education integrated with professional role.

Early entry could follow the lines of the Association of American Medical Colleges' *Project 3000 by 2000* (1991b). Although this project is aimed at the recruitment of underrepresented minorities, it merits broader application. The program emphasizes, among its objectives, (1) development of sustained, long-term relationships with high schools, (2) advocation of assistance for the creation of magnet high schools in the health sciences, and (3) nurturance of the creation of a "seamless" education curriculum. Seamless curriculum is a concept initiated in corporate education, and it is eminently applicable to all of the professions. Essentially, in a well-functioning enterprise, one should never be quite certain whether one is working or learning. Seamlessness implies not only a smooth transition between one stage of learning and another but also a lack of seams between one's work and one's development as a professional. Seamlessness implies continuity of experience, a natural progression. And it implies natural divisions of learning and labor: not two calendar years of a fixed sequence of courses followed by six weekly rotations in clinical specialties, and not six weeks in torts followed by six weeks in constitutional law, followed by six weeks in contracts.

Conclusion

In this chapter, I have discussed five concepts that appear to be influential in solving three problems facing the education of professionals for the twenty-first century: (1) greater emphasis on both management training and sound management of professional skills within the context of developing complex organizations for the delivery of professional skills, (2) just-in-time training, (3) accounting for the value of the student's time in computing the cost of education and training, (4) making more use of current knowledge about learning in the design of instruction, and (5) increasing the continuity and specificity of continuing learning in the development of professionals. In these times of rapid change, unstable futures, and insecure support, educators, individual professionals, and corporate organizers and deliverers of professional services might well hang more closely together in preference to hanging separately. It is important that we look favorably on such a union, or, at least, a mutual exploration. I believe that we have much to learn from one another.

PART THREE

Professional Education
and Practice
in Lifelong Partnership

The objective of this third section is to reflect on conceptual and attitudinal changes necessary for professions to realize and maintain closer linkage between professional education and professional practice throughout the careers of involved professionals, both academics and practitioners.

In Chapter Ten, William C. McGaghie discusses possible revisions in the concept of and the attitude toward identifying initial levels of appropriate competence at the point of entry to professional practice. Nancy L. Bennett and Robert D. Fox, in Chapter Eleven, continue this line of thought in their discussion of changing expectations and structure to maintain professional competence throughout a practice career.

In Chapter Twelve, R. Eugene Rice and Laurie Richlin broaden the role of the academic, or the university-based arm of the professions. They suggest an expanded role that could more appropriately and more effectively sustain the four distinct purposes expected of professional school faculty: contributions to discovery in the profession, contributions to integrating professional knowledge, contributions to optimizing teaching and learning within the professional field, and contributions to professional practice.

This wider view of the structural, attitudinal, and conceptual change necessary to the evolution of professional education forms the basis of Chapter Thirteen, wherein Lynn Curry and Jon F. Wergin trace the significant themes repeated throughout the book: proactivity, integration of technical and practical knowledge, and reflection on practice. They conclude by suggesting a series of principles and strategies to support fundamental change in professional education.

CHAPTER 10

Evaluating Competence for Professional Practice

William C. McGaghie

This chapter addresses why and how the competence of professionals is evaluated. It treats the topic broadly and amplifies earlier writing (McClelland, 1973; McGaghie, 1991b; Menges, 1975). Features of the professional and social context of competence evaluation are emphasized. Some issues about educational measurement are also covered, but not in great detail.

The four main sections of the chapter address basic issues that appear simple but are actually complex. The issues involve four overlapping topics: social issues, central ideas, technical problems, and professional meetings. The chapter closes with a consideration of implications for practice and research.

The idea that professionals should be evaluated before starting practice is not new. For example, Christian tradition endorses criteria expressed by Saint Paul to another first-century missionary about the consecration of bishops: "Appoint elders in every town as I directed you, men who are blameless, married only once, whose children are believers and not open to the charge of being profligate or insubordinate. For a bishop, as God's steward, must be blameless; he must not be arrogant or quick-tempered or a drunkard or violent or greedy for gain, but hospitable, a lover of goodness, master of himself, upright, holy, and self-controlled; he must hold firm to the sure word as taught, so that he may be able to give instruction in sound doctrine and also to confute those who contradict it" (Titus 1:5–9).

These criteria for professional practice are matched by more recent questions, from the eighteenth century, that Methodist bishops are required to ask of all prospective clergy (United Methodist Church, 1980, para. 425). Originally composed by John Wesley, the nineteen questions seek an affirmative response from candidates about spiritual and secular matters. The questions include inquiry about basic Christian faith, belief in ultimate perfection (afterlife), knowledge of general church rules, intent to instruct children, endorsement of fasting or abstinence, both by precept or example, and freedom from financial debt.

Pentecostal evangelist Jimmy Swaggart was unfrocked in 1988 by the Assemblies of God denomination. The church announcement cited "unspecified sin" (presumably, sexual misconduct) as the reason Swaggart was stripped of his multimillion dollar television ministry ("Church Defrocks Swaggart . . . ," 1988). Clearly, criteria specifying personal qualities needed for practice of Christian ministry in the late twentieth century are nearly identical to those of the eighteenth century or even of the first century A.D.

Competence evaluation for the medical profession also has clear-cut historical precedent. The by-laws of the Royal Colledge of Physicians (1693) state as follows:

> Before anyone be admitted either into the Order of the Fellows or Candidates, let him be examined thrice in lawful Meetings, whether greater or lesser, according to the pleasure of the President and Censors. . . .
> Let the form of the examination be after this manner.

First, let him be examined in the Physiologic part, and the very Rudiments of Medicine. . . .

Secondly, let him be examined in the Pathologic Part, or concerning the causes, differences, symptoms, and signs of diseases, which physicians make use of to know the essence of diseases. . . .

Thirdly, let him be examined concerning the use and exercise of medicine, or the reason of healing.

This sequential, three-part format is identical to the approach used to evaluate the fitness of candidates for U.S. medical licensure in the 1990s (National Board of Medical Examiners, 1990, 1991). Today, the evaluations are named the National Board Comprehensive Part I, II, and III Examinations. The titles are different but the purpose is the same. For more than three centuries, students of Western medicine have submitted to knowledge assessments of basic sciences, clinical sciences, and clinical practice, respectively. The examination content has evolved due to scientific and technical advances. The examination format, by contrast, appears immutable.

Beyond the clergy and medicine, there are today hundreds of occupational groups that claim professional status (American Educational Research Association, American Psychological Association, and National Council on Measurement in Education [AERA-APA-NCME], 1985; Freidson, 1986). The groups are disparate as they are numerous. There is, however, no gold standard to separate true professionals from aspirants. Distinctions are arbitrary, yet writers such as Freidson (1986) argue that a requirement for training in an accredited institution of higher education is the real arbiter.

Groups claiming professional status include chiropractors and clinical psychologists, attorneys and accountants, systems analysts and soldiers, divas and defensive tackles. The four categories of helping, entrepreneurial, technical, and performing professions constitute a simple but useful scheme to organize the groups. What unifies the professional groups is that they all aim to somehow evaluate and certify the fitness of individuals before those persons can work autonomously. Certification methods vary in focus, formality, and rigor but their purpose is the same. One needs to be a "card-carrying" member of a profession to be a bona fide practitioner.

Several definitions are needed here. A *profession,* according to *Webster's New Collegiate Dictionary,* is "a calling requiring specialized knowledge and often long and intensive academic preparation," and a *calling* is "a strong inner impulse toward a particular course of action, esp. when accompanied by conviction of divine influence." Pious overtones are evident here as well as in another definition of profession, "the act of taking the vows of a religious community." A profession, clearly, is not just a job or an artifact of chance. It is one's primary life's work, involving concrete knowledge and skill components joined with ineffable qualities of personal character, behavior, and spirit. The learning and practicing of a profession require large investments of one's time, effort, education, and ego.

Ideas about evaluating an individual's *competence for professional practice* are embodied in the AERA-APA-NCME *Standards for Educational and Psychological Testing* (1985, p. 63): "For licensure or certification [credentialing] the focus of test standards is on levels of *knowledge and skills* necessary to assure the public that a person is competent to practice" (emphasis added). Note that this statement does not include assessment of one's personal qualities, life-style, or private interests.

Assessment refers to the measuring instruments and procedures used to obtain data about an individual's competence for professional practice. *Evaluation* extends assessment by imposing policies (for example, education requirements) and standards (for example, a minimum passing score) on assessment methods. The policies and standards are expressions of prevailing values about basic requirements for competent professional practice.

These four terms—profession, competence for practice, assessment, and evaluation—coalesce to form the theme of this chapter. The theme can be expressed as two questions: How shall we go about assessing, evaluating, and credentialing the fitness of individuals for autonomous professional practice? How do we know that our motives and methods are right?

Three more thoughts need expression. First, competence evaluation always involves certification by a professional association or agency (for example, American Guild of Organists, 1988). However, professions under government regulation, such as veterinary medicine, also require licensure. Second, competence evaluation may or may not occur at the end of formal training. In medicine, most states grant a license for unsupervised practice during a physician's first of at least three years of postgraduate education, after Part III of the National Board Comprehensive Examinations is passed. Third, forms of professional credentialing vary widely. All it takes to become a university professor is an advanced degree, a good reputation, and a job offer. Sometimes, degree requirements are waived. This is very different from obtaining a military commission, becoming ordained, making the final cut for a National Basketball Association team, or getting a part in a Broadway play after an audition.

The title of professional may be obtained formally or informally, by competitive examination or competitive performance, for a lifelong career or for as long as one's body holds up (for example, ballerinas). Credentialing approaches are matched to the unique requirements of each profession.

Social Issues

Evaluation and credentialing of professionals has important social consequences in at least three ways: maintenance of social hierarchies, effects on income and status, and the behavior of professional schools (see Abbott, 1988; Berlant, 1975; Derber, Schwartz, and Magrass, 1990; and Freidson, 1986; for thorough treatments of the sociology of professionals).

Social Hierarchies

Sociologists of the professions, especially Freidson (1970), argue that the professional credentialing process supports a rigid caste system. This support is particularly the case in the health professions, although similar arguments have been made about other professions such as the military (Moskos, 1970). Scholars point out that once an individual earns an entry-level professional credential, that person is usually locked into a professional caste. Few nurses, physicians' assistants, or allied health professionals become M.D.s. Paralegals rarely attend law school and pass the bar exam. Seldom do enlisted men or women earn an army, navy, or air force commission. The professional status one achieves early in a career is often fixed. Individual mobility is rare.

Professional personnel evaluation plays a role in maintaining social hierarchies by governing access to education opportunities. Admission to prestigious professional schools, and progress through their curricula, depends more on high norm-referenced test scores (for example, Dental School Admission Test) than on practical experience in a lower-status professional role (for example, dental hygienist). Individuals who perform well on assessments of acquired knowledge gain access to professional training and opportunities to earn credentials.

Income and Status

For some professions, especially high-status professions like medicine, achievement of a credential is a ticket to a high income. Reference to the 1990 *Statistical Abstract of the United States* shows that receipt of the M.D. degree from an accredited U.S. medical school virtually guarantees a six-figure income. This financial fact, together with the recognition that approximately 1.4 percent of students leave medical school for academic or nonacademic reasons (Jonas, Etzel, and Barzansky, 1991), leads to an important conclusion. The most important evaluation decision made about the career of most physicians is the decision to admit them to medical school (McGaghie, 1990).

Other professions such as school teaching, accounting, and law enforcement do not enjoy these financial and social advantages for a variety of reasons. The reasons include the supply of the professional labor pool, demand for professional services, whether nonprofessional (or nonspecialized) persons can provide services, the rigor and cost of the professional education program, and the extent to which professional bodies control market forces.

Professional income is not necessarily a correlate of professional status. The income of professionals is directly linked to the market value of their skills. Professional status is granted according to the social value given to one's work. Trial lawyers and cardiovascular surgeons are among the highest salaried professionals. University professors and Supreme Court justices, by contrast, have much lower earnings yet equal or higher status due to public perceptions of the social value of their work.

Behavior of Professional Schools

Professional schools are the first source of professional credentials. This is particularly true for learned professions in the helping, entrepreneurial, and technical categories. Without a diploma or certificate from an accredited professional school, an individual is rarely eligible for later evaluation and certification by a professional body. One has to earn a professional degree as a prerequisite to obtaining a license to practice as a clinical psychologist, certified public accountant, or civil engineer. There are, of course, exceptions to this rule in such professions as international finance where neither a diploma nor a license is a work requirement. Beyond demand and competitive merit, few rules govern the evaluation of performing professionals (for example, actors, athletes) to practice their crafts.

Professional schools usually cannot issue credentials to candidates unless the schools are accredited. Accreditation involves fulfillment of institutional certification criteria similar to the individual criteria that candidates must achieve. To gain accreditation, a professional school must satisfy minimum requirements in such areas as curriculum, faculty credentials, financial stability, admissions and records, student evaluation, and administrative practices. Accreditation requirements are imposed by peers—institutions and persons. They are valid by consensus and zeitgeist.

External accreditation requirements do not always match the internal policies set by a professional school or university faculty. In extreme cases, conflict can become so bitter as to cause a school to voluntarily forfeit or involuntarily lose its accreditation. A recent illustration is the decision by the University of Wisconsin at Madison to abandon the journalism accreditation process that is imposed by the Accrediting Council on Education in Journalism and Mass Communications ("Madison Shuns Journalism Accrediting . . . ," 1991). The university and the Accrediting Council disagree about distribution requirements for liberal arts courses and journalism courses needed for the baccalaureate degree. A high administrator at another journalism school comments about the case, "This is a big deal because this isn't Podunk U." The same external official interprets the university's position toward the Accrediting Council as, "This rule is a straitjacket, and rather than put ourselves into it, we have the confidence in our product that we don't need accreditation."

Journalists are not required to be certified or licensed to pursue their profession. The marketability of Wisconsin graduates, and the journalism school's ability to attract new students, will likely determine if the university ultimately prevails.

Central Ideas

Professional competence evaluation requires thoughtful attention to several key ideas. One idea concerns how professionals perform at the beginning of their careers and throughout the career continuum. A second idea concerns the nature of professional competence, including the skills, knowledge, and personal qualities that require evaluation and, by inference, those that can be ignored. The third idea is whether competence is a lasting trait or if judgments about one's competence are shaped by variables involving practice setting, time, and other conditions. Finally, evaluators need to consider whether the competence of professional persons can be judged independently of their ability to achieve desired outcomes with clients, patients, or others who receive service.

Evaluation Continuum

The literature on professional competence evaluation tends to focus on evaluations for credentials that are made at the conclusion of professional school and the beginning of practice (Shimberg, 1983). This is shortsighted because evaluation and certification of an individual's competence for professional practice is rarely a "one-shot" event. Competence evaluation takes place throughout professional life, although with much variation in format and in what is at stake for an individual's career.

An illustration of a continuum of competence evaluation for one of the learned professions—medicine—is presented in Figure 10.1. This example shows that professional competence evaluation is sequential, beginning very early in a physician's career. It indicates that significant evaluations occur before and after the four years of undergraduate medical education. Evaluation addresses not only the outcomes that result from periods of formal education but also the screening and admission tests that grant access to more advanced medical training. Norcini and Shea (this volume) discuss the role of evaluation for recertification and relicensure, another location on the professional career continuum.

Stevens (1983) makes a similar case about the sequential character of competence evaluation in the legal profession. This is echoed throughout the chapter contributions to Hunt, Hinkle, and Maloney (1990). Evaluation of an individual's competence for professional practice is frequently a career-long enterprise.

Criterion Problem

What are the features of an individual's knowledge, skill, and personal qualities that need to be evaluated and approved

Figure 10.1. Continuum of Medical Learner Evaluation.

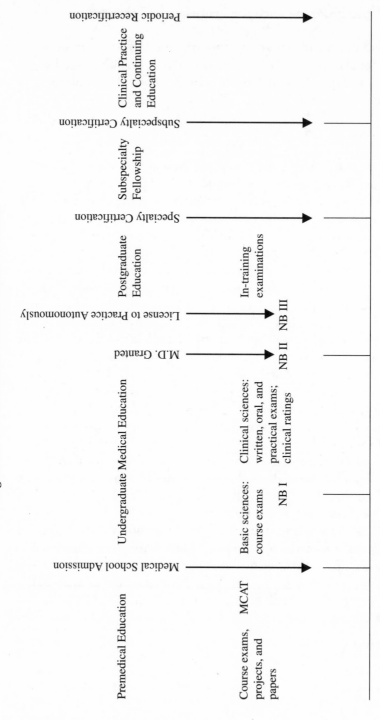

Note: NB = National Board Comprehensive Part I, II, and III Examinations; MCAT = Medical College Admission Test.

Source: McGaghie, 1986, p. 131. Reprinted with permission.

before a credential is granted? What are the boundaries of professional practice that define limits for evaluation? Test developers wonder about the breadth and organization of content and skill domains from which content is sampled to prepare questions, checklist items, interview schedules, practical problems, and other materials (Millman and Greene, 1989).

This is the knotty and persistent criterion problem that for decades has vexed scholars of professional competence evaluation (Menges, 1975; Hunt, Hinkle, and Malony, 1990) and scholars in other fields, including personality measurement (Wiggins, 1973). The problem is vexing because, as noted in AERA-APA-NCME (1985, p. 64), "People who take licensure or certification tests . . . are seeking to be deemed qualified for a broad field, rather than for a specific job. This distinction has important implications for the content to be covered in licensing or certification tests." Wiggins (1973, p. 39) further clarifies the criterion problem: "The 'problem' resides in the considerable discrepancy that typically exists between our intuitive standards of what criteria of performance should entail and the measures that are currently employed for evaluating such criteria."

The criterion problem has theoretical and practical features. Theoretical matters surface whenever professional practice or education addresses problems that do not have straightforward, algorithmic, one-best-answer solutions. This is the realm of professional judgment, temperament, insight, and style, approaching what Wagner and Sternberg (1986) call "tacit knowledge." Tacit knowledge is neither visible nor tangible, cannot be evaluated using multiple-choice questions, yet is the touchstone of competent professional practice. Descriptive statements about knowledge and skill requirements for professional practice that fail to acknowledge its tacit, qualitative features are incomplete. Professionals are adaptive, can identify and frame issues that laypersons do not even recognize, understand problems in depth, and work fast. Eisner's (1991) approach to evaluation, which places much reliance on "connoisseurship," is probably the only way to evaluate the tacit knowledge of professionals.

In practice, of course, competence evaluations for most professions do not include assessments beyond probes of knowledge, and sometimes practical skill. This is because most of today's assessment technology is limited to measurement methods that only permit right or wrong answers to specific questions keyed to test blueprints covering professional knowledge. The domain of professional practice for an airline pilot, rabbi, or social worker encompasses much more than the knowledge base of each profession. However, until evaluation practices grow to embrace a broader conception of professional work, and assessment methods that have more than one-best-answer items, competence evaluations will retain a narrow scope.

Thorndike (1949), Wiggins (1973), and Menges (1975) separate immediate, intermediate, and ultimate criteria. Immediate criteria are bits of knowledge and skilled behavior needed to reach a short-run goal like passing a test, or achieving a high grade point average during the first year of professional school. Intermediate criteria go beyond acquired knowledge and skill to include one's ability to complete a required program of study, interact with clients tactfully, and preserve confidentiality. Ultimate criteria refer to value judgments about one's technical skill, professional manner, or character and life-style: being a good doctor, teacher, salesman, or funeral director. These are behaviors very distant in time and quality from those measured at the point of assessment for a credential. To illustrate, one needs to pass a written test to become a licensed mortician. But Shakespeare reminds us that an undertaker's graveside manner is different from his or her fund of knowledge: "HAMLET: Hath this fellow no feeling of his business, that he sings at gravemaking? HORATIO: Custom hath made it in him a property of easiness" (*Hamlet*, act 5, scene 1, lines 65–67).

The criterion problem will not go away. It will persist because what professionals think and understand and how they act is far more complicated than what today's assessment technology can probe. Competence evaluations cover a small fraction of the real domain of practice for nearly all professions.

Trait Versus State Approaches

Is a professional's competence in practice a stable, enduring trait or a variable that changes with time, practice setting, client or patient characteristics, or phase of service or treatment? Is the attribution of competence to a professional person something permanent, or does it change due to location, service requirements, time available, and whether or not a crisis exists?

Research in several fields, including psychotherapy, medicine, and military combat, indicates that professional competence is not a general trait (Shaw and Dobson, 1988; Stillman and others, 1986; Shavelson, Mayberry, Li, and Webb, 1990). Instead, an individual's professional effectiveness is governed by the content and severity of clients' or patients' needs, the amount of professional preparation time, client or patient difficulty, and chance. In short, professional effectiveness is frequently case or situation specific, at least as assessed by current measurement technologies. Shavelson, Mayberry, Li, and Webb (1990, p. 129) state about military performance that "the major source of measurement error in job performance measurements is the heterogeneity of tasks that comprise the job."

Most evaluations of competence for professional practice assume that professional fitness is stable and does not change. A passing score on a test of acquired knowledge is an acceptable datum for establishing that a professional person is effective and safe, despite evidence that a much broader behavioral sample is required (Sternberg and Wagner, 1986). Valid evaluation of professional competence stems from performance assessment against a wide variety of practical problems and situations rather than just tests of what one knows (Engel, Wigton, LaDuca, and Blacklow, 1990).

Can Competence Be Evaluated Independently of Outcomes?

A key issue in professional personnel evaluation is whether individuals' competence can be evaluated separately from their effectiveness with clients, patients, or other recipients of service. Today's competence evaluations, chiefly tests of acquired knowledge, assume that there is a link between standardized test performance and behavior in practice. However, a metanalysis of thirty-five studies that assessed the link between performance in education settings and performance in professional practice did not find a strong correlation. Teaching, engineering, business, nursing, medicine, the military, and civil service were the professions covered in the metanalysis. The authors of the report concluded that "the overall variance accounted for makes grades or test scores nearly useless in predicting occupational effectiveness and satisfaction" (Samson, Graue, Weinstein, and Walberg, 1984, p. 320).

Several professions have adopted more lifelike evaluation approaches to tighten the link between behavior evaluated on competence tests and behavior needed to practice. In medicine, objective structured clinical examinations (Petrusa and others, 1991) and other practical examination formats (Barrows, Williams, and Moy, 1987) are growing in popularity due to their realism and congruence with what doctors actually do. Medical accreditation bodies are beginning to tighten standards to force education institutions to move testing in this direction (Langsley, 1991). An analogous technique in business is the assessment center (Gangler, Rosenthal, Thornton, and Bentson, 1987), chiefly used to evaluate middle and top managers. The military, of course, also has a long history of using assessment centers (Tziner and Dolan, 1982) and other practical examination formats for personnel evaluation (Shavelson, Mayberry, Li, and Webb, 1990; Webb, Shavelson, Kim, and Chen, 1989).

These examination formats are, of course, only approximations of the real world of patient care, managerial savvy, and combat effectiveness. In actual practice, professionals encounter such a wide variety of clients, settings, and unforseen pressures that no approach to competence evaluation can completely capture professional work. For example, psychotherapy research has shown that due to variation among patients in terms of motivation and responsiveness to treatment, it would be unfair to judge therapists solely by patient improvement (Schaffer, 1983; Shaw and Dobson, 1988). A similar situation exists for treatment professionals who work with alcohol-dependent persons. Here, base rates for patient relapse are often 50 percent within one year (Marlatt, 1985). An individual therapist's competence can only be judged in this context, recognizing that for many patients backsliding is an inevitable phase in recovery.

Can competence be evaluated independently of outcomes? An honest answer is maybe, because today's evaluations for professional certification and licensure are distant approximations of actual practice. Results from competence assessments need to be interpreted and used with an understanding of the limits (not failure) of current assessment technologies.

Technical Problems

Research and writing about professional competence evaluation tends to dwell on technical problems in personnel evaluation because most authors are education evaluators or psychometricians. The current technical state of the art for the assessment and evaluation of professionals is embodied in the AERA-APA-NCME (1985) standards and their sequels (for example, Linn, 1989). Occasionally, such minimum standards for evaluation are amplified to suit the specific needs of a specific profession. For example, candidates for the Roman Catholic priesthood not only must submit to education evaluations that meet minimum technical standards, they must also "commit themselves to lives of service through the vows of obedience, poverty, and chastity" (Hall, 1990, p. 191).

Technical requirements for evaluations of professional competence typically focus on the twin concerns of reliability and validity. Historically, *test* reliability has been the minimum technical requirement for measures of professional fitness. This is because high test reliabilities are easy to achieve through item analysis and by increasing test length (Feldt and Brennan, 1989). Recent applications of generalizability theory extend classical approaches to reliability estimation for test scores

(Shavelson, Mayberry, Li, and Webb, 1990; van der Vleuten and Swanson, 1990; Webb, Shavelson, Kim, and Chen, 1989). This approach permits estimation of the dependability of assessment results across various contextual factors, including occasions, test forms, and different administrators or observers. Generalizability theory is gaining popularity as the cutting edge among approaches to reliability estimation for education assessments (Shavelson and Webb, 1991).

Approaches to test validation are also undergoing transformation. It is now widely acknowledged that validity is an inherent property not of education measurements but rather of the way in which measurements are developed, used, and their results interpreted in specific contexts. Customary descriptions of content, criterion-related, and construct validity are now held insufficient (Messick, 1989). Newer and richer approaches to validation of education measurements attend to such factors as their consequences, fairness, transfer and generalizability, cognitive complexity, content quality, content coverage, meaningfulness, and cost efficiency (Linn, Baker, and Dunbar, 1991).

Measurement Methods in Competence Evaluation

Measures of professional competence, especially for the purpose of credentialing, have historically involved assessments of acquired knowledge and observations of professional behavior. More recent assessments include the use of open-ended problems and various types of simulations of professional practice.

Knowledge Assessment. Measures of professional knowledge acquisition have a long-established historical precedent. Paper-and-pencil knowledge assessments, using essay and multiple-choice formats, date to the early twentieth century (Levine, 1976). Oral examinations were used earlier. Such evaluations reflect an emphasis on educational efficiency and presumed objectivity that still exists in the 1990s. Measures of acquired knowledge are a well-established tradition in professional competence evaluation, especially in the health-related fields (Langsley, 1991).

The advantages of using knowledge measurements are straightforward. They are relatively simple to create, can be administered and scored with great efficiency, and are suitable for use with large groups of candidates. However, knowledge measurements also have limits. They can only tap one's existing fund of knowledge, not how professional work is actually done in terms of focus or quality, or how knowledge is acquired or organized. Knowledge assessments enumerate sins of commission, that is, total number of questions correct and incorrect. They rarely probe for sins of omission, that is, "What would you do if . . . ?"

Observation of Professional Behavior. Direct and indirect observations of professional behavior are widely used as a part of competence evaluation plans in many professions. Direct observations are made under conditions of actual work performance, frequently with supervision. Examples include in-flight training, judgments about a young surgeon's skill at suturing, and evaluation by a jury of a vocalist's performance. Direct observations are often guided by a checklist or structured rating scale that specifies key evaluation criteria. Checklists yield nominal data about the evaluation criteria (for example, medical maneuver done or not done). Rating scales, by contrast, provide ordinal or interval data that express judges' views about the quality of professional performance (for example, high, average, or low skill at conducting a client interview). Careful attention to checklist or rating scale development and calibration is a key step in the use of direct observation as a facet of professional competence evaluation. Stiggins (1987) provides practical advice about the creation and use of these instruments.

A common pitfall in the use of direct observation for professional personnel evaluation is the lack of interrater agreement (Linn, Baker, and Dunbar, 1991; Liston, Yager, and Strauss, 1981; Shaw and Dobson, 1988). This happens when two or more evaluators observe the same professional activity yet disagree either about what was seen or about the quality of a professional performance. Since an independent gold standard or benchmark for evaluating professional competence frequently does not exist, evaluators rely on consensus among judges as the best available option. Problems arise when consensus is not achieved, even for such public skills as conducting a psychotherapeutic interview (Liston, Yager, and Strauss, 1981; Shaw and Dobson, 1988). Moreover, data from legal circles clearly show that the reliability of eyewitness testimony, of which direct observation of professional behavior is a special case, is highly suspect (Loftus and Schneider, 1987). Eyewitness testimony yields suspicious data unless the conditions of observation are managed tightly and evaluators are specifically prepared for the task.

Rater training is the single best way to boost the interrater reliability of professional performance observations. Research data support this generalization. Rater training under controlled laboratory conditions significantly increases judgmental accuracy, in contrast with untrained controls (Thornton and Zorich, 1980). Field studies reinforce this conclusion. Rater training in the context of managerial evaluations in business settings (Pulakos, 1986) and in evaluations of the fitness of military personnel (Shavelson, Mayberry, Li, and Webb, 1990; Webb, Shavelson, Kim, and Chen, 1989) clearly demonstrates its utility in improving data quality.

Numerous anecdotal reports also address the importance of selecting, training, and regularly calibrating professional persons who judge consumer products, animals for work and show, world-class athletic competition, and beauty contests. Descriptive reports give detailed accounts about the training and experience needed to qualify as a U.S. Department of Agriculture meat inspector (Miller, 1958), or as a judge of farm and show horses (Daniels, 1987), men's Olympic competition (International Gymnastics Federation, 1989), or the Miss America pageant (Goldman, 1990). These reports show that evaluations of hamburger, horseflesh, horizontal bar, and female chutzpah are not left to chance. This is in stark contrast with other fields such as clinical medicine where faculty who rate and judge medical students and residents are rarely prepared for the task (Herbers and others, 1989).

Indirect observations about professional behavior of trainees is another source of evaluation data. Indirect observations are notes for the record drawn from general impressions, comments about critical incidents, and global ratings about an individual's technical skill, character, or reliability that are made on occasions remote from the pressures of the practice setting. Examples include post hoc ratings of medical residents for submission to a specialty board and letters of recommendation for graduate study or employment. Indirect observations are subject to bias and distortion for many reasons, especially the fallible memories of evaluators who presumably render fair and honest judgments. Medical evaluators, in particular, have raised doubts about the utility of indirect observations for any meaningful purpose. Herbers and others (1989, p. 202) conclude from a rigorous education study that even under moderately controlled conditions, "Faculty internists vary markedly in their observations of a resident and document little." This circumstance has led physician Richard Friedman (1983) to call the act of interpreting dean's letters about medical students seeking residency training a "fantasyland," suggesting they are no more informative than a Ouija board.

New Assessment Formats. Several new approaches to the evaluation of competence among professional persons are growing in popularity. This is in response to widespread sentiment that current methods of competence evaluation—chiefly, tests of acquired knowledge—are far too narrow to capture the richness of professional practice. Linn, Baker, and Dunbar (1991) have discussed the need for more complex, performance-based assessments, with special reference to validation criteria. Two categories of these assessments are now being used as major parts of the credentialing schemes for several learned professions. The categories are open-ended problems and simulations.

Open-ended problems present candidates with cases or situations that are not defined completely. The initial task for each candidate is to frame and define the boundaries and elements of a problem. Later, the candidate must figure out a strategy to reduce the problem to a sequential series of tasks; rank the task series in order of priority; exercise judgment in developing and evaluating alternatives and proposing practical solutions; communicate effectively with clients, patients, or customers; and keep cool under pressure. The task of responding to such ill- or partially defined problems is similar to what real professionals do everyday.

Despite their realism and face validity, open-ended problems give professional evaluators fits because they cannot accommodate an algorithmic, one-best-answer approach to scoring. Just as there is frequently no one best way to approach practical problems in professional life, evaluation problems need to leave room for a variety of scoring systems. This means that judges must act as "connoisseurs," to paraphrase Eisner (1991). The selection and training of judges for high-stakes evaluation take on added importance when their role as connoisseurs is acknowledged.

One professional association that has pioneered the large-scale use of open-ended problems and qualitative (yet very rigorous) judgment of candidate responses is the Canadian Institute of Chartered Accountants (1991), through use of its Uniform Final Examination (UFE) (McGaghie, 1991b). Validation research is under way to evaluate the inferences drawn from UFE data about the competence of accountants in practice.

Architecture is another profession that employs open-ended problems as a feature of its national certification program. The problems are embedded within the National Council of Architect Registration Boards site design subtest. Candidate responses to the evaluation problems, which call for creation of prototype architectural site designs, are scored by panels of expert jurors. The jurors judge proposed site designs according to the presence or absence of various design features such as landscape contours and the spatial arrangement of a cluster of buildings. While the judgments are intuitive, research has shown that they are reliable. Work is now under way to computerize the scoring of the site design problems by capturing jurors' implicit judgment policies (Bejar, 1991).

The use of simulations of job performance has grown in popularity as a means of evaluating professional practice. Simulations are popular because they can mimic the problems and conditions that professionals encounter, from routine to crisis. Simulations vary in fidelity, from highly realistic devices used to train and evaluate commercial and military pilots to written patient management problems used in the health professions. Variation in the fidelity of simulations is linked to their utility for professional personnel evaluations. A growing body of data, chiefly from the health professions, indicates that low-fidelity written and computer-based simulations are inappropriate for competence evaluation (Jones, Gerrity, and Earp, 1990; Swanson, Norcini, and Grosso, 1987). Low-fidelity simulations remain a controversial issue and more validation research is needed about their utility for personnel evaluation.

High-fidelity simulations, by contrast, are being used with great success for competence evaluation in many professions. These are devices (for example, flight simulators), highly trained people (for example, standardized patients), and environments (for example, assessment centers for business and industry) that place competence evaluation candidates in extremely lifelike professional situations. Problems that vary in difficulty and urgency are presented to candidates, whose responses and nonresponses are recorded and judged. Descriptions of high-fidelity simulations used for personnel evaluation in several professions have been published. They include commercial aviation (Holahan, 1991), management (Thornton and Cleveland, 1990), and clinical medicine (Barrows, Williams, and Moy, 1987; van der Vleuten and Swanson, 1990).

One of the most ambitious uses of high-fidelity simulations for professional training and evaluation exists in the nuclear power industry. Power plant operators must be certified by industry and licensed by the U.S. Nuclear Regulatory Commission. In addition, the power plant simulators used for training and personnel evaluation must also be certified before use and recertified annually. The simulators are site specific. There is no presumption that training, certification, and licensure obtained for one power plant can be generalized to another nuclear power facility (American Nuclear Society, 1985).

Nuclear power plant simulators are required to have minimum capabilities. "The response of the simulator resulting from operator action, no operator action, improper operator action, automatic plant controls, and inherent operating characteristics shall be realistic to the extent that within the limits of the performance criteria the operator shall not observe a difference between the response of the simulator control room instrumentation and the reference plant" (American Nuclear Society, 1985, p. 2). The simulator performance criteria are complicated. They include steady-state operations, transient operations such as start-up and minor malfunctions and alarms, and major disasters. Given the potential consequences of real-life nuclear power plant malfunctions, it is reassuring that competence evaluations of plant operators and plant simulators are done with great rigor.

Unresolved Problems

Despite the advances that are being made using open-ended problems and performance simulations, professional competence evaluation faces a persistent set of unresolved problems. These problems are not unique to professional credentialing. They are noteworthy, however, because they define an agenda for thought and research in professional education.

Base rates or pretest probabilities of success should receive careful attention when professionals receive credentials to practice. Following admission to professional education, if attrition rate is very low (as in the case of U.S. medical schools), the use of *any* method of personnel evaluation may result in more wrong decisions about candidates than will no evaluation at all. The reason is that no method of personnel evaluation is flawless. The use of assessments that have imperfect reliabilities under circumstances where base rates of success are very high increases the odds that evaluators will make false-negative decisions about candidates.

Algina (1978) made this argument, cast in formal Bayesian terms, fifteen years ago. However, few programs of professional certification or licensure have taken his advance into account when making decisions about candidate credentialing.

Standard setting, which is most often expressed as a minimum passing score on an achievement test, is a problem that defies simple solutions. Many prominent education researchers have addressed this question, including Jaeger (1989) and Millman (1989). These authors conclude that while all approaches to setting education standards are arbitrary, they need not be capricious. Systematic and thoughtful approaches are superior to haphazard standard-setting methods. This is especially important when candidates undergo competence evaluation after one or more failures, increasing the likelihood of false-positive decisions (Millman, 1989).

Fitzpatrick (1989) presents a reminder that decisions about minimum passing standards on all evaluations are not made in a black box. There are, instead, many social and political factors that affect judgments about how well the minimally competent candidate should perform on professional assessments. Evaluators in all professional fields should take heed of social pressures when decisions about passing standards are made.

Rules of evidence are rarely established for the purpose of evaluating the competence of professional persons. Such rules would set inclusion and exclusion criteria about the admissibility of data when the fitness of candidates is judged. What are good data for the decision problem at hand? Are they numbers such as quantitative test scores or grade point averages? Conversely, are good data words in the form of qualitative expressions like a letter of recommendation?

Rules of evidence are commonly used in legal proceedings. One of a trial judge's chief responsibilities is to rule on the admissibility of evidence into the formal record. The purpose, of course, is to prevent information derived from bias, heresay, or privileged communication from affecting the jury's verdict (*Federal Rules of Evidence for United States Courts and Magistrates,* 1989). No such formal rules exist about the admissibility of evidence for professional competence evaluation.

Experts, even in the same profession, disagree about the utility of different types of evidence in reaching competence decisions about candidates. Data revered by some professionals are shunned by others. For example, some theologians, including John Westerhoff (McGaghie, 1991a), dismiss outright the objective, quantitative data used as primary evidence in the Readiness for Ministry Project of the Association of Theological Schools of the United States and Canada (Schuller, Strommen, and Brekke, 1980). This research project was undertaken to define the qualities needed for effective practice in the Christian ministry.

Westerhoff's logic is simple. Because the research data are secular, they have no meaning for the certification of professional ministers. Westerhoff says that numbers simply will not work here. On grounds of eschatology, real predictive validity cannot be quantified.

The issue of objectivity versus subjectivity stems directly from the rules-of-evidence question. Thoughtful persons readily acknowledge that assessment of many key features of professional competence must be subjective. They defy quantification. For example, regarding the education and certification of psychotherapists, Shaw and Dobson (1988, p. 667) assert, "Although the definition of learning objectives is a necessary part of pedagogy, competency evaluations are often subjective, global, and dichotomous (that is, pass/fail)."

The real problem here is not recognition of the value of subjective data for professional competence evaluation. Instead, the problem concerns which subjective data to consider and how to fold such information into decision making in a fair and unbiased manner. Maybe this problem cannot be solved. There are, however, numerous opportunities for research, writing, and spirited argument on this topic for professional education in general and personnel evaluation in particular.

Summary

Earlier it was noted that four terms—profession, competence for practice, assessment, and evaluation—coalesce to form the theme of this chapter. The current portrait of evaluation of competence for professional practice has been painted deliberately with a broad brush. This is to argue that the psychometric details that usually dominate discussion about competence evaluation need to be understood in social, educational, and historical context. Glass (1978, p. 237) had it right when he wrote, "A common experience of wishful thinking is to base a grand scheme on a fundamental, unsolved problem." One hopes that fundamental, unsolved problems will receive more attention as the practical affairs of professional competence evaluation continue.

Professional Matters

Several general professional matters bear on the evaluation of individuals for practice. The matters include demographics, individual personal qualities and life-style, importance of professional experience, and validation research.

Demographics

Professions evolve. Sometimes they die. Professions change in focus and character due to social and technological change. Blacksmiths and scribes are no longer in great demand. By contrast, other professions were unheard of fifty years ago. They include anesthesiology, astronautics, family therapy, and operations research. Just as the definition of competence in practice of various professions can shift over time, so too must the substance of competence evaluation.

Another demographic factor that shapes the character of practice and competence evaluations of individuals is the changing racial and gender composition of the learned professions. Barriers that once prevented minorities and women from gaining access to professional education and subsequent evaluation have crumbled. In medicine, for example, Petersdorf, Turner, Nickens, and Ready (1990) document the rapid growth in enrollment and graduation of underrepresented minorities since the early 1970s. Data published by Jonas, Etzel, and Barzansky (1991) show that the number and percentage of women in medicine has mushroomed in the same time frame. In the 1970–1971 academic year, there were 827 female graduates of U.S. medical schools, 9.2 percent of the total. By 1990–1991, there were 5,584 female medical graduates, 36 percent of the total.

Not all professions have been as aggressive as medicine in recruiting, educating, and credentialing female candidates. The clergy, in particular, has been quite conservative about the involvement of women in professional leadership roles. This is in spite of the case that female seminarians typically have stronger academic credentials than their male peers. O'Neill and Murphy (1991, p. 5) assert, "Resistance to the entry of women, while it may exist in other professions, does not seem to have slowed the flow of women into medicine and law as much as it has into the ranks of the clergy. Women are becoming doctors and lawyers at a much faster rate than they are becoming ministers, priests, and rabbis."

How do increased numbers of women and minorities affect competence evaluations in the professions? Certainly not by altering the contents of knowledge tests or expectations about practical professional behavior. Instead, the real difference is new opportunities for women and minorities to gain access to professional education and, later, to professional credentials. Admissions assessments made and interpreted to determine an individual's readiness for professional education are now seen as a major thread in the fabric of professional competence evaluation. This is especially true in professions like medicine where education attrition is rare and the decision to admit an individual to professional school is tantamount to a decision to grant that person a license to practice.

Personal Qualities and Life-Style

No one doubts the importance of personal qualities and life-style habits as basic elements of professionalism. Who wants to be treated by a surgeon who is a cocaine addict? Why would anyone confide in a pastoral counselor with a reputation as a gossip? What intelligent family would entrust its financial estate to a dishonest accountant?

Honesty is only one of the personal qualities that are usually taken for granted when a layperson entrusts a lawyer, psychiatrist, or architect. Honesty is also expected of persons in the performing professions, where point shaving or association with gamblers can ruin a professional athlete's career. Other personal qualities and life-style habits are also basic facets of professionalism: reliability, sobriety, holding of confidences, placement of service to clients or patients before self-interest. In professional life, these traits are as important as knowledge and skill and are most conspicuous by their absence. They are rarely addressed in selection, education, or credentialing unless a problem becomes evident.

Most professions have a code of conduct or set of ethical principles that embody the personal qualities and life-style habits that are expected of practitioners. Some professionals, including clergy and physicians, must swear an oath about conformity to standards of personal and professional conduct. In education settings, failure to uphold standards of appearance or behavior are sufficient grounds for student dismissal without regard to academic progress (Irby and Milam, 1989). In practice, failure to uphold standards can lead to such consequences as revocation of one's license or disbarment for conduct unbecoming a professional.

There is no doubt that a professional's personal qualities and life-style are a basic part of competence. Everyone knows that these traits are judged constantly, usually by subjective means. Despite recent (and largely unsuccessful) attempts to impose "integrity tests" on professionals in business and industry (Sackett, Burris, and Callahan, 1989), evaluations of professional competence in terms of personal qualities and life-style are qualitative. Norcini and Shea (this volume) address in depth the significance of personal qualities and life-style in the context of professional recertification and relicensure.

Does Experience Matter?

Intuition and folklore hold that an individual professional's competence becomes broader and deeper as a result of experience with clients or patients. Seasoned professionals, in contrast with newcomers, use their experience to identify and frame problems quickly and apply solutions efficiently. Early research on expertise among chess grandmasters demonstrated that the abilities to structure the contest and to visualize game conditions several moves ahead are some of the skills that distinguish experienced from novice players (de Groot, 1965). Recent research in clinical medicine shows that experts differ from novices in terms of such intellectual skills as problem comprehension, diagnostic accuracy, coherent and focused explanations, and selective use of findings (Patel, Evans, and Groen, 1989).

All of us know at a gut level that the seasoned professional, whether a diplomat, real estate salesperson, molecular biologist, or paratrooper, is more likely to produce a successful result than a rookie in the same field. But are there research data to support this generalization?

The research data, it turns out, are sketchy, probably because common sense and opinion suggest that experience does matter. But the little data available tell a different story. To illustrate, a series of reports have been published on the comparative effectiveness of professionals and paraprofessionals in providing mental health services (Durlak, 1979; Hattie, Sharpley, and Rogers, 1984; Berman and Norton, 1985). Professional therapists are presumed to be more skillful than paraprofessionals due to longer training, supervised internships, and years of experience with troubled clients. However, the weight of the evidence in these reports, two of which are metanalyses, shows there are no reliable differences between the two groups on a variety of client outcomes measures. If experience in psychotherapy matters, these studies show it cannot be detected, perhaps due to methodological weaknesses in study designs (Schaffer, 1983).

A similar picture exists for another profession, clinical medicine. Proxy measures of clinical competence with patients—multiple-choice tests and patient management problems—show that professional performance falls sharply with experience (Ramsey and others, 1991; Webster, 1979). In regard to setting passing standards on today's internal medicine certification tests and applying the standards to experienced doctors, one research group notes, "If this standard were applied to the subjects [doctors] who had received initial certification 14 to 15 years previously, approximately 68% of these individuals would have failed the examination" (Ramsey and others, 1991, p. 1106).

How can such results be interpreted? Can such findings be applied to other professional fields where increments in experience seem to yield ever richer professional results? What about Isaac Stern, Pablo Picasso, Isaac Bashevis Singer, Henry Moore, Jessica Tandy, and George Blanda?

Research showing that professional competence declines quickly after initial certification is probably measuring competence poorly. The proxy measures used in such studies, especially multiple-choice tests, are simply invalid indicators of the work that physicians, psychotherapists, or other professionals perform on behalf of their clients. Kirschenbaum (1992) reinforces this point in a study on the influence of experience on the professional competence of naval officers. The real problem resides with the assessments believed to be indexes of professional competence, not with the persons who submit to evaluation. The assessments may be reliable but the evaluations are probably invalid.

Validation Research

Real progress in professional competence evaluation will chiefly stem from a vigorous and sustained program of validation research (Kane, 1982). The measures used to select individuals for professional education and to confer professional credentials fall short of what is needed to fulfill either purpose. Sound validation research calls for clear thinking about such basic questions as the criterion problem, gold standards in competence evaluation, and whether professional performance is due to enduring traits or is an artifact of measurement methods (Messick, 1989; Forsythe, McGaghie, and Friedman, 1986). Broader and richer approaches to validation research should also be used to move beyond the worn-out notions of content and predictive validity (Linn, Baker, and Dunbar, 1991).

Implications for Practice and Research

This chapter raises a number of implications about the practice of professional competence evaluation and about research on the subject. Some implications are obvious, others are subtle. What follows are short lists of suggestions that derive from this work.

Implications for Practice

First, organizations that accredit programs of professional education should insist that methods of learner evaluation closely match what professionals do in the practice setting. Several professions, including commercial aviation, nuclear power plant operators, and accountancy in Canada, already use evaluation procedures that simulate professional practice. In medicine, the Liaison Committee on Medical Education of the American Medical Association revised its medical school accreditation standards in 1991. The standards now specify that "institutions must develop a system of assessment which assures that students have acquired and can demonstrate on direct observation the core clinical skills and behaviors needed in subsequent medical training" (Liaison Committee on Medical Education, 1991, p. 14). Policy statements like this need to be prepared and implemented by other professional accreditation bodies.

Second, those responsible for professional competence evaluation should give increased attention to assessments of individuals for the purpose of admission to professional school. This is especially the case for professions like medicine with low school attrition rates. Assessments made prior to professional school admission are an integral feature of competence evaluation to the extent that nearly everyone who is admitted eventually graduates and is credentialed to practice.

Third, more attention should be devoted to personal, qualitative variables that are crucial to professional practice: tact, reliability, honesty, confidentiality, humor, judgment, to name a few. Granted, these qualities are very difficult to judge systematically and without bias, thus fairly. There is, however, widespread agreement that professionals should be evaluated against such criteria, probably using elements of Eisner's (1991) connoisseurship model. Bold steps should be taken in this direction.

Fourth, serious work should begin on the preparation of individuals to be evaluators of professional practice. The professional community can no longer presume that possession of an advanced degree warrants an individual's evaluation skill. This is especially true for medicine, where the evaluation situation is scandalous, and other health professions. At minimum, preparation would involve training faculty members to be raters of skilled performance and accurate interpreters of assessment data.

Fifth, an individual's professional competence should be reported and judged as a profile of skills, acquired knowledge, dispositions, and other achievements. Such a profile might look like a Minnesota Multiphasic Personality Inventory report, although the scales would be completely different. Competence evaluations must move beyond reports of cognitive test scores as the sole or primary source of assessment data. One's competence profile, perhaps maintained by a board or agency, could be updated and extended at planned career milestones.

Sixth, use of assessment centers should be expanded to professions beyond business, commercial aviation, and the military. Some progress has been made in using the assessment center approach for the comprehensive evaluation of competence in medicine (Vu and others, 1992). The method has also been proposed as a key feature of a national certification system for elementary and secondary school teachers (National Board for Professional Teaching Standards, 1991). Other professions should weigh the benefits (and costs) of using the assessment center approach to competence evaluation.

Seventh, competence evaluations should become an integral feature of continuing education in the professions. There is no reason why continuing education programs should focus exclusively on instruction with almost no attention to assessment.

Implications for Research

First, a sustained program of validation research should begin to shed light on assessment methods used in professional competence evaluation. Rich and new suggestions about approaches to validation research made by Linn, Baker, and Dunbar (1991) and by Messick (1989) should be heeded. More studies using the multitrait-multimethod matrix (Forsythe, McGaghie, and Friedman, 1986) are needed to better understand the relative contributions of professional traits versus measurement methods when competence evaluations are done.

Second, one part of a validation research program should address the persistent criterion problem in professional competence evaluation. This line of research would aim to better define domains of professional practice and rules for sampling content that form the basis of competence assessments. Content inclusion and exclusion rules should be considered along with new ways to generalize an individual's performance across domains of practice. Attention to the criterion problem would also encourage studies on the linkage of the immediate criteria that are commonly measured to the more elusive intermediate and ultimate criteria that represent professional practice (Menges, 1975; Wiggins, 1973).

Third, longitudinal research is needed to better understand competence evaluations that are made at different stages on the professional career continuum. Such studies would involve variables assessed prior to and during professional school admission, throughout professional education, and at planned career intervals. By following cohorts of individuals in a variety of professions, research would clarify the cascaded inferences that are involved in attributing competence to professional people at different career stages.

Fourth, studies need to be done on approaches to scoring and judging responses to ill-defined professional problems, especially when the problems have more than one right answer. Bejar's (1991) work provides a point of departure in architecture, and the methods used by the Canadian Institute of Chartered Accountants (1991) to score its UFE provide a model from business. This research will probably lead advocates of objective scoring methods into partnership with colleagues who endorse Eisner's (1991) connoisseurship model of evaluation.

Fifth, on a broader scale, more research and writing should be encouraged on the sociology of professions. This scholarship is obscure to most educational evaluators and students of professional education. Sociological analyses in the manner of Abbott (1988), Berlant (1975), Derber, Schwartz, and Magrass (1990), Freidson (1970, 1986), and Moskos (1970) bear directly on the work and interests of professional educators. Topics such as the division of professional labor, power and authority relations, methods of credentialing, school accreditation, and the social context of professional education have been studied by sociologists. Educators can be enriched from a comprehension of this research.

CHAPTER 11

Challenges for
Continuing Professional Education

Nancy L. Bennett
Robert D. Fox

Performance is the central theme and the central challenge of continuing professional education (CPE). While continued learning has always been integral to the professions, its shape and form have varied. In the past decade, a body of research has proliferated on such issues as how professionals learn and make changes, what experience contributes to learning, and when continuing educators can best contribute to that process. In this chapter, we assess where the field of CPE is going, based on recent knowledge about how work is linked to experience, change, and learning; how continuing professional educators help professionals perform; and how these trends might lead educators in professional schools to think differently about their own goals.

The promise and the dilemma facing those who labor in CPE are defined by five themes that emerge from the recent literature:

- Performance: The object of teaching and learning in CPE is performance, the actual behaviors of the professionals in practice.

- Experience: A significant proportion of changing and enhancing professional performance is a function of learning embedded in the day-to-day experiences of professional practice.
- Learning and change: Practicing professionals prefer learning as the agency of change; changes accomplished through learning are enduring and consistent.
- Change agents: Planned and purposeful change in performance is the outcome expected from the efforts of many actors in society, including those in CPE; continuing professional educators are agents of change.
- Self-directed curricula: Although some changes accomplished through learning are a consequence of traditional CPE programs, most are a function of the professionals' own self-directed learning curricula.

Each of these themes presents challenges to the form and functions of CPE in the arenas of research and practice. In the following five sections, we describe how these themes play out in practice and reflect on ways that CPE can be changed to meet the ensuing challenges.

Performance and CPE

Professionals perform various services in our society. The framework of the workplace and specific work roles define how each profession contributes. Nowlen (1988) represents the framework as a double helix. The values and expectations of a culture, its mission, and the available resources intertwine with each professional's experiences, attributes, and limitations. The context or culture gives meaning to a personal history. The work role is shaped within an individual's own history by its function in society. By understanding the influence of each strand of the double helix, the complex meanings of work are better defined. An understanding of these complex meanings undermines the assumption that changes in performance can result from a single variable rather than from the interactions of several. Knowing the job description of a manager, for example, is not enough to know how to help plan effective CPE. An understanding of the formal and informal networks, experiences, and future expectations of the manager is required to place learning within a specific context.

Professionals respond to societal needs. Cervero (1988) talks about those societal needs and expectations by contrasting two viewpoints, arguing for a shift from a "functionalist" view of professional performance to a "critical" view.

Functionalism views professionals as a group who use a specific body of knowledge to address problems that are important to society. The work of a professional is technical or specialized, so that more expertise or more knowledge provides a basis for solving more problems more effectively. If elementary school teachers learn more about how to teach science, children will learn more about science. If a dentist buys new equipment, the result will be better performance, leading to better patient care. A new computer system and knowledge of its applications will improve response time in filling orders for a company that sells by catalogue.

When the functionalist viewpoint underlies the creation of CPE activities, deficiencies in the profession are corrected by expanding the knowledge base, recruiting good people to the profession, or enhancing training. CPE is a technical process to help professionals provide better service to clients. Helping a journalist learn new desktop publishing skills expands expertise. A social worker broadens services to new immigrants by learning a second language or finding resources for translation.

Functionalism has been the prevailing view of the professions for the last several decades, but Cervero (1988) describes a recent shift toward the critical view. Professionals must make choices about how to view each practice situation because the problems may be poorly defined and conditioned by situational variables. Everyone in a profession does not necessarily understand problems in the same way, nor is a common understanding expected by those within the profession. Standardized solutions may not fit the context of a specific problem. Creative use of the knowledge base is a regular and essential part of practice. Judges look for alternative sentencing ideas. Lawyers present arguments for reinterpretation of older laws given the norms of today. Architects design large buildings that users perceive as manageable and friendly. A physician helps an eighty-five-year-old man decide whether to have heart surgery considering age, resources, family support, cost, and patient wishes.

CPE based on a critical viewpoint says that the knowledge base builds, in part, on experience gained from specific cases or examples in a professional practice. Knowledge is not applied in a predefined fashion; rather, previous cases or examples help to shape the response to the current problem. There is no consensus about defining the problem or solving it, although there are usually professional standards and societal norms that define the boundaries of acceptable practice. Technical expertise is not enough to practice effectively. Ways to look at questions and answers by case or example may be built in as part of the learning. Learning a language used by clients is only one step for a social worker to provide better services. If good housing and schooling are not available, conditions may not change even though communication may be better. When architects create plans for buildings that are within budget and meet all legal requirements, they may not be used as planned by the intended group if they are not seen to meet the group's needs. Children may not learn more about science if the school does not support more teaching of science. And the ways to create that support may be complex.

Although studies of professional performance suggest that the immediate environment and culture of the profession influence professional practice, contemporary CPE often fails to consider this relationship in its programs. Moreover, providers of CPE often do not understand the integral role of CPE in connecting societal demands to professional performance. CPE providers also fail to understand how CPE strengthens a sense of professional affiliation and lends meaning to professional life by providing a focus on learning, a group-defined professional identity, and a common understanding of how the group solves problems. CPE helps shape the boundaries of the profession by strongly influencing the ways in which professional roles are refined, expanded, compared, or limited.

Experience and CPE

Learning from experience is part of professional practice. When physicians, architects, or school teachers perform their roles with an eye toward improving and expanding their repertoires of answers, learning and changing are part of the regular routine. As Cavanaugh (this volume) observes, this integration of performance, learning, and change ought to be the aim of preprofessional education and CPE. CPE has the added challenge of facilitating this process as it unfolds. While practice performance is the basic theme of CPE, a clear definition of performance is difficult to provide. The most obvious purpose of CPE is to provide a system for helping professionals improve performance by updating knowledge and adapting skills and attitudes based on what is new and better.

The question of how individual professionals can enhance performance is the subject of much discussion in the literature. Schön (1987), for example, describes how reflective practitioners can enhance performance by using experience. A professional uses a specific knowledge base, incorporating experience, to formulate and generate professional work. This approach contrasts with "technical rationality," the foundation of the functional model described earlier, which holds that professionals are technicians who select optimal solutions for a given problem. Increased technical expertise solves more problems. However, real problems often cannot be well defined. Indeterminate situations may be the usual rather than the unusual. So increased technical expertise does not clarify the problem, and there may not be a single or simple solution.

Instead, professionals define problems according to the solutions available to them. They choose what to see according to what they can solve, and what they can solve depends on their discipline, training, background, and interests. Thus, the indeterminacy of many problems may result in different views of the problem, and different actions by different professionals.

Professionals often agree on who the experts are within a profession, but they do not necessarily understand the criteria of expertise. Such clichés as the "art of medicine," or the "creativity of science" are ways to describe professional knowledge when it is difficult to define more clearly what we mean. The labels close off discussion or analysis because they lack specificity. But, if made more explicit, this kind of knowing allows learning.

Here is what we mean. How one frames professional problems and the range of solutions available is what differentiates an expert from a novice. Examples of how to learn problem framing and solutions are common in the education of professionals, and they are often made clear by the terminology we use to describe learning. Athletes are "coached" to improve performance. The work of musicians, dancers, and artists is "critiqued" by faculty. Medical interns and residents treat real patients with "guidance" from senior physicians. Student professionals in all of these settings perform or execute productive practice for review by expert professionals acting as teachers. Performance problems direct learning. Teachers guide or coach performance rather than engage in a traditional form of lecturing on facts and theory, removed from situations of practice. Students learn by doing. They enter into the art of specific professional learning by working in the field next to a professional as teacher or coach.

Schön (1987) talks about the "right kind of telling" that takes place when students work closely with faculty, learning to frame questions and responses as practitioners in the profession. His explanation for reflective learning begins with knowing-in-action, which is presumed or implied knowledge. It is the knowledge base available to a professional at work. Surprise may interrupt knowing-in-action. An unexpected finding or unusual twist to the usual practice stops the process. Reflection-about-action is the process of reviewing what is known and why a case does not fit. Experimentation follows. Will this work, or does it seem to make sense to try that? The search for a solution is not a random process; rather, one tries to find an answer based on experience gained by working with other surprises. The results of experimentation lead to reflection-about-action. Why did it work or fail to work? What is it about the surprise that would suggest this solution? To complete the loop, reflection-about-action feeds back into the knowing-in-action bank. The whole process may be internal, occurring so rapidly that it is invisible to others. It may involve weeks, months, or years of activities. Increased experience with reflection in the learning process helps performance and artistry grow over the course of a career. Performance is the centerpiece of development for the reflective practitioner.

The model of the reflective practitioner is one view of performance. It is, however, not usually incorporated into CPE program planning. Rather than address specific issues of performance, often professional schools or associations address learning by providing experts to review new information or preferred practice. Individuals must integrate their own interpretation into actual performance. They must adapt a general theme to the specifics of their own situations.

Learning and Change in CPE

CPE in the past has based its efforts on principles of teaching rather than principles of learning. The notion has been that it is possible to teach knowledge and skills because the system of teaching is well designed, methods and techniques are appropriate and systematic, and resources are carefully constructed through a system of educational and instructional design. Although there is little doubt that principles and procedures based on sound theories of education practice are necessary, they may not be sufficient. We need to know about the *natural* process of learning and how these fit into CPE.

Professionals are complex and sophisticated learners. They have systems for incorporating new information into competence and performance. These learners are not blank slates or empty disks. They come with ways and means as sophisticated as the knowledge base that they use in practice. Performance is adapted, modified, refined, or altered to meet new demands, incorporate new information, or react to improved ideas.

The CPE literature on change focuses on new ways of thinking. Houle (1980, p. 32) defines change in professional performance as the process of internalizing an idea or making practice routine so that it becomes fundamental to the way in which professionals think about how to approach their work. While this definition helps determine what constitutes a "change," it does not explain why or how changes are made.

A comprehensive study on how physicians make changes (Fox, Mazmanian, and Putnam, 1989) lays out clues about how and why those changes in performance are initiated. Forces that most commonly drive professional performance changes toward increased competence are the desire to excel, the presence of an innovation, and the growing dissatisfaction with a current procedure or practice. The desire to excel tied to the presence of an innovation is a particularly powerful combination, accounting for more than half of the changes identified in this study.

Changes to enhance competence almost always involve conscious learning strategies, and these strategies often seem to occur in phases. In the study by Fox, Mazmanian, and Putnam (1989), three separate phases were observed, each using somewhat different learning resources. First, physicians identified the desired change and prepared to effect it. Participation in a formal CME activity was the most frequently used way to prepare for the change. Formal CME activities included small, hospital or department programs, meetings of professional associations, and coursework. These activities were used to gain specific information, gather new information, or to hear a range of ideas. Other learning resources were journal reading, interaction with other physicians, use of other instructional materials, and interactions with nonphysicians.

The second phase was to make the change. When preparation seemed sufficient, physicians used fewer learning resources and shifted to interaction with other physicians. CME programs moved to second place, followed by other instructional materials, journal reading, and interaction with nonphysicians. Physicians experimented and tested the new information or skill in actual practice. Fewer resources were used in this phase, but they were used more intensively.

The third phase solidified the change. Even when physicians feel competent to use a given procedure or new drug, for example, the change must become a habit. Habits come from practice and evaluation. Shifts in thinking, adaptations for a specific setting, and use of a technique in different ways are part of developing a habit or integrating a change into practice. Learning continues during the solidifying stage. Resources, in order of use, include interaction with other physicians, continuing medical education, journal reading, and teaching.

Knowledge about the phases of change suggests how CPE can be more effective. For example, formal programs can be particularly helpful in providing a comprehensive view of change for those thinking about trying a new idea in practice. The background can be provided. Those already in the process of making a change—the second phase—are more apt to find small group discussion useful.

Other conclusions from Fox, Mazmanian, and Putnam (1989) add to our understanding of how to link preparation for change to performance in practice. The study showed that professional and social forces, rather than personal forces, are more likely linked with conceptually oriented learning. When the force for change or the effect of change was clear and unambiguous, learning was more likely to be directed toward solving concrete problems than toward broadening conceptual understanding.

CPE in the future must base its program decisions on an understanding of the dynamics of learning as they exist in professionals. Like performance, learning is a product of the environment and the personal history of the learner. It is also the product of the culture of professional education, the "frame of the problem," and the point of application. Learning is natural. It is a requisite part of living. As such, learning patterns are templates used to make changes in practice. In the future, continuing professional educators must be able to integrate changes into learning through education planning, design, and evaluation. Resources must support learning rather than hinder the process. In effect, there must be a transformation of the role of educator, from distributor of knowledge and skill to collaborator and facilitator of learner-controlled changes in performance.

Change Agents in CPE

Continuing educators are agents of change. To work more effectively in that role, each educator must begin with knowledge about how change occurs. While a common understanding of change is basic to acting in the role of change agent, the specific setting for CPE will interpret the mission of learning. There are four types of providers: professional associations, institutions of higher education, employers, and private companies. Professional associations, for example, are concerned with the boundaries of the profession and education for the group as a whole. Their focus is on performance issues as they relate to defining and expanding the profession. Higher education institutions focus on the individual. They act as a change agent for improved practice for each professional and often provide a way to continue learning beyond initial preparation. They have many resources and high credibility. Employers act as change agents to meet corporate or agency goals. Budgets may be a major concern. Learning is often tied very closely to on-the-job performance. CPE providers in this setting are responsible to the company or agency rather than to individual learners. While CPE may address specific performance issues, the perspective may be narrow or fail to keep pace with new findings in other settings. Private companies usually intend to make a profit from learning activities. They may be flexible and able to offer new activities quickly, but the budget limits what will be done. Resources may be limited, and credibility is often not high.

A perusal of program brochures and pamphlets in medicine, law, social work, or any other profession readily reveals that most CPE programs, regardless of the type of provider, focus on knowledge and skill without regard for the practice environment. If there is attention to the culture of the profession, it is merely to borrow terminology of teaching (for example, "grand rounds" or "professional development days") rather than to engage in culture-sensitive programming. This failure to accommodate culture and context in design in any meaningful way means that the professional practitioner may find it difficult to connect knowledge and skills to application. The end result is often no effect.

Nowhere is the failure to attend to performance more evident than in the ways commonly used to assess needs and evaluate programs. Often, the professionals receive a survey form that lists topics and asks for opinion related to their knowledge of or skill in a given area. The survey asks the professional to tease out the connections among personal performance, knowledge, and skills. This request would be reasonable if each of us understand our own behavior perfectly and the environment within which that behavior occurs.

There are some notable exceptions, where performance is the object of assessment and education. One example is the Physician Remediation and Enhancement Program (PREP) of McMaster University, sponsored by the Ontario Medical Association. Its objective is to identify and remediate performance problems of physicians in Ontario. It uses a variety of assessment procedures, including review of clinical cases, simulated patient care episodes, and structured interviews related to physicians' practice performance, knowledge, and skill. Information gathered before and after the program supports the design and redesign of education efforts to enhance clinical performance. This system is a valuable departure from traditional lectures and seminars based on participant reactions to lists of topics and speakers. However, this remedial program is not the main path but rather a side path in contemporary CPE. Procedures used in such programs could be adapted and incorporated into the menu of education for any group of practicing professionals.

CPE providers could also base investigations of need and evaluations of effect on a more current understanding of professional performance. For example, assessment of performance in simulations of professional practice problems of nurses, lawyers, or accountants could illuminate education design. Actual case histories could capture the effects of culture and environment on performance. CPE could develop ways to embed programs within existing problem frames, or the ways in which professionals assess problems, so as to enlarge and reshape those frames to better meet the needs of professional practice. Although there are examples where performance occurs, they are rare.

An understanding of performance is not enough, however. CPE practitioners must also be able to view change in performance as the object of their efforts. They must become expert in the complications and solutions associated with the adoption of innovations, the elimination of outdated performance, and the exchange of professional actions of lesser value for those of greater value. This means that programs must fit into and complement professionals' efforts to continuously improve practices. The role of agents of change requires that continuing professional educators become skilled and knowledgeable about the processes of change. They must be able to describe the forces at work in the change process, that is, the elements of culture that give meaning to performance and change in performance, and manage the cultural bias that can inhibit the change process. They must be in the culture of practice without losing their position as facilitators of change.

Among the implications for the future of CPE is the effect of the role of change agent on the ethics of CPE. Because the continuing professional educator is acting to help bring about change in professional practice, he or she must provide informed consent to clients, those whose performance may change. Informed consent of participants in CPE can occur in two ways: (1) Brochure material and objectives must be explicit about the change fostered by the education effort. This allows professionals, who are most often voluntary participants in education, to make an informed decision to participate. (2) Planning and implementation should include adequate representation of the audience for change. This allows the education effort to take its place in the culture and environment of application as well as ensure that the perspective and values of the client are in the design. Each of these actions shows ways that continuing professional educators may fulfill the role of change agent without assuming control of the process.

Another dimension of the activities of the change agent involves working as a partner for change with other agencies:

examples include working with basic science faculty to translate the latest information on tumor immunology for physicians in practice or helping a local engineering society develop a self-study option on new materials. Cooperative efforts with others are especially important when making large changes such as those that may be necessary for geriatric care, improvement of the functions of court systems, or the design and development of large-scale industrial or civic projects.

A change agent must also work with regulatory agencies. As reflections of societal uneasiness with the ways in which professionals perform, requests for regulation have resulted in a system of quantifying CPE activities. Many professionals either receive a mandate or voluntarily choose to participate in groups that regulate their professional practice. Regulations are designed to assure the public that professionals within a given group continue to attend CPE activities in order to perform competently. Some regulations are developed at the urging of members within the group, and others are responses to concerns by government and consumer agencies.

Mandatory requirements for participation gained prominence during the 1970s, especially in the health care field. The assumption was that the performance of a group could be better regulated through regular participation in learning activities designed to enhance performance. The commitment to learn has always been central to the identity of a professional group. The translation to mandated participation in CPE, however, has not been universally accepted. And the system relies on attendance as an indirect measure of learning.

Regulations may take the form of licensure, certification, or registration. A license, for example, is designed by a political body such as a state legislature. Renewal may require participation in CPE. Physicians and dentists must have a state license to practice, and about half of the states require documentation of participation in CPE for renewal.

Certification, also set up by legislative groups, usually requires completion of a specific education program. In some states, teachers must have a certificate to teach in public schools. In Illinois, there is one certification process for school teachers, and another for school principals. A professional certificate given by a professional association requires participation in a program outlined by that group. Renewals of certification may require participation in CPE.

Registration is designated by a professional group, usually after successful completion of an examination. Medical technologists may be registered with the Board of Registry of the American Society of Clinical Psychologists or with the National Certification Agency for Medical Laboratory Personnel under the American Society for Medical Technology. Both groups require medical technologists to take an examination after completing an approved education program. Dietitians can register with the American Dietetic Association. Some states have registration systems for professionals. Architects in Massachusetts must pass an examination after completing an education program and three years of apprenticeship under a registered architect.

Some professional associations, state chapters, or societies may list, among their criteria for membership, a specified number of credits hours of CPE. Other professional associations or groups suggest participation in CPE but leave the form of participation to the individual.

Self-Directed Curricula in CPE

Most learning associated with changes in practice is directed by professionals as opposed to curriculum planners in CPE. The challenges to those in CPE are to develop ways (1) to enhance the abilities of professionals to plan and manage their own learning and (2) to fit formal education into the patterns of professionals' self-directed learning activities. To meet the first challenge, CPE cannot continue to offer programs that inhibit rather than foster independence. CPE in the future must offer opportunities to learn that both maximize the autonomy and independent actions of learners and also provide systematic feedback on ways to approach learning. For example, computer-assisted practice audits accompanied by programs can guide learners from need to preferred design, to realistic evaluation.

The second challenge is to build education for professionals that fits easily into their own strategies for learning and changing. This requires continuing professional educators to investigate, document, and understand how professionals manage learning and change in their professional practices. When we understand the patterns of self-directed curricula, formal CPE can fit into those patterns and make the process of learning and changing more efficient and more effective. For example, in examining a teacher's attempts to develop a new method of classroom management, we may discover that there is a need to obtain both expert and collegial feedback. A CPE program designed for this part of the self-directed curriculum would thus focus on the need to gain structured feedback, perhaps by using activities that allow for observation and comparison with others. This would provide one element of the learner's self-directed curriculum that might otherwise be difficult to acquire.

At the heart of the challenge of aiding professionals in their individual curricula to learn and change is the development of better ways and means of explaining and predicting curriculum patterns in learning projects. Modern CPE must build strategies for scientific and applied research, as well as better ways to disseminate findings, conclusions, and recommendations to other change agents. Journals and articles, books, and CPE for continuing educators must be part of the system. In effect, there must be a planned and purposeful system for the development of CPE that includes research strategies and projects to discover patterns of self-directed curricula. It must also include procedures to bring those who practice CPE with different groups of professionals together to discuss common and unique aspects of this work.

Changing the System

In the future, successful CPE practices must be pliable enough to change as situations change but firm enough to be safe and predictable. For CPE to fulfill its mandate of helping professionals to continue professional development, it must find ways to help professionals as they encounter their clients and apply their knowledge and judgment to nonroutine situations. This task may be the greatest challenge of the future for CPE programs. In part, the task is difficult because practice is complex and, to some extent, spontaneous. And, in part, it is difficult because the traditional system of CPE looks to knowledge rather than practice performance for its organizing principles. Finally, most CPE looks at the parameters of a group rather than the swampy areas of individual professional practices.

CPE must approach this task of reform on two fronts at the same time. It must develop an understanding of the ways in which professionals integrate knowledge from their disciplines into the contexts of their practice, and it must develop new models of education that are directed toward the process of learning from professional practice.

Each of these mandates requires that a new partnership in education evolve around the practice of the profession. This means reducing the traditional authority of the academic power that comes from the numbers of students enrolled moving toward greater equality between learner and teacher. New dilemmas will face CPE practitioners, dilemmas about the role they play in shaping not only the professional practices of individuals but also the entire professions. The aims of education must change to encompass the ways in which professionals think and act while constantly dealing with unique, conflicted, and ambiguous circumstances of professional practice. CPE must depart from education based on certain knowledge (scientifically valid or technically correct) and move into the swamps of "maybe" and "sometimes." When one is in a swamp, structured knowledge and skills from formal education may not be helpful. Appropriate knowledge and action are embedded in each case. Information and education will need to be as fluid as practice problems and as malleable as the contingencies that add to the ambiguity, conflict, and unique nature of each case.

The form and function of such a system of CPE is not detailed here because little is certain about this new perspective on education. This is the frontier of CPE. It needs exploration.

We need to understand how knowledge organizes and shapes actions if we are to develop education that fits like a missing puzzle piece into the practices of professionals. We need to know how professionals distinguish between the usual and the unusual in order to help them adopt new areas of practice or improve existing practices. We need to know how professionals think back over their actions, critique themselves, and reorganize their knowledge and information to fit the problems faced in day-to-day experience. We need to be able to help them look for spontaneous new ways of practicing that are safe and effective as they adjust to the nonroutine nature of specific professional problems. We need to find methods and techniques that professionals can use to look back over a series of similar practice events in a way that leads them to new needs and opportunities to develop. Research can answer these questions if we can develop a system of investigators and studies to serve that purpose.

In the future, CPE must change its structure and function. Each of these challenges requires stronger connections between investigations of the practice of a profession and education systems for professional development. To meet the challenge and opportunity that CPE currently faces, we must have a new definition of the field based on the needs of individual practitioners, the profession, and society. CPE in the future will link these needs and participate in new solutions to integrate education and learners and to enhance professionals' ability to change their performance.

CHAPTER 12

Broadening the Concept
of Scholarship
in the Professions

R. Eugene Rice
Laurie Richlin

American higher education is engaged in a fundamental reassessment of scholarly work of faculty. The established European—essentially, German—model of scholarship, imported to the United States in the late nineteenth century, is under assault. Legislators, boards of trustees, professional clients, students, and scholars are questioning the appropriateness of the current notion of scholarly work for a society so heavily reliant on the production and utilization of knowledge. And nowhere is this assault more vigorous than in the professional schools.

Responding to this widespread dissatisfaction with the dominant view of scholarship, The Carnegie Foundation for the Advancement of Teaching launched a national project on the topic and issued a report (Boyer, 1990) that has focused the debate and led to the serious consideration of a broader conception of scholarship: one that is congruent with the rich diversity that is the hallmark of American higher education; one that is more appropriate, more authentic, and more adaptive for both our institutions and the day-to-day working lives of faculty.

It is fitting that The Carnegie Foundation should lead the way in addressing the issue of scholarship, for in the opening decade of this century it helped put into place a view of the role of scholarship in professional education that is still with us and that reinforced the view currently being vigorously questioned. In 1910, Abraham Flexner revolutionized professional education by publishing his report on medical education, under the auspices of The Carnegie Foundation. As a result of the Flexner report, schools of medicine were moved into the research universities and the scientific component of medical education was greatly increased. Two years of study in the basic sciences were prescribed as the necessary foundation for later clinical training. The medical school curriculum was separated into two disjunctive stages, the preclinical and the clinical, reflecting the division between theory and research, on the one hand, and practice, on the other.

The significance of structuring the elements of professional knowledge in this hierarchical way was felt not only in medicine but across the professions. The Flexner report established the pattern for medicine, and the other professions followed medicine's lead. The Flexner report inspired Reed's (1921) report on legal education (also published by The Carnegie Foundation) and the Gies's (1926) report on dental education. Both reports recommended stratified, research-based programs, and, as a result, schools of law and of dentistry were moved into university settings if at all possible.

The medical model of professional education was greatly strengthened by the prestige that the medical profession enjoys in the occupational status system of America. That medical education in the early years of the century required reformation is abundantly clear—the Flexner report was much needed—but the framing of the issue in a way that denigrated practice in favor of research in the quintessential profession of the society had a ripple effect of lasting consequence across schools of professional education as they were developing throughout the remainder of the century.

The result of moving professional schools into research universities was that practical competence was regarded as professional when grounded in systematic, preferably scientific knowledge. The application of knowledge took on value— rigor and prestige—only when derived from original research. In the most utilitarian society in the world, scholarship was conceptualized as independent of, and prior to, practice. Jencks and Riesman (1977, p. 252) pointed out that the affiliation of professional schools with universities had, over the years, damp- ened the schools' occupational commitments and stressed "a more academic and less practical view of what . . . students need to know." Normative for almost all of our career-oriented programs are the assumptions that learning precedes doing and that practice is the application of theory.

Today, the divergence between theory and practice and between professional preparation and application in the work- place continues to plague professional schools. Much of this can be traced to the kind of scholarship required of faculty working in these programs and to the scholarly criteria used to evaluate them for tenure and promotion.

In this chapter, we, first, place the issue of scholarship within the wider context of American higher education and set forth the four dimensions of scholarly work proposed by the Carnegie report (Boyer, 1990), with attention to the scholar- ship of practice. We then turn from a general consideration of the dominant view of scholarship in the American professori- ate—what it means to be an academic professional—to the professional schools and their struggle, across various fields, to articulate an appropriate approach to the scholarly work of faculty in the professions. Our effort concludes with an exami- nation of what it would mean for professional education if a broader conception of scholarship were institutionalized. In pressing for this enlarged view of the scholarly work of profes- sional school faculty, we recognize that much is already being done and that this is a particularly propitious time for a reex- amination of this critical issue.

Scholarship in Context

To understand what is happening to faculty across American higher education—and, particularly, to professional school faculty—we must attend to the symbolic, the dominant image of what it means to be a scholar and a professional in this society. Much about life is defined by socially constructed patterns of meaning that cohere in a particular time and place.

Nowhere in the contemporary world do socially constructed meanings have more power than in the professions. Burton Bledstein (1976), in his important book *The Culture of Professionalism* has demonstrated the significance of professional status for Americans and has related the rise of professionalism to the development of higher education in this country. In this highly mobile, democratic society, we have little sense of identity, class, or even place. In being a professional, we acquire identity and status. And there is no profession that takes its own professional imagery more seriously than academics. References need only be made to the years of graduate school socialization and the power that academics have in the lives of their protégés to make the argument.

Sometime after the mid-1950s, following the impact of the G.I. Bill of Rights and the launching of *Sputnik*, a major shift took place in the image of what it meant to be an academic professional. American higher education went through a dramatic period of expansion that brought with it a new conception. The constituent parts of this new professional image existed in nascent form throughout the early history of American higher education, with roots going back to Britain, Scotland, and Germany. But it was only in the heady days of what seemed to be limitless growth, affluence, and societal influence that the constituent elements fused to form a powerful and dominant new conception.

In a 1968 essay on the professions, Talcott Parsons (1968) described the education revolution that he saw coming to full fruition in American society after World War II. Fundamental to this revolution was the process of professionalization, a process that he regarded as the most important single component in the structure of modern societies. According to Parsons's elaborate theory, the keystone in the arch of the professionally oriented society is the modern university, and the profession par excellence is the academic. He also described the impact of professionalization or the role of the faculty member: "The typical professor now resembles the scientist more than the gentleman-scholar of an earlier time" (p. 542). As a result of the process of professionalization, achievement criteria are now given the highest priority, reputations are established in national and international forums rather than locally defined, and the center of gravity has shifted to the graduate faculties and their "newly professionalized large-scale research function" (p. 542).

What is most striking about this statement is that what he describes is not the typical professor of today. What he articulates is the dominant fiction by which typical American professors measure themselves and their colleagues as professionals. The image of the academic professional that emerged during the expansionist days of higher education not only shaped the self-conceptions of faculty but also informed institutional policies and largely determined who received promotion, tenure, and such amenities as leaves of absence and funding for travel and research. Clustering around this dominant professional image were the following basic assumptions:

- Research is the central professional endeavor and the focus of academic life.
- Quality in the profession is maintained by peer review and professional autonomy.
- Knowledge is pursued for its own sake.
- The pursuit of knowledge is best organized according to discipline (that is, according to discipline-based departments).
- Reputations are established through national and international professional associations.
- The distinctive task of the academic professional is the pursuit of cognitive truth.
- Professional rewards and mobility accrue to those who persistently accentuate their specializations.

This scholarly vision and the interrelated complex of assumptions on which it was built contributed to an extraordinary advancement of knowledge. The increased specialization, the new levels of funding for research, and the rigorous exchange and critique of ideas produced undeniable benefits. So much was achieved that toward the end of the 1960s, Jencks and Riesman (1977) could join Parsons (1968) in proclaiming that an academic revolution had actually occurred.

During the same expansionist, post–World War II period, another academic revolution took place, equally as significant and certainly as dramatic. An already diverse system of higher education exploded with growth and innovation, changing in size, complexity, and capacity to meet the rich variety of education needs across the states and regions of the nation. These two dramatic transformations in American higher education could be contained as long as budgets were expanding, enrollments were increasing, and programs were being added. It was soon evident, however, that these two remarkable revolutions encompassed serious contradictions and were not easy to reconcile. At the heart of the tension created by these significant changes were the role of faculty and the meaning of scholarship.

We want to challenge the cluster of assumptions, listed earlier, emerging from the first of these revolutions, not because it is inappropriate in itself—in fact, most of the elements have been fully institutionalized in the present-day research university. Rather, we question this conception of the academic scholar because it became normative, and continues to be so, for the majority of the American professoriate, dominating faculty thinking about themselves professionally in institutional contexts where it is no longer appropriate and causing faculty to see themselves disenfranchised as scholars.

The interrelated elements that we have identified were woven into a fabric of consensus that became the assumptive world into which the large number of new faculty from the rapidly expanding graduate schools were initiated. What has evolved is a hierarchical conception of scholarly excellence that is tied to the advancement of research and defined in zero-sum terms. This restricted, one-dimensional view places research in competition with other important scholarly responsibilities and leads to their devaluation. Faculty find themselves divided within, set against one another, and profoundly disheartened when confronted with the disparity between the mission driving their institutions and their own professional self-understanding.

A Broad View of Scholarship

Enlargement of our understanding of scholarship became a central concern of The Carnegie Foundation for the Advancement of Teaching during the two-year period between 1988 and 1990. Drawing heavily on the previous work of Lynton and Elman (1987), Shulman (1987), and others, Boyer's *Scholarship Reconsidered* (1990) opened a vigorous debate about the scholarly work of faculty and the activities that are rewarded. As a part of this process, four forms of scholarship were identified.

Scholarship of Discovery

The first element in this broader conception of scholarship, and still a key element, is the discovery of knowledge. The place of pure research, the pursuit of knowledge for its own sake, needs to be assiduously defended, particularly in a society primarily committed to the pragmatic and too often concerned more with whether something works over the short term than with whether it is of lasting value. There is no disputing that if scholarship is to be sustained in our day, the advancement of specialized knowledge is required.

Scholarship of Integration

The extension of the frontiers of knowledge is, however, not enough. The second element in scholarship is the integration of knowledge, an undertaking as critical to the understanding of our world as the discovery of knowledge that is new. In fact, the extension of specialization itself requires new forms of integration. Without a continuous effort at reintegration, we have fragmentation. Scholars are needed with a capacity to

synthesize, to look for new relationships between the parts and
the whole, to relate the past and future to the present, and to
ferret out patterns of meaning that cannot be seen through
traditional disciplinary lenses.

Scholarship of Teaching and Learning

This is the most difficult form of scholarship to discuss because
we do not have the appropriate language. In the working lives
of individual faculty, scholarship and teaching are often seen as
antithetical—competing for one's time and attention. This is a
reflection of the way in which both tasks are conceptualized. We
want to challenge this understanding and argue that quality
teaching requires substantive scholarship that builds on, but is
distinct from, original research, and that this scholarly effort
needs to be recognized and rewarded. The scholarship of
teaching and learning is a special kind of scholarship that has
for too long been implicit, unacknowledged, and virtually
unnamed. Some are now willing to talk about "a missing
paradigm."

This third dimension of scholarship has an integrity of its
own but is deeply embedded in the other forms. In addition,
the scholarship of teaching and learning has three distinct
elements: first, a *synoptic capacity*, the ability to draw the strands
of the field together in a way that provides both coherence and
meaning, to place what is known in context and open the way
for connections to be made between the knower and the
known; second, what Shulman (1987) calls "pedagogical content knowledge," the capacity to represent a subject in ways that
transcend the split between intellectual substance and the
teaching process, usually having to do with the metaphors,
analogies, and experiments used; and third, *what we know about
learning*, scholarly inquiry into how students "make meaning"
(Perry, 1981) out of what the teacher says and does.

Scholarship of Practice

This is the most distinctly American form of scholarship. The
great land grant institutions were established during the nine-

teenth century precisely for the purpose of applying knowledge to the enormous agricultural and technical problems confronting society. These schools and their utilitarian missions matched the mood and needs of an emerging nation. In the academic profession today, however, there is a disturbing gap between what is valued as scholarship and the pragmatic needs of the larger world.

From the struggle with this issue, there is an emerging recognition of the legitimacy of another kind of knowing: knowledge that emerges from practice. The dominant view of scholarship has research and theory standing in a hierarchically superior relation to practice. Practice has been seen as the passive recipient of developed knowledge. The alternative view suggests that in many applied fields knowledge emerges from the complexity and rigors of practice. Rather than a hierarchical relationship, this view holds that theory and practice are complementary and mutually enriching.

This form of scholarship relates most directly to the work of faculty in professional schools. In assessments and rewards of the scholarship of professional school faculty, the tension between theoretical reflection and active practice is immediately joined. As professional schools became more firmly ensconced in the research university, faculty in practice-related fields became subject to the same centrifugal pressures toward narrow research as experienced by arts and sciences faculty. In fact, the more prestigious the university, the more the programs became concerned with research and scholarship in the narrowest sense than with the "practical view of what their students need to know" (Jencks and Riesman, 1977, p. 252). Successful integration into the academic research culture varied, however, based on how able and willing the faculty members were to conduct the kind of research required.

Scholarly Work in Professional Schools

The place of scholarship and what is valued as scholarly work varies across professional fields. As a result, there have been different responses from the different professional schools.

Factors Influencing the Development of Scholarship
in the Professional Schools

To understand what counts as scholarly work by professional
school faculty, several key variables must be considered. One
primary influence has been whether or not faculty members
continue to practice within their fields. Two methods for describing a field's relationship to knowledge help us understand
the backgrounds of diverse types of scholarship: Biglan's (1973)
classification by amount of disciplinary agreement on a central
paradigm and on a field's concern with life systems and Kolb's
(1984) classification of learning styles. Other important factors
are the mission of the profession, the length of study required
to obtain the field's professional degree, and the relative numbers of female and of male faculty members in the field.

Active Practice

Not only do faculty in the professions face the necessary division of time and effort among the traditional categories of
research, teaching, and service, they also must incorporate
professional practice. In order to define the appropriate types
of scholarship for professional school faculty, it is important to
focus on how professional practice and theory are integrated.
Education for the professions creates a "triangular relationship
between the academics, and practitioners, and the students"
(Barnett, Becher, and Cork, 1987, p. 51). Although faculty in
most programs have completed a doctorate (usually a Ph.D.) at
a research university, they may or may not currently practice in
the field. In some cases (for example, medicine and architecture), ongoing practice is intrinsic to the faculty member's
intellectual life; in other fields (for example, education, nursing, and pharmacy), faculty members teach but usually do not
practice the profession (Dinham, 1987).

Freidson, a leading scholar in the sociology of the professions, states that "the differentiation of members [of a profes-
sion] into practitioners, administrators, and teacher-researchers
is thus a central characteristic of the organization of profes-

sional occupations. It also represents a critical division bearing on both professional powers and the use of formal knowledge. Located in different positions in the system, with different duties, each has different interests and perspectives" (1986, pp. 211–212).

The Professional Preparation Project, supported by the Fund for the Improvement of Postsecondary Education at the University of Michigan, found that the differences inherent to generating and using research actually broaden the gap between research and practice (Stark, Lowther, and Hagerty, 1987). The question asked regarding professional identity and professional preparation is, Should the nature of education be determined by practitioners? The choice is whether graduate education for the professions should be dominated by abstract consideration of a field's theories or should be focused on training students in the skills necessary to practice their profession in the real world. For faculty scholarship, the decision is between creating theory that could, eventually, inform application and observing the impact of current practice on clients and patients in order for practice to inform theory. In law, for instance, this is the difference between using Socratic legal reasoning and studying the effects of storefront law clinics on precedents.

Biglan Classification

Biglan (1973) proposed three scales on which academic disciplines can differ: *pure* or *applied,* based on concern with application; *hard* or *soft,* based on the amount of agreement on a paradigm within the discipline; and *life* or *nonlife,* based on "concern with life systems," which include both biological and social systems. Nearly a dozen studies (Biglan, 1973; Smart and Elton, 1975, 1976; Eison, 1976; Hesseldenz and Smith, 1977; Smart and McLaughlin, 1978; McGrath, 1978; Muffo and Langston, 1979; Creswell, Seagren, and Henry, 1979; Creswell and Bean, 1981; Roskens, 1983) have tested Biglan's model and found differences along the dimensions using independent variables as diverse as research production, job satisfaction, social connectedness, need for professional development, initiation into disciplines, number of books checked out of the library, and response rates to surveys.

Table 12.1 shows how professional schools can be classified under the Biglan model. All professional programs are considered applied fields. The hard/life division includes the professions of dentistry, medicine, and pharmacy, in which there is high agreement among the disciplinary paradigms, combined with a concern for life systems. The soft/life quadrant includes the fields of business, education, law, nursing, and social work, which focus on life systems but in which the paradigms are less fixed. The fields of accountancy, architecture, and engineering are classified as hard/nonlife because they have high agreement on the disciplinary paradigms and focus on nonlife systems. No profession is classified as soft/ nonlife.

Kolb Learning Styles

Kolb (1984) developed a four-step system of experiencing and understanding, describing how learners move from *concrete experience* to *reflective observation,* create *abstract conceptualizations*

Table 12.1. Professional Schools Classified According to Biglan's Model of Faculty Culture.

	Applied Fields	
	Agreement with Dominant Paradigm	
	Hard	*Soft*
Life	Dentistry	Business
	Medicine	Education
	Pharmacy	Law
		Nursing
		Social work
Nonlife	Accountancy	
	Architecture	
	Engineering	

Source: Based on Biglan, 1973.

and then test their theories through *active experimentation.* The Kolb model of experiential learning has two axes: preference for grasping experience either through concrete or abstract means, and preference for transforming knowledge through reflection or active experimentation. The points on the learning cycle are ways in which different people prefer to deal with information: different types of learners can be placed at various points around the circle.

Figure 12.1 places professional school faculty in the classification for their dominant learning styles. The first group, *accommodators,* grasps through concrete experience and transforms knowledge through active experimentation. Faculty in education, nursing, and social work are most often accommodators. The second group, *divergers,* also grasps through concrete experience but transforms knowledge through reflective observation. This is a secondary focus for architecture

Figure 12.1. Professional School Faculty Classified According to Kolb's Dual-Axis Model of Learning Styles.

Concrete Experience

Accommodators	*Divergers*
Education	Architecture[b]
Nursing	
Social work	

Active Experimentation ——————————————————— Reflective Observation

Convergers	*Assimilators*
Accounting	Business
Architecture[a]	Medicine[a]
Dentistry	
Engineering	
Law	
Medicine[b]	
Pharmacy	

Abstract Conceptualization

[a]Primary focus.
[b]Secondary focus.
Source: Based on Kolb, 1984.

faculty, whose dominant mode tends to be converger. *Convergers* grasp experience through abstract conceptualization and transform it through active experimentation. This group includes the bulk of professional school faculty; it is the primary style of accounting, architecture, dentistry, engineering, law, and pharmacy, and the secondary style for medicine. The fourth group, *assimilators*, is the most abstract and reflective type of learners and includes business and medicine.

Although no one style is innately preferable to others, those utilizing more abstract and reflective methods lend themselves more readily to scientific research, whereas more concrete and active methods are more applicable to practice.

Professional Mission

The University of Michigan Professional Preparation Project conducted a massive study of twenty-nine hundred journal articles on professional preparation that were published between 1979 and 1984. From that work, and subsequent investigations on related issues, the project has created professional clusters based on the primary missions of the fields. Stark, Lowther, and Hagerty (1986) identified three emphases: *helping* (dentistry, medicine, nursing, pharmacy, and social work), *enterprising* (architecture, journalism, and library science), and *informing* (education, journalism, and library science). Recently, after further discussion with representatives of the fields, they have refined the system into the clusters shown in Exhibit 12.1: *helping professions* (dentistry, medicine, ministry, nursing, pharmacy, social work, and teaching), *entrepreneurial professions* (business, journalism, and law), and *technical professions* (architecture, engineering, and military).

Professional Degree

Through the influence of professional associations and university departments, certification for entry into the professions has become the responsibility of the professional schools. Only business remains a profession in which a member may practice

Exhibit 12.1. Professional Schools Classified by the Professional
Preparation Project's Professional Clusters.

Helping Professions

Dentistry
Medicine
Ministry
Nursing
Pharmacy
Social work
Teaching

Entrepreneurial Professions

Business
Journalism
Law

Technical Professions

Architecture
Engineering
Military

Source: Adapted from Stark, Lowther, and Hagerty, 1986.

without degree or certification; the other professions require
some sort of official blessing in the form of being granted a
degree, passing an examination, or meeting hiring criteria.
This usually means a college degree, although this may not yet
be necessary in all cases for entry to journalism, the ministry,
and the military. A bachelor of arts or science remains the
terminal degree in some nursing, education, and social work
programs, although there is continuing pressure in those fields
to require more education. Pharmacy is in the process of
dropping certification of undergraduate programs for entry
into the profession (Blum, 1991b).

The primary instrument for acknowledging readiness for
practice in most professional fields remains the master's degree (Glazer, 1986). Law, a soft field, upgraded its terminal
degree to a doctorate of jurisprudence (J.D.), imitating the
degrees of the hard fields of dentistry and medicine. In some
professional areas, such as accountancy, law, medicine, and

dentistry, additional certification is necessary through a national board or association examination. A recent report commissioned by the Council of Graduate Schools calls the master's degree a "silent success" (Conrad, Hayworth, and Miller, forthcoming). Between 1970 and 1990, there was a 48 percent increase in master's degrees awarded annually, with most of the growth in professional fields such as engineering, education, nursing, and business. Recipients reported that the master's degree "sharpened their ability to connect theory and practice, refined their analytical and communication skills and helped them develop a 'big picture' perspective in their field" (Blum, 1991a, p. A32). Provision of a master's degree education focused on practice becomes problematic when the faculty in these programs are themselves educated as research doctorates rather than as practitioners, and when the academic reward system demands more abstract than applied work from them. The resulting mismatch results from the desire of "full-time academics to make the discipline more academically and theoretically credible and less like practical training" (Brown and Gelernter, 1989, p. 64). In architecture, for example, research has "modeled itself after the natural and social sciences and stressed the internal logical and elegance of the research more than its practical application" (Brown and Gelernter, 1989, p. 64). The bias of the professor then becomes the recreation of the researcher rather than the education of the up-to-date practitioner, or learning from practice itself.

Feminization of the Field

Seemingly, a determining influence on the type of scholarship in which professional school faculty engage is the proportion of women faculty in the programs. As discussed below, the fields in which women have the highest proportion of practitioners and faculty members (education, nursing, and social work) have focused on a more client-centered type of scholarship than have the fields in which there are proportionally more men.

Current Status of Scholarship in the Professions

What has the move from an apprentice system to the academy meant for scholarship in the professional schools? The professions have had four responses. Some have separated discovery research from application and practice. Others have focused instead on client-centered practice or pragmatic application. And several fields currently are in transition, with ongoing discussion regarding the place of research and practice. Table 12.2 displays the grouping of eleven professional schools, with the six influences on scholarship discussed above.

Separation of Discovery and Practice

One response to the move to the academy has been the separation of functions into discovery and research versus clinical and applied areas. Both of the professions in this category—engineering and medicine—are nonfeminized, hard Biglan fields in which the faculty usually continue professional practice.

It was the Flexner (1910) report, described earlier, that moved medical education into the research university, where training is divided between a preclinical, basic science curriculum and a clinical stage focusing on practice. Scholarship in medicine has been divided along those lines, with preclinical or strictly research faculty publishing basic research and clinical faculty emphasizing applied medicine.

Investigation of research productivity of family medicine practitioners found twelve characteristics of "productive" (that is, publishable) researchers: in-depth knowledge, research methods, socialization to the academic profession, experience with research mentor, early scholarly habits, supportive network, productive colleagues, multiple simultaneous research projects, adequate time, activities both inside and outside of the institution, autonomy with institutional commitment, and an organizational environment supportive of research (Bland, Hitchcock, Anderson, and Stritter, 1987). If medical schools want their faculty to publish basic (discovery) research, they

Table 12.2. Approaches to Scholarly Work and Factors Influencing Scholarship in Professional Schools.

Approach to Scholarly Work	Professional School	Do Faculty Practice?	Biglan	Kolb	Professional Mission	Professional Degree	Is Field Feminized?
Separation of discovery and practice	Engineering	Yes	Hard/Non	Converger	Technical	Master's	No
	Medicine	Yes	Hard/Life	Assimilator/Converger	Helping	Doctorate	No
Client-centered practice	Education	No	Soft/Life	Accommodator	Helping	Bachelor's/Master's	Yes
	Nursing	No	Soft/Life	Accommodator	Helping	Bachelor's/Master's	Yes
	Social work	No	Soft/Life	Accommodator	Helping	Bachelor's/Master's	Yes
Pragmatic application	Accountancy	Usually	Soft/Non	Converger	Entrepreneurial	Master's	No
	Architecture	Varies	Hard/Non	Converger/Diverger	Technical	Master's	No
	Business	Varies	Soft/Life	Assimilator	Entrepreneurial	Master's[a]	No
Fields in transition	Dentistry	Yes	Hard/Life	Converger	Helping	Doctorate	No
	Pharmacy	No	Hard/Life	Converger	Helping	Doctorate[b]	No
	Law	No	Soft/Life	Converger	Entrepreneurial	Doctorate	No

[a] No degree necessary for entry to field.
[b] Phasing out bachelor's degree programs.

must emphasize those academic qualities. Especially important in sustaining productivity of this sort is the socialization of physicians into academic research culture (Bland and Schmitz, 1986).

In response to the call for scientific research, the field of engineering was divided into two components: engineering (which is really "engineering science") and engineering technology. In the rush toward science following the launching of *Sputnik*, major engineering programs began to focus more on conceptual and theoretical aspects (including design theories) than on practice. In response, a four-year technology degree was developed by faculty whose real interest was in engineering practice. The Accreditation Board for Engineering and Technology established different criteria for accreditation of the two subfields, and for over twenty-five years the two have functioned separately. Stephen R. Cheshier, president of the Southern Technical Institute, relates that

> the research-oriented faculty of such [engineering science] programs regarded themselves as engineers, although many were conducting scientific investigation rather than practicing engineering in the industrial sense. Some had not spent any time in the practice of engineering outside of academe, yet they viewed themselves as engineers and the students they were preparing as learning engineering. This new direction towards abstraction, engineering theory and engineering science would have been fine had it not displaced some of the still-needed aspects of most engineering schools. When these aspects were preserved in emerging engineering technology colleges, the problem of building an educational process separate from engineering education began [1985, p. 707].

Partly in response to industry's needs and partly due to the shrinking number of engineering students, engineering (science) programs have begun to move closer to engineering technology programs by reemphasizing practical rather than theoretical design content in the curriculum. Many academic and professional leaders are calling for a realignment of programs under an overarching engineering accreditation, with the technology programs relabeled as *applied engineering*. If engineering does move back to a single type of program, the diversely prepared faculty in the technical programs will once again be confronted with the need to demonstrate the scholarship of application within the bounds of the research university.

Client-Centered Practice

Three fields, education, nursing, and social work, have focused on client-centered practice rather than scientific research. This group of professions is similar on all six classifications shown on Table 12.2. They have a high percentage of female faculty, their faculty do not continue to practice, they operate with soft paradigms in areas focused on life systems, they are all helping professions, the main style of knowing is accommodation, and they remain some of the easiest fields to enter, often with only a bachelor's degree required.

Nursing is classified as a *soft* Biglan field because it is more client than science oriented, more like social work than medicine. Graduate nursing programs were originally organized to prepare nursing faculty and were often found in departments of education. It was not until the 1960s that master's programs were revised to focus on practice (Glazer, 1986). As a result, "faculties of nursing . . . bear responsibility for the whole range of intellectual endeavor, from basic research to testing-in-practice to serving and training nurses in the field. While the traditional academic disciplines are concerned almost exclusively with developing knowledge, nursing as an applied field must also be concerned with the attitudes and skills necessary for genuinely professional practice" (Newell, 1989, p. 73). Unlike physicians, nurses usually do not continue to practice when they become faculty. The focus has been on the application of nursing theory to client care, rather than on purely theoretical aspects of nursing.

Glazer (1986) found that the identity of graduate schools of education was more ambiguous than that of other professional schools (for example, medicine, law, and business). Their main function has been to train and credential kindergarten through high school teachers, with little credit given by other arts and science or professional departments for the scholarship of educators.

In their study of the earlier problems of the School of Education at the University of California, Berkeley, Clifford and Guthrie (1988, p. 301) attributed the lack of importance given to education research to the status of the School of Education: "Low-status groups tend to be ambivalent about their group, and try to demonstrate commitment to the norms of those higher in the stratification system. These efforts never achieved parity for education at Berkeley. Education faculty were given tenure and promoted for doing research and publishing it. But this, like the hiring of non-education-trained faculty, did not convince campus opinion leaders that the scholarship was equal to that done in cognate departments."

Recently, schools of education in research universities have been called on to learn from the wisdom of practice, to get faculty into this nation's schools, and to focus on the student as client. In particular, more credence is being given to learning from interactions in the classroom and with students who learn in different ways. The quality of our schools depends on our ability to take seriously the scholarship of practice and a different kind of interaction between research and practice.

Reporting on the extent to which social work educators are adopting traditional university criteria, McNeece (1981, p. 18) found that a large majority of the tenured faculty were not active in publishing, lending credence to the observation that "publication in refereed journals has not, as yet, been accepted by schools of social work." Tenured faculty, however, published more than untenured faculty, leading to the conclusion that "during this transitional period, a few social work educators have moved toward the acceptance of traditional academic values regarding research and publication" (p. 18). Although social work is a feminized field, men are more likely than women to be faculty members rather than practitioners; of faculty members, men are more likely than women to be senior faculty. In part, this is a direct result of scholarship production: Kirk and Rosenblatt (1984, p. 67) found that "faculty members are more likely than social work practitioners to publish articles" and "senior faculty are more likely than junior faculty to publish articles." This is in contrast to 1934–1938, when men wrote only a third of the published articles.

Citation analysis of six major social work journals found that faculty in schools with doctoral programs published much more than those in schools without. There was considerable difference in the number of citations between the top-ranked school (sixty-two citations) and fifteenth-ranked school (eighteen citations) (Thyer and Bentley, 1986). Studies on the publication rates of social work educators show that their overall productivity is low, and that a relatively small number are doing most of the publishing (Faver, Fox, Hunter, and Shannon, 1986). Overall, although it is accepted in social work that practice should be empirically based, there is still the feeling that scientific research should not alone determine practice. One problem in stimulating more traditional research that was identified by the Council on Social Work Education is the anxiety of faculty who have no preparation for research (Smith, DeWeaver, and Kilpatrick, 1986).

Pragmatic Application

Pragmatic application constitutes the third category of reaction to the call for academic scholarship in professional schools. Two of the professions in this group, accountancy and business, are classified by the Professional Preparation Project as entrepreneurial. The third, architecture, is considered technical, although it certainly has entrepreneurial aspects. It is noteworthy that faculty in all three areas continue to practice at some level.

Business is an anomaly because it is the only profession

in which a practitioner can enter and succeed without any degree or certification from a college, university, or accreditation organization and without having to meet an employer's criteria to practice or be promoted. Although usually a part of a business school, accountancy differs from business in an important respect: it requires considerable certification to practice. Both business and accountancy are considered *soft* fields, although there are good arguments that accountancy could just as easily be put in the *hard* category.

One way in which pragmatic scholarship has been developed is through the innovative teaching strategy of *case method* adopted by business schools. This combination of real-life practice with theoretical consideration has led to a practicum-based curriculum for the students and an application-based scholarship by the faculty. As a result, the ties between faculty research interests and student preparation have been strengthened.

In many ways, architecture has faced the same problems as engineering, with a tension between theoretical, design aspects of the field and practical considerations of the real world. As in engineering, the movement of architecture schools to the university was particularly difficult because "their subject matter traditionally dealt with practical knowledge, not abstract principles or empirical research" (Brown and Gelernter, 1989, p. 62). In architecture, as in business, one of the ways that scholarship has remained useful to professional education has been through a teaching method, in this case workshops (sometimes called clinics), that help students become "reflective practitioners" (Schön, 1983, 1987). Schön uses the term knowing-in-action to describe the way that novices become experts in the application of theory. The teacher models, rather than describes, the appropriate actions; students learn by imitating, doing what they cannot understand until they have done it successfully. The task of educating the reflective practitioner is a complicated, iterative process, requiring patience and trust by both faculty and students (Schön, 1987).

The growing number of architecture doctoral programs poses a threat to this pragmatic thrust because the new faculty will be selected with a "research orientation rather than with substantial professional experience and qualifications" (Steward, 1988, p. 10). The dilemma of appropriate education for the field's mission remains, both in curriculum and scholarship, how to "accommodate a profession that values design education, yet wants more technical and practice-oriented instruction" (Fisher, 1989, p. 17).

Fields in Transition

Three professions are involved in spirited discussion on the place of "narrow" scholarship: dentistry, pharmacy, and law. All three fields now require a doctoral degree for entry. Faculty in all three tend to be convergers who combine an abstract, analytical way of knowing with active practice.

Gies's (1926) report was to dentistry what the Flexner (1910) report was to medicine. After the Gies report, dental schools became affiliated with universities, even though through the mid-1960s dental school faculty were drawn from practice settings. In an important discussion of the problem, Albino (1984, p. 509–510) states that "the result was that the dental faculty in clinical disciplines had considerable practical experience, but little appreciation for the academic traditions of scholarship and publication. . . . Nowhere in the academy do we find individual faculty members more poorly equipped for the demands of traditional scholarship than in clinical dentistry. . . . In short, many of our clinical faculty do not possess even modestly developed research skills." He states, however, that "career advancement in academic dentistry appears to demand success in . . . three areas [teaching, scholarship, and service], but first and foremost in research and scholarship. . . . As a result, many dental faculty believe they face an ethical as well as practical dilemma: they are forced to choose between providing excellent professional preparation for their students or ensuring their own academic careers" (p. 509).

Whether the profession of pharmacy is a life or nonlife Biglan field is under considerable discussion by the groups representing pharmacists. Originally a nonlife profession concerned with chemical and physical properties of drugs, as pharmaceutical companies have taken over most of the necessary compounding, pharmacists have become more "patient-oriented, clinical, and therapeutic" (Blum, 1991b, p. A18).

Currently, there is a five-year bachelor of science program that awards the B.S.P. and a six-year doctorate that awards the Pharm.D. The American Council on Pharmacy Education has stated its intent to make the six-year doctoral program the only degree that it accredits (Blum, 1991b, p. A18). The move to upgrade the requirements for entry into pharmacy parallels those in medicine and dentistry. However, there is considerable opposition from the National Association of Chain Drug Stores, which believes a doctoral program will "overtrain" pharmacists in community practice while "under-training the people who go into practice at a hospital or other settings" (Blum, 1991b, p. A18). Supporters of the change include the American Society of Hospital Pharmacists (with a membership of 23,000 pharmacists), National Association of Retail Druggists (NARD) (owners and employees of 40,000 retail pharmacies), and the American Pharmaceutical Association (representing 150,000 pharmacists, pharmaceutical scientists, and pharmaceutical students).

Scholarship in pharmacy also is in the process of changing from a hard-science orientation to a greater focus on clinical care. With the move toward a single doctorate degree, the system is likely to become more like medicine, with separation between basic science and practice.

The history of preparation for a legal career has been remarkably similar to the history of preparation for the medical profession. In addition to passing a bar examination, requirements moved from apprenticeship alone to apprenticeship *or* law school, to law school only, to a law school approved by the American Bar Association (ABA) after a college education. Stevens (1983, p. 113) reports that "the Flexner Report may have been galling to the ABA, but, because of this indignation and the report's success, it also deeply impressed the association. Three years after the Flexner Report was published, the ABA decided enough was enough, and the members of the

Committee on Legal Education and Admissions to the Bar announced that it was 'most anxious to have a similar investigation made by The Carnegie Foundation into the conditions under which the work of legal education is carried on in this country.' "

The Flexner report on medicine inspired Reed's (1921) report on legal education, which also was published by The Carnegie Foundation for the Advancement of Teaching. However, Reed's recommendations did not lead to a scientific consensus among legal scholars but instead left the field in a state of "increasing conflict, contradiction, and confusion" (Kimball, 1988, p. 465). Kimball (1988, p. 464) attributes the different response to the "differing nature of law and medicine." Because medicine was able to develop a "germ theory" and treat the same disease in the same way at different times in difficult situations, medical education became "one of increasing consensus, reliability, and predictability" (p. 464). Law, on the other hand, developed less uniformly: "American law became associated with precedents rather than principles and with ad hoc rationalizations, as the judges moved from case to case. Instead of attempting to discover 'the underlying theory of law,' the American lawyer looked 'for cases "on all fours," ' cases whose facts duplicated as closely as possible the ones from the case at hand" (Stevens, 1983, pp. 132–133).

This difference between what is possible in medicine and in law is the difference in what can be replicated:

> Wills get executed, property conveyed, and trials conducted, of course. But underlying and even within the various branches of case law, statutory law, constitutional law, and administrative law, there is no systematic theory that ensures that a legal germ today in Massachusetts will yield to the same remedy as it did in California in 1920 or will in Iowa in 2003. Lawyers, like educators, can take some comfort in the fact that, as Aristotle indicated, theirs is a "practical science," from which one cannot expect the certainty that one finds in

the natural sciences. This is because human voli-
tion is involved in a "practical science." Such com-
fort, however, is small in a century that honors
natural science and has come to expect reliability,
consistency, and predictability in matters where
professionals are concerned [Kimball, 1988,
p. 465].

Schuck (1989, p. 323) avers that "law is preeminently a
practical profession. Law teaching seeks to prepare students for
the world of practical affairs. Legal scholarship is supposed to
clarify truths about the world even though (indeed precisely
because) such truths are often elusive and contingent. Yet
empirical research—the uncovering of facts about how individuals and institutions within our legal culture actually be-
have—is a decidedly marginal activity in the legal academy
today." He states the "widespread conviction that the gap
(perhaps 'chasm' would be more accurate) between the legal
academy and the real world of practice and public policy is
already alarmingly wide" (p. 325).

Summary

Faculty in the professional schools have been torn between the
worlds of practice, education, and scientific disciplinary research. Two fields with hard paradigms, medicine and engineering, have dealt with the move to the academy by dividing
into discovery and application areas. In the feminized, soft/life
fields of education, nursing, and social work, the focus has
remained on the client and practice. Fields in which faculty
continue their professional practice—accountancy, architecture, and business—have adopted a more pragmatic view of
research and have focused on what would improve professional
practice. And other fields, including dentistry, pharmacy, and
law, are still engaged in debate about the appropriate types of
research for their faculties. One way to resolve the dissonance
between the traditions of the academy and the needs of professional education is to broaden our conception of scholarship to
include practice.

Toward a Broader Conception of Scholarly Work

Including the wisdom of practice in the scholarly work of professional school faculty does not eliminate the importance of the other types of scholarship. Rather, there need to be opportunities for faculty to pursue a broader range of scholarly activities.

Discovery with Purpose

When the professional schools entered the university, the initial impulse of faculty was to ape the scientists and to publish for legitimacy. Freedom of inquiry—the opportunity to question critically, to follow an argument where it leads—is fundamental to the life of the university and college. There is no tenet in the academic profession that has endured longer than the commitment to knowledge for its own sake, to the value of dispassionate reason, to the objective study of nature, society, and the individual.

The commitment to scholarship for its own sake must be sustained, but in a broader, more inclusive context. The dissenting voices must be heard, not excluded or silenced, and the realities about the relationship of knowledge and power confronted, not masked. While affirming the importance of the advancement of knowledge and supporting faculty research, we are concerned about the distortions introduced into American higher education by the prominence of the research function, the inordinate prestige associated with it and the narrowness of the specializations. Research efforts that were supposed to be pursued freely, for the purpose of advancing knowledge, have become means to ends with little scholarly connection. The pressure to publish has become so intense in some institutions that many junior faculty publish in order to qualify for tenure and promotion, not because they have something significant to say to their peers. Work is published prematurely and journals proliferate to meet an extraneous need. Research and the advancement of knowledge must be seen as a significant part of scholarship, but not the whole of it. For its own vitality, research needs to be pursued within a more comprehensive scholarly context, one that is concerned not only with the advancement of knowledge but also with its integration, application, and mutual relevance to subsequent generations.

Integrating Context

Without a broader conception of scholarship providing for integration and a sense of the whole, intense specialization— as important as it is—gets cut off, losing its meaning and even its legitimacy. We are particularly concerned that many of our most talented young people, who at an earlier time would have been drawn to the challenges of an academic career, are finding the research ethos uninviting—divisively competitive and inconsequential. Across higher education, there is a profound need for scholars with the capacity to bridge disciplines, to integrate, to synthesize, and to look for new relationships. This is not a call for the "gentleman scholar" of an earlier time, or for the dilettante who dabbles here and there, but rather for broadly educated men and women who are serious about making the kinds of scholarly connections so much needed in our time. Substantial interdisciplinary endeavors are the most obvious examples.

A new appreciation for the scholarship of integration is particularly pressing in the highly specialized disciplines. Fundamental reforms that are both comprehensive and pervasive will require a different conception of scholarship. Until faculty are encouraged to give time and energy to the integration of knowledge, most of the reforms currently recommended for American higher education will flounder. For instance, the dominant view of scholarship, where integration and the synthesis of knowledge are not particularly valued, encourages dependence on the text; at the same time, those most capable of writing richly textured comprehensive texts are discouraged from doing so. According to the prevailing view, *real* scholars in most fields do not write textbooks; such activity is regarded as a serious detraction from research.

The current view of scholarship also has discouraged the exploration of broader ethical implications or value themes. The fields that traditionally have been responsible for maintaining a larger perspective and presenting an integrative view have been pressed by the dominant mode of inquiry to narrow their purview. A view of scholarship that consistently honors the integration of knowledge would raise the ethical questions in a systematic way. For example, a rich interdisciplinary approach would place research questions within their historical and social contexts, and broader philosophical questions would be raised. We would be spared the ethics traumas that confront professional fields on an all too regular basis. Predictably, what has emerged from these sporadic activities are specializations in ethics: biomedical ethics is now established and business ethics is struggling for recognition. It is clear that the specialized effort to apply ethics to the professions is sorely needed, and we applaud the recent developments. But this specialized work is often procedural in character, dealing with issues that are narrowly technical and functional, and needs to be grounded in a broader, substantive approach to ethics.

Intellectually, the case for a broader view of scholarship is already being made. That knowledge is relational—grounded in communities of commitment and belief—is widely acknowledged. The call for a view of scholarship that includes the integration of knowledge, as well as its advancement, must be supported by more flexible structural arrangements for developing multidisciplinary programs and for rewarding faculty scholarship that is integrative.

Teaching for Learning

The tiresome teaching versus research debate reflects the way in which both tasks, at present, are conceptualized. We want to challenge this understanding and argue that quality teaching requires substantive scholarship that is embedded in and builds on specialized research but is qualitatively different in kind. This important form of scholarship remains implicit, unacknowledged, and usually neglected given our current definitions and priorities. The teaching-research polarity sets intellectual substance and educational process at odds. And not only are disciplinary content and teaching methods separated, they also are hierarchically arranged so that research is always viewed as superior to teaching. As a result, the rigorous scholarship required for effective teaching is unrewarded and often neglected. The view of teaching as a generic process, disconnected from intellectual substance, has reinforced the tendency to view teaching and research in either/or terms.

One of the reasons legislators, trustees, and the general public do not understand why ten or even fifteen hours of teaching a week is a heavy work load is that we have systematically separated scholarship from teaching. Under the current conception, there is no way to account for or understand the extensive scholarly effort, the hard intellectual work, that undergirds fine teaching.

This dimension of scholarship has an integrity of its own; it can be pursued, evaluated, and rewarded with the same confidence with which we support research. The representation of knowledge—teaching—is the active ingredient that bonds the multiple aspects of scholarship together. Of all of the efforts to enhance the quality of teaching in higher education, those having the largest impact and the most enthusiastic acceptance by faculty are those that focus on the nexus of intellectual substance and teaching process.

In teaching, more than in research, the need for faculty to prepare students for the real world of the profession has led professional schools to implement teaching methods that honor application. Chief among those methods is the use of cases, particularly in business, medicine, law, and social work. Foremost among the schools that are developing student-centered, experiential learning activities are the business schools at Harvard, Syracuse, and Pace universities, which have integrated the case method of teaching. Architecture schools have moved to utilize assessment and portfolio methods in design studios, with students actively bringing critical review to their work.

Taking Practice Seriously

The contemporary equivalent of the nineteenth-century land grant college might well be required if higher education is going to again move to center stage in the struggle to address the nation's pressing economic and technological problems. In many ways, the needs of the knowledge society into which the United States has recently evolved are strikingly similar to those of the agricultural society of a century ago. But the connection between knowledge and economic development is even more direct now than it was then. Knowledge is now commonly acknowledged to be a primary economic force.

Professional schools are beginning to challenge the hierarchical conception of scholarship that makes application of knowledge derivative and, consequently, second best. Schön's (1983, 1987) work on the reflective practitioner calls for a reassessment of the relationship between scholarship and practice—a new "epistemology of practice." His work is especially influential in the field of architecture where the relationship with the research university and its established definition of scholarship has been one of perpetual tension. Even in medicine, the connection between basic research and practice is being realigned. Harvard Medical School, following the lead of problem-based programs elsewhere (especially McMaster and Southern Illinois universities), has instituted the New Pathway program that attempts to build clinical practice into medical education from the very beginning.

In the behavioral sciences, the traditional approach to influencing practice is to conduct research, formulate theories or principles based on the findings of well-controlled studies, and then prescribe those principles as the proper basis for grounded practice. Cognitive psychologists interested in information processing are developing an alternative approach. Instead of the established pattern of moving from research to theory to practice, these psychologists begin with practice—the practice of an accomplished expert, artist, or problem solver—and attempt to understand how complexity and nuance are encompassed in creative practice. They would argue that any theory designed to account for the genius of Godel's Proof or the Sistine Chapel must take seriously the subtleties of practice.

It is not uncommon in this time of enormous complexity of professional responsibility and shifting contexts of professional education for the best practice to surpass theory in a number of applied fields. Shulman (1987), drawing on his work with both practicing physicians and teachers, contends that in addition to the established ways of moving from research and theory to practice, we need also to study variations in practice in order to more adequately understand the deeper reasons for and causes of action.

A number of professional programs are moving toward a broader view of scholarly work. For instance, the School of Social Service Administration at the University of Chicago has integrated research and practice through a conceptual and operational definition of "empirically based practice" (Siegel, 1984, p. 325). From their analysis, a typology of five views of how research and practice can be integrated in both social work education and practice emerged: (1) research activities can be a part of clinical interventions, (2) research findings can be used to shape interventions, (3) research and practice are both problem-solving processes, (4) research concepts can be useful as practice concepts, and (5) research and practice are both applied logic (Siegel, 1984, p. 327). By this account, an ideal social worker engages in empirically based practice by (1) making "maximum use of research findings," (2) collecting "data systematically to monitor the intervention," (3) demonstrating "empirically whether or not interventions are effective," (4) specifying "problems, interventions, and outcomes in terms that are concrete, observable, and measurable," (5) using "research ways of thinking and research methods in defining clients' problems, formulating questions for practice, collecting assessment data, evaluating the effectiveness of interventions, and using evidence," (6) viewing "research and practice as part of the same problem-solving process," and (7) viewing "research as a tool to be used in practice" (p. 329).

The American Assembly of Collegiate Schools of Business (1991) approved new standards for business and accounting accreditation that divided the "intellectual contributions" of faculty members into three categories: basic scholarship (creation of new knowledge), applied scholarship (application, transfer, and interpretation of knowledge to improve management practice and teaching), and instructional development (enhancement of the educational value of instructional efforts of the institution or discipline).

Schools of education, in research universities particularly, are being called on to take practice more seriously. From his major survey of schools of education, Goodlad (1990, p. 177) reports that emphasis on research "leaped forward for many public universities with each transition in classification—from normal school, to teachers' college, to regional college, to regional university." Goodlad found that one response, primarily by major private universities, has been to retain a school of education while going "out of (or almost out of) the teacher education business" (p. 173). In order to incorporate the wisdom of practice into the teacher preparation process, several states have enacted bills requiring faculty who teach methods classes to spend time in regular school classrooms. Goodlad placed the focus of university-school collaboration in the education school faculty member's *service* rather than research category. He states that "recognizing the work [of school improvement] as fundamental, intellectual, and entirely appropriate for serious faculty engagement is the first step that our institutions of higher education must take" (p. 181). In the recommendations for "enhancing teaching as a profession," Goodlad found that ranked after increases in the salary and power of teachers, respondents agreed on the need for "higher standards for entry into programs, provision of a solid knowledge base, programmatic blending of theory and practice, and stress on the moral imperatives of teaching and being a teacher" (p. 187).

Schön has devoted much of his career to the study of professionals in practice as they go about the day-to-day work of solving problems. After looking closely at a variety of fields, ranging from architecture and engineering to psychotherapy and town planning, he is convinced that the universities are not devoted to the production and distribution of knowledge in a general sense. As he puts it, "They are institutions committed, for the most part, to a *particular* epistemology, a view of knowledge that fosters elective inattention to practical competence and professional artistry" (1983, p. vii).

An important kind of knowing is implicit in professional practice. In the act of developing a medical diagnosis, working with a client in psychotherapy, or creating an architectural design, a special kind of knowing is developed. Polanyi (1967) speaks of "tacit knowing"; for Schön (1983) it is "knowing-in-action." Knowledge is generated from the practice itself. The advancement of knowledge builds on disciplined inquiry—research and the construction of theory—but a qualitatively different kind of knowledge is generated out of the struggle with the uncertainty, uniqueness, conflict, and even "messiness" of practice.

There is a way in which the phrase "application of knowledge," so often used in academic contexts, suggests the dominant hierarchical pattern that we are questioning, where knowledge is generated in a scholarly research setting and then applied in standardized form to practical problems. This referent is not what we intend when we refer to the scholarship of practice. We want to recognize fully the knowledge generated out of practice: research about practice, evaluation studies, the "action research" that Kurt Lewin sought to promote, and what is learned from clinical work and, for architects, from the design process. In other words, we want the scholarship embedded in professional practice to be acknowledged and rewarded.

The Hughes (1986) report on faculty in architecture, for instance, draws a careful distinction between what might be regarded as scholarly practice and the routine. As Dinham (1987, pp. 9–10) clarifies, "In sum, the relationship of practice to scholarship is mixed. When the faculty member's professional work is defined as 'distinguished design accomplishments recognized by awards and publication,' or as 'exemplary practice recognized by peers,' practice takes its place with research and criticism among the forms of scholarly inquiry found in the academic architect's repertoire. When practice is seen as 'mere practice,' a conflict with the faculty member's 'commitment to the school,' an activity 'outside their academic obligations,' it moves to the realm of entrepreneurship."

Albino (1984), in writing about dental education, also addresses this issue. Albino suggests a redefinition of research to include scholarly practice: "A broad definition of the re-search responsibility within a university includes any activity that treats the substance of one's discipline in a creative and scholarly manner, and communicates the knowledge gained from the work so that it is available to the discipline or profes-sion as a whole" (1984, p. 511). Mackenzie (1984, p. 496) also argues for "broadening the definition of scholarship [in dental schools because it] will encourage better clinical teaching, clinical judgment, and clinical assessment of student perfor-mance, and will result in more satisfied teachers, students, and alumni, and ultimately in better health care through improved judgments and decision processes."

In our press for an enlarged view of scholarship, we are not attempting to elevate the study of practice above research and theory. The "art" of practice has often been so mystified that the traditional academic pursuits of research and theory have been summarily dismissed. We want these pursuits to be seen on a more equal plane, each interacting in a dialectical fashion and enriching the other. What we are calling for is a conception of scholarship large enough to encompass both.

The view of scholarship being proposed here is more inclusive, encompassing a wider array of scholarly activities than does the present conception. While being more inclusive, however, this enlarged view has its own boundaries; the four aspects of scholarship—discovery, integration, teaching, and practice—are discrete types but form a conceptual whole that is every bit as important as the parts.

Implied here are assumptions about the kind of scholar-ship appropriate for colleges and universities. For instance, teaching that is *not* grounded in the most recent theoretical development and empirical research in the field and is obliv-ious to the interconnections with other disciplines is not appro-priate for a college or university setting. On the other hand, it is important that narrow, specialized research takes place in a broader context—a university—where critical questions are raised and scholars are reminded by students and colleagues that academic freedom carries with it special responsibilities. The recent debate over genetic engineering underscores the point. As Alfred North Whitehead (1929, pp. 137–139) observed in his essay on "Universities and Their Function," "At no time have universities been restricted to pure abstract learning. . . . The justification for a university is that it preserves the connection between knowledge and the zest for life, by uniting the young and the old in the imaginative consideration of learning."

We know that what is proposed here challenges a hierarchical arrangement of monumental proportions, a status system that is firmly fixed in the consciousness of the present faculty and the academy's organizational policies and practices. What we are calling for is a broader, more open field where these different forms of scholarship can interact and thus inform and enrich one another, and where faculty can follow their interests, build on their strengths, and be rewarded for what they spend most of their scholarly energy doing. All faculty ought to be scholars in this broader sense, deepening their preferred approaches to knowing but constantly pressing, and being pressed by peers, to enlarge their scholarly capacities and encompass other, often contrary, ways of knowing.

CHAPTER 13

Setting Priorities for
Change in
Professional Education

**Lynn Curry
Jon F. Wergin**

For at least the past thirty years, the professions in North America have been indulging in rhetoric about the necessity of change and doing very little about it. They have announced a changed itinerary in a particular direction, but all of their structures, processes, and support mechanisms continue to be oriented in the opposite direction. Southbound horses reach northern destinations the long way.

Our associates have presented a strong case for change in this book. The forces for change are many, from external ones such as societal calls for greater professional accountability, to internal ones such as shifting concepts of professional roles and faculty skills. In this concluding chapter, we attempt a synthesis of what our colleagues have had to say and then shift the focus, from the *substance* of change to the *process of* and *prospects for* change as we approach the next century. Accordingly, we begin by positing three central themes of the previous twelve chapters, and casting them as priorities for professional schools. We then suggest ways of bringing about the needed changes and note the difficulties in doing so. We end with a plea for reform, before the issues described in this book become crises.

Emerging Priorities for Professional Education

The preceding twelve chapters, while written by different authors from widely diverse settings, are remarkably complementary in their implications. Taken together, they point to three fundamental ways in which professional education needs to change.

Take a Proactive Stance with Regard to Public Accountability

Each profession holds an implicit contract with the society it serves, a contract that provides the profession with certain exclusive rights in exchange for the assurance of quality and the effectiveness of professional services. Because of the technical and complex nature of professional service, ordinary citizens, or their representatives (government), have historically felt unable to pass judgments on issues of quality and effectiveness; consequently, the people, through their governments, have entrusted the accountability function to the professionals themselves, as Ozar (Chapter Seven) has noted. A general human tendency toward bureaucracy, perhaps, has resulted in the establishment of "within-profession institutions" to oversee these accountability demands on behalf of the professions. These institutions are of two types. The first type, the professional schools, has developed over time a particular culture and set of mutually reinforcing beliefs. Increasingly, as Cavanaugh (Chapter Five) has pointed out, this culture and belief pattern has diverged from the realities of professional practice, resulting in a discontinuity between institutional and societal views of professional competence. The second type, the organized registration of licensing bodies, enjoys various degrees of legislative protection. These licensing institutions are organized at present to ensure professional competence, primarily at the point of entrance to professional practice, although, as Norcini and Shea (Chapter Four) have noted, the demand for recertification is increasing. Licensing and registration bodies do investigate public complaints and review some aspects of professional practice to detect gross deviation from accepted norms; and, recently, they have been making available practice parameters for particular limited conditions and settings. There exists, however, little surveillance of these standards in practice and thus there are few sanctions for violating them.

This approach to quality assurance and effectiveness in professional behavior is designed to detect and correct individual practitioners whose patterns of practice are sufficiently divergent from the usual patterns of practice pursued by their local peers. This approach does little to improve the average performance of all practitioners, nor does it consider the possibility that the usual norms of practice may be deficient, erroneous, or simply ineffective.

The public is asking for much more than this level of oversight. People want more than to be assured that they are protected from truly incompetent individuals; they are concerned about the rising cost of professional involvement in all aspects of life, and the possibility that proffered services may not all be necessary, appropriate, or effective. Society is now demanding some method of continuous assessment, both of the individual professional's ability to use professional knowledge in ways that clearly accomplish desirable ends and, more broadly, of the entire profession's impact as a group on society's well-being.

Society is also no longer content with the assumption that increased professional involvement results in improved outcomes, or, as McGaghie (Chapter Ten) has noted, with the assumption that professional schools produce individuals capable of tackling societal problems. Evidence is accumulating that while professional work is an admirable commodity, it is not the major determinant of society's well-being. Other factors such as distributed wealth, levels of education, sense of personal control, and levels of social support all appear to have at least as much effect, if not more cumulative effect, as expenditures in the professional sector have on any of the standard measures of population success: economic well-being, quality of life, mortality, or morbidity.

Government policy in public regulation can be expected to proceed under assumptions and beliefs that roughly match those of the general public. For this reason, we are witnessing more discussion throughout Western society of a whole range of increased public regulation devices within the professional sector. Discussion of budgetary caps, professional redistribution, empowerment of alternative professionals, ensurance requirements for second opinions, downsized training institutions, and myriad other examples of increased restriction (see McGuire, Chapter One) are evidence of this mood for change in the public contract.

The ensurance of competence is the profession's part of the bargain with society. How that competence is defined, inculcated, and ensured throughout a practice career is the crux of the intellectual problem currently facing professional education. These definitions are increasingly open to public scrutiny, and those who advance them are increasingly held accountable to the public. These pressures to redefine competence throughout a professional career come from litigation, third-party payers, government oversights, and a multitude of other changes in the professional environment.

Integrate Technical with Practical Knowledge in Professional Curricula

Just what is competence? Authors in this volume discuss three emerging conceptions of what it means to practice competently as a professional, all of which will require that professional schools broaden their curriculum goals far beyond those that speak to the development of technical prowess. Harris (Chapter Two), by enlarging on Schön's (1983) seminal work on the reflective practitioner, discusses the self-consciousness and continual self-critique crucial to competent professional practice and describes how such reflection ought to drive professional curricula as well. Part of this continued commitment to improvement comes, as Armour and Fuhrmann (Chapter Six) describe, from the view that competence in professionals should be defined as more than competent technical action. Their suggestion is that professional competence include evidence of the fruits of liberal learning: evidence of active thinking, employment of an intellectual and social context for that thought, the questioning of established values, and the skills to communicate the results of the thought process. Ozar (Chapter Seven), in his analysis of the nature of professional obligation, suggests that because ethical standards are rarely fixed or explicit, practitioners need not only to be sensitive to shifting societal demands but also to think critically about values, precisely in ways consistent with the nature of liberal learning.

There is considerable rhetoric about making higher education, particularly professional schools, more "businesslike." Everyone from Lee Iacocca to the Club Rome has gone on record bemoaning the detriment to national and global competitiveness when technical and practical knowledge are not integrated in the work force. Rippey (Chapter Nine) examines the corporate approach to this necessary integration and points out areas and practices that could be effectively adopted and modified for professional education.

Thus, these chapters converge in their view that, in an increasingly complex society, successful professional practice can no longer be defined simply as the application of a mastery of technical and abstract information. Indeed, this has never been the sole defining characteristic of "professional," as we noted in the Preface of this volume, but too often professional schools have acted as if it were. It is time to redress the imbalance.

Adopt a More Reflective Educational Practice

The nature of the discontinuity between education and practice, and some specific ways in which professional schools need to change, is the third theme in this volume. A restructuring is necessary to bring about greater communication between the practice of a profession and the education and recruitment for that practice. All sides stand to benefit from greater interdigitation, and better understanding of problems, constraints, and perceived opportunities. Cavanaugh (Chapter Five) discusses the evidence and implications of this rapprochement in detail. For her, a more reflective educational practice will require three substantive changes in professional curricula: helping students "learn how to learn" more effectively, providing contextual problem-solving experiences throughout the curriculum via both formal instruction and apprenticeship experiences, and implementing systematic and continuous evaluation of the curriculum.

Other chapters expand on these points. Wales, Nardi, and Stager (Chapter Eight) outline a practical method of modeling professional problem solving as part of initial professional education and show how this method inculcates the "habits of mind" that must be maintained well into professional practice. McGaghie (Chapter Ten) presents a compelling case for broadening the criteria used to evaluate competence for professional practice, particularly the personal qualities and other less tangible characteristics so critical to modern practice, and he discusses how these criteria ought to serve as the locus of congruence between the academic and professional worlds. Bennett and Fox (Chapter Eleven) continue this discussion by describing what practitioners stand to gain from maintaining closer relationships with the professional schools throughout their practice careers. Finally, Rice and Richlin (Chapter Twelve) propose a different paradigm for scholarship in the professions, one that allows for closer linkage between education and practice. Their message, echoing previous authors, is that we need not just better measurement and different methods of teaching but also a much more comprehensive *cultural* shift in how professional faculty view their roles as teachers, scholars, and practitioners.

What, then, are the characteristics of reflective educational practice as enunciated in this book? We and our colleagues suggest that how we approach the tasks of designing, implementing, and evaluating professional education ought to mirror the principles of reflective practice: by adopting the principles of deliberative curriculum inquiry, as spelled out by

Harris (Chapter Two), by acting proactively to set standards for professional competence that are isomorphic with societal needs and to revisit those standards regularly, by linking more closely prepractice curricula and continuing education programs, and by putting into practice a *process* for promoting reflection via a well-integrated program of curriculum assessment. In order for all of this to work, professional faculty need to reflect on their own professional practice: how their teaching, research, and service activities take place not in an academic sanctuary but in an environment that models the kind of professional expertise increasingly demanded by the larger society.

Possibilities for Change

The authors contributing to Part One of this book outline significant features of the changing environment for professional education and practice. The question is not *whether* the professions will adapt to this changing environment, but *how.* Alfred North Whitehead is said to have counseled that the "art of progress is to preserve order amid change, and change amid order." Change induces anxiety due to the ambiguity and uncertainty with which people must live as they create a new equilibrium. Thus, change is almost always resisted at institutional and personal levels. Colleges and universities are probably more resistant to change than any other type of organization. Societal changes always seem to occur at a more rapid pace than changes in professional practice, and changes in practice always seem to occur more quickly than corresponding changes in professional education. Before we can begin to suggest strategies for change, we need to understand why professional schools are so conservative in the first place.

Change is difficult in these settings for two principal reasons (Wergin, forthcoming). First, professional schools are *political systems.* Shifts in alliances and coalitions, all undertaken to protect and enlarge one's own turf, often result in organizational gridlock. The inertia is strengthened by the low priority given to organizational and governance issues by professional faculty. The principal interests of faculty appear to lie in furthering their career aspirations and meeting the pressures to publish, to take on increasing student advisement and teaching loads, and to fund portions of their own, their students', and their support staffs' salaries by winning competitive research grants and contracts. Thus, widespread participation only occurs when individual interests are threatened, or when the organization itself faces a crisis of survival. Even then, the tendency is to regress to business as usual when the crisis is over. Second, professional schools, like other colleges and universities, have a *culture that inhibits change.* The nature of professional work revolves around individual expertise, and thus professional faculty usually wish to be left alone to practice their craft. Administrators in professional schools are generally viewed with suspicion as a threat to individual autonomy, and they are often regarded more as hindrances than as facilitators of professional work. In this context, collective decision making is difficult at best.

Useful lessons about the consequences of organizational conservatism are plentiful in the corporate world. Rosabeth Moss Kanter, in her book *The Change Masters* (1983), describes a group of companies that were consistently noninnovative, even when faced with years of evidence that their economic and performance indicators were slipping. These companies tended to be traditional, formerly successful companies that had slipped into complacency. They had a view of themselves and their products that honored the history of their development more than the currency, utility, and market share of their products. Their comfortable formula had worked well in the past, and they were, therefore, "doomed to replicate it, handing over their operations to people who control things so that there are no deviations from the formula" (Kanter, 1983, p. 70).

This description applies equally well to the structure and value position of most of our professions. The structure of most professions was last changed in the early 1900s by the Flexner (1910) report (medicine) and its sequels, the Reed (1921) report (law) and the Gies (1926) report (dentistry). Each of these studies was conducted by a member of the respective profession, and each stimulated the move of professional education into university settings that carefully separated "foundation" learning from "practical application," and that equally carefully separated university-based academic professionals from rank-and-file practitioners. These structures have been honored, for good or ill, ever since. Initial results were positive in improving standards of education and training. For the past thirty years, however, these traditions have been perceived as barriers to more appropriate evolution. The Panel on the General Professional Education of the Physician (GPEP) (1984) discussed these yearnings and the frustrations of creating change from within the traditions of medicine. A follow-up project, supported by the Macy Foundation (Barrows, 1984) and designed to assess the implementation of the GPEP recommendations, found only pockets of change, which only reinforced the frustration about the glacial nature of the process.

What can be done? A wide range of recent works have suggested strategies that can be applied to professional education. These studies include Kanter (1983), Mohrman and others (1989), and Kets de Vries and Associates (1991). The strategies suggested vary by level and time frame required, ranging from a grand strategy for a profession as a whole, a plan for the professional schools as a group, and a strategy for individual institutions or programs.

An example of change of the first type, a grand strategy, is the program undertaken by the College of Family Physicians of Canada, the voluntary professional body of family physicians in that country. This profession is developing and implementing plans that will have profound effects not only on the practice of Canadian family physicians but also on the recruitment, training, licensing, dispersal, and continued competence of that group. These plans are the result of a careful strategic planning process that investigated and articulated changes in the opportunities and environmental conditions of this particular profession.

An individual institution can undertake a change strategy that will reach to all segments of the organization, all products and processes. This level of change is undertaken, for example, when a law school changes the structure of legal education and competence assessment, as occurred at the University of Calgary Law School. In place of the more usual case recitation model for both learning and evaluation, this institution employs a series of professional work simulations that become increasingly more real, culminating in the upper-year criminal law course, which assigns students as public defenders, under supervision, in the public law courts. Part of the grade in that course is based on the student's written analytical review of and reflection on the experience and the points of law involved in an assigned case. An institution can undertake these changes as long as the processes and results are sufficiently supported by other segments of the profession. In this case, the law firms who are the potential employers of the Calgary graduates were carefully involved in the rationale, substance, and monitoring of this change strategy.

Individual professional programs and services can also develop strategies for active change. The continuing professional education department can, for example, initiate a range of change strategies that represent more authentic and productive approaches than can be undertaken at that time by the school as a whole. For example, the continuing medical education group at Dalhousie University, a traditional medical school environment, recognized a need ten years ago to make available just-in-time professional upgrading. The group developed a mechanism of clinical traineeships that facilitated rural physicians negotiating short-term, focused skills and knowledge training in any of the teaching hospitals in any area of specialization. At the time, these short-term interventions did not exist due to the logistical difficulties involved in securing hospital privileges and changes in licensure status and in arranging locum tenens coverage for the practice temporarily abandoned. When the Continuing Medical Education Division took on these logistics, it was in a position to improve the quality of the professional education involved, rather than leave it up to ad hoc arrangements among physicians: the nature (depth) of the "learning contract" was improved; the access to training no longer depended on personal contacts, which limited sources;

and the quality of the trainers chosen was monitored and those trainers were formally acknowledged within the university reward system.

Regardless of the level at which change is sought, the potential change agent is well advised to operate with several key principles:

- Change is political, and thus not necessarily logical, and thus requires political strategies.
- Change is incremental and adaptive, not immediate and precipitous.
- As Marshall (Chapter Three) has noted, change moves successively through several layers of support, thus making it imperative that "innovators" and "early adopters" be identified early and supported.
- Planning and implementing of change require participation by those most affected by it.
- Change requires persistence and flexibility from those who champion it.

At every level, the change required in the professions at this time is profound. This is not a time for tinkering with adaptations. A continuation of what we have been doing in the professions—only pursued harder, longer, or with more publicity—will not satisfy the various stakeholders: the public, the funders, the members of the profession in practice, and the students in training. Fundamentally, what is required here is, in Kanter's (1983) terms, a "renaissance" in the archetypes of professions, professional organization, and professional education. The attitudinal and conceptual shift required is of a magnitude comparable to Galileo's achievement in eventually convincing the physics establishment that their geotropic model of the universe was discordant with emerging observations, whereas a heliotropic model was not only concordant with observed facts but also a wellspring for creativity and new thought in other areas, such as the sister profession of mathematics. A shift in paradigm is a fundamental change, destabilizing the older order of things. In Galileo's time, the professions of physics and mathematics were comfortable with their old conceptions and actively resisted Galileo's observations and his new ideas for most of his professional life. Eventually, however, the value of the new paradigm became undeniable, a generation of established professional physicists and mathematicians died, and the world changed.

This book has presented a range of concrete ideas about how the current professions can avoid the ignominious fate of resisting fundamental structural, attitudinal, and conceptual change as the evidence for the necessity of that change continues to mount. The route maps are available to reach the rhetorically desired destinations. The professions, the designated leaders, and the innovators must first understand the need to change direction structurally and in all procedures; then they must act on it. Professional schools are no longer insulated, privileged sanctuaries; they must either become agents of their own reform or face becoming the increasingly vulnerable targets of a skeptical society.

REFERENCES

Abbott, A. D. *The System of Professions: An Essay on the Division of Expert Labor.* Chicago: University of Chicago Press, 1988.

Albino, J. E. "Scholarship and Dental Education: New Perspectives for Clinical Faculty." *Journal of Dental Education,* 1984, *48* (9), 509–513.

Alderman, D. L., Evans, F. R., and Wilder, G. "The Validity of Written Simulation Exercises for Assessing Clinical Skills in Legal Education." *Educational and Psychological Measurement,* 1981, *41,* 1115–1126.

Algina, J. "On the Validity of Examinations for Making Promotions Decisions in Medical Education." *Medical Education,* 1978, *12,* 82–87.

American Assembly of Collegiate Schools of Business. *Accreditation Standards for Business and Accounting Programs.* Saint Louis, Mo.: American Assembly of Collegiate Schools of Business, 1991.

American Council on Pharmaceutical Education. *Accreditation Standards and Guidelines.* (8th ed.) Chicago: American Council on Pharmaceutical Education, 1984.

American Educational Research Association, American Psychological Association, and National Council on Measurement in Education. *Standards for Educational and Psychological Testing.* Washington, D.C.: American Psychological Association, 1985.

American Guild of Organists. "Professional Certification Requirements for 1989." *American Organist,* 1988, *22* (7), 31–35.

American Law Institute–American Bar Association Committee on Continuing Professional Education (eds.). *Continuing Legal Education and Professional Competence and Responsibility:*

Since Arden House II. Philadelphia: American Law Institute–American Bar Association Committee on Continuing Professional Education, 1984.

American Law Institute–American Bar Association Committee on Continuing Professional Education. *1990 Report of the Executive Director.* Philadelphia: American Law Institute–American Bar Association Committee on Continuing Professional Education, 1990.

American Library Association Presidential Committee on Information Literacy. *Final Report.* Chicago: American Library Association, 1989.

American Nuclear Society. *Nuclear Power Plant Simulators for Use in Operator Training.* La Grange Park, Ill.: American Nuclear Society, 1985.

Anderson, J. R. *The Architecture of Cognition.* Cambridge, Mass.: Harvard University Press, 1983.

Armour, R. A., and Fuhrmann, B. S. (eds.). *Integrating Liberal Learning and Professional Education.* New Directions for Teaching and Learning, no. 40. San Francisco: Jossey-Bass, 1989.

Association of American Colleges. *Integrity in the College Curriculum: A Report to the Academic Community.* Washington, D.C.: Association of American Colleges, 1985.

Association of American Colleges. *Liberal Learning and the Arts and Sciences Major.* 2 vols. Washington, D.C.: Association of American Colleges, 1991.

Association of American Medical Colleges. *Annual Report.* Washington, D.C.: Association of American Medical Colleges, 1991a.

Association of American Medical Colleges. *Project 3000 by 2000.* Washington, D.C.: Association of American Medical Colleges, 1991b.

Atkins, E. "The Deliberative Process: An Analysis from Three Perspectives." *Journal of Curriculum and Supervision,* 1986, *1,* 265–293.

AT&T Quality Assurance Center. *Quality by Design: A Quality Assurance Manual.* (2nd ed.) Murray Hill, N.J.: Bell Laboratories, 1989.

Barnett, R. A., Becher, R. A., and Cork, N. M. "Models of Professional Preparation: Pharmacy, Nursing, and Teacher Education." *Studies in Higher Education,* 1987, *12* (1), 51–63.

Barrows, H. S. *How to Design a Problem-Based Curriculum for the Preclinical Years.* New York: Springer, 1985.

Barrows, H. S., and Peters, M. J. (eds.). *How to Begin Changing a Medical Curriculum.* Springfield: Southern Illinois University Press, 1984.

Barrows, H. S., and Tamblyn, R. *Problem-Based Learning: An Approach to Medical Education.* New York: Springer, 1980.

Barrows, H. S., Williams, R. G., and Moy, R. H. "A Comprehensive Performance-Based Assessment of Fourth-Year Students' Clinical Skills." *Journal of Medical Education,* 1987, *62,* 805–809.

Bebeau, M. "Ethics and the Practicing Dentist: Can Ethics Be Taught." *Journal of the American College of Dentists,* 1991, *58,* 5–15.

Bejar, I. I. "A Methodology for Scoring Open-Ended Architectural Design Problems." *Journal of Applied Psychology,* 1991, *76,* 522–532.

Bell, D. "Teletext and Technology: New Networks of Knowledge and Information in Postindustrial Society." In D. Bell, *The Winding Passage: Essays and Sociological Journeys.* New York: Basic Books, 1980.

Benner, P. *From Novice to Expert: Excellence and Power in Clinical Nursing Practice.* Reading, Mass.: Addison-Wesley, 1984.

Bennett, W. J. *To Reclaim a Legacy.* Washington, D.C.: National Endowment for the Humanities, 1984.

Benson, J. A., Jr. "Certification and Recertification: One Approach to Professional Accountability." *Annals of Internal Medicine,* 1991, *114,* 238–242.

Berlant, J. L. *Profession and Monopoly: A Study of Medicine in the United States and Great Britain.* Berkeley: University of California Press, 1975.

Berman, J. S., and Norton, N. C. "Does Professional Training Make a Therapist More Effective?" *Psychological Bulletin,* 1985, *98,* 401–407.

Berner, E. S. "Paradigms and Problem Solving: A Literature Review." *Journal of Medical Education,* 1984, *59,* 625–633.

Biglan, A. "Relationships Between Subject Matter Characteristics and the Structure and Output of University Departments." *Journal of Applied Psychology,* 1973, *57* (3), 204–213.

Bird, C. *The Case Against College.* New York: McKay, 1975.

Bland, C. J., Hitchcock, M. A., Anderson, W. A., and Stritter, F. T. "Faculty Development Fellowship Programs in Family Medicine." *Journal of Medical Education,* 1987, *62* (8), 632–641.

Bland, C. J., and Schmitz, C. C. "Characteristics of the Successful Researcher and Implications for Faculty Development." *Journal of Medical Education,* 1986, *61* (1), 22–31.

Blanshard, B. *The Uses of a Liberal Education and Other Talks to Students.* LaSalle, Ill.: Open Court, 1973.

Bledstein, B. J. *The Culture of Professionalism.* New York: Norton, 1976.

Bloom, A. *The Closing of the American Mind: How Higher Education Has Failed Democracy and Impoverished the Souls of Today's Students.* New York: Simon & Schuster, 1987.

Bloom, B. S. *Taxonomy of Educational Objectives: Cognitive Domain.* New York: McKay, 1956.

Bloom, S. W. "Structure and Ideology in Medical Education: An Analysis of Resistance to Change." *Journal of Health and Social Behavior,* 1988, *29,* 294–306.

Blum, D. E. "Master's Degree Is 'Silent Success' for Many Students and Employers." *Chronicle of Higher Education,* Dec. 11, 1991a, pp. A31–A32.

Blum, D. E. "Three Big Pharmacy Groups Call for New Doctoral Program to Be Adopted as Entry-Level Requirement for Profession." *Chronicle of Higher Education,* Dec. 11, 1991b, pp. A15, A18.

Bonser, S., and Grundy, S. "Reflective Deliberation in the Formulation of a School Policy." *Journal of Curriculum Studies,* 1988, *20,* 35–45.

Borchardt, D. A. *Think Tank Theatre.* Lanham, Md.: Unipub, 1984.

Borgman, C. "The User's Mental Model of an Information Retrieval System." *International Journal of Man-Machine Studies,* 1986, *24* (1), 47–64.

Borovansky, V. T. "Educating Engineers in Information Utilization." *European Journal of Engineering Education,* 1987, *12,* 147–158.

Bowie, N. "The Law: From a Profession to a Business." *Vanderbilt Law Review,* 1988, *41,* 677–807.

Boyer, E. L. "Forward." In N. Eurich, *Corporate Classrooms: The Learning Business.* Princeton, N.J.: Carnegie Foundation for the Advancement of Teaching, 1985.

Boyer, E. L. *Scholarship Reconsidered: Priorities of the Professoriate.* Princeton, N.J.: Carnegie Foundation for the Advancement of Teaching, 1990.

Bratchell, F. F., and Heald, M. *The Aims and Organization of Liberal Studies.* Oxford, England: Pergamon Press, 1966.

Brinkerhoff, R. O., Brethower, D. M., Hluchyj, T., and Nowakowski, J. R. *Program Evaluation: A Practitioner's Guide for Trainers and Educators.* Boston: Kluwer-Nijhoff, 1983.

Bronson, D. E., Pelz, D. C., and Trzcinski, E. *Computerizing Your Agency's Information System.* Newbury Park, Calif.: Sage, 1988.

Brooks, T. J. *Comparison of the Features of Mandatory Continuing Legal Education Rules in Effect as of July 1991.* Albany: New York State Bar Association, 1991.

Brown, G., and Gelernter, M. "Education: Veering from Practice." *Progressive Architecture,* 1989, *3,* 61–62, 64, 66–67.

Brown, J.H.U. "Medical Schools in Crisis." *Evaluation and the Health Professions,* 1988, *11,* 147–171.

Brown, J. S. "Toward a New Epistemology for Learning." In C. Frasson and J. Gauththiar (eds.), *Intelligent Tutoring Systems at the Crossroads of AI and Education.* Norwood, N.J.: Ablex, 1990.

Brown, J. S., Collins, A., and Duguid, P. "Situated Cognition and the Culture of Learning." *Educational Researcher,* 1989, *18* (1), 32–41.

Buchler, J. *The Concept of Method.* New York: Columbia University Press, 1961.

Buchmann, M. "The Use of Research Knowledge in Teacher Education and Teaching." *American Journal of Education,* 1984, *92,* 421–439.

Bugelski, B. R. *The Psychology of Learning Applied to Teaching.* New York: Bobbs-Merrill, 1971.

Bush, V. "As We May Think." *Atlantic Monthly,* 1945, *176,* 101-108.

Butterfield, P. S., and Pearsol, J. A. "Nurses in Resident Evaluation: A Qualitative Study of the Participants' Perspectives." *Evaluation and the Health Professions,* 1988, *11,* 453–473.

Campbell, D. T., and Stanley, J. C. *Experimental and Quasi-Experimental Designs for Research.* Skokie, Ill.: Rand McNally, 1966.

Canadian Institute of Chartered Accountants. *Uniform Final Examination Report, 1990.* Toronto, Ontario: Canadian Institute of Chartered Accountants, 1991.

Carline, J. D., Wenrich, M., and Ramsey, P. G. "Characteristics of Ratings of Physician Competence by Professional Associates." *Evaluation and the Health Professions,* 1989, *12,* 409–413.

Carpenter-Huffman, P. *MODIA.* Vol. 2: *Options for Course Design.* Santa Monica, Calif.: Rand Corporation, 1977.

Carter, G. L. "A Perspective on Preparing Adult Educators." In S. M. Grabowski (ed.), *Strengthening Connections Between Education and Performance.* New Directions for Adult and Continuing Education, no. 18. San Francisco: Jossey-Bass, 1983.

Cashin, F. J. "President's Address." In Accreditation Board for Engineering and Technology, *1989 Annual Report.* New York: Accreditation Board for Engineering and Technology, 1989.

Cervero, R. M. *Effective Continuing Education for Professionals.* San Francisco: Jossey-Bass, 1988.

Cervero, R. M. "Professional Practice, Learning, and Continuing Education: An Integrated Perspective." *Professions Educator Research Notes,* 1989, *11,* 10–13.

Chapman, S. "Boesky, Takeovers and the Value of Rewarding Greed." *Chicago Tribune,* May 1, 1987, Section 5, p. 3.

Cheshier, S. R. "A Modest Proposal Regarding the Future of Engineering Technology Education in America." *Engineering Education,* 1985, *75* (8), 706–712.

Chi, M.T.H., Glaser, R., and Farr, M. J. (eds.). *The Nature of Expertise.* Hillsdale, N.J.: Erlbaum, 1988.

"Church Defrocks Swaggart for Rejecting Its Punishment." *New York Times,* Apr. 9, 1988, p. A1.

Clark, C. M., and Peterson, P. L. "Teachers' Thought Processes." In M. D. Wittrock (ed.), *Handbook of Research on Teaching.* (3rd ed.) New York: Macmillan, 1986.

Clement, J. "A Conceptual Model Discussed by Galileo and Used Intuitively by Physics Students." In D. Gentner and A. Stevens (eds.), *Mental Models*. Hillsdale, N.J.: Erlbaum, 1983.

Clifford, G. J., and Guthrie, J. W. *Ed School: A Brief for Professional Education*. Chicago: University of Chicago Press, 1988.

Cognition and Technology Group at Vanderbilt. "Anchored Instruction and Its Relationship to Situated Cognition." *Educational Researcher*, 1990, *19* (5), 2–10.

College of Architecture and Urban Studies. *Architectural Program Report, 1991–1992*. Blacksburg: Virginia Polytechnic Institute and State University, 1991.

Collins, A. "Principles for a Theory of Cognitive Apprenticeship." Paper presented at the annual meeting of the American Educational Research Association, Washington, D.C., April 1987.

Communications, Computers, and Networks: How to Work, Play, and Thrive in Cyberspace. Special Issue of *Scientific American*, 1991, 265 (entire issue 3).

Conrad, C. F., Hayworth, J. G., and Miller, S. B. *A Silent Success: Master's Education in the United States*. Baltimore: Johns Hopkins University Press, forthcoming.

Coscarelli, W., and White, G. *The Guided Design Guidebook: Patterns in Implementation*. Morgantown: Center for Guided Design, West Virginia University, 1986.

Creswell, J. W., and Bean, J. P. "Research Output, Socialization, and the Biglan Model." *Research in Higher Education*, 1981, *15*, 69–92.

Creswell, J. W., and Brown, M. L. "Understanding How Department Chairpersons Enhance the Research Performance of Faculty." Paper presented at the annual meeting of the Association for the Study of Higher Education, Portland, Oregon, November 1990.

Creswell, J. W., Seagren, A. T., and Henry, T. C. "Professional Development of Training Needs Departmental Chairpersons: A Test of the Biglan Model." *Planning and Change*, 1979, *10*, 224–237.

Curry, L., Fried, B., and McQueen, R. "Preparing for Accreditation: An Opportunity for Faculty Development and Curriculum Renewal." *Journal of Health Administration Education,* forthcoming.

Curry, L., and Purkis, I. E. "Learning Preferences of Specialists." *Annals of the Royal College of Physicians and Surgeons of Canada,* 1982, *15,* 407–414.

Curry, L., and Putnam, R. W. "Continuing Education in Maritime Canada: The Methods Physicians Use, Would Prefer and Find Most Effective." *Canadian Medical Association Journal,* 1981, *124,* 563–566.

Dahlgren, L. O., and Pramling, I. "Conceptions of Knowledge, Professionalism, and Contemporary Problems in Some Professional Academic Subcultures." *Studies in Higher Education,* 1985, *10* (2), 163–173.

D'Amour, G., and Wales, C. (eds.). *The Nature of Evidence.* Morgantown: Center for Guided Design, West Virginia University, 1979.

Daniels, L. J. *Tales of an Old Horsetrader.* Iowa City: University of Iowa Press, 1987.

Dawson-Saunders, B., and others. "Patient Management Decision Making in Ambulatory Care." Paper presented at the annual meeting of the American Educational Research Association, San Francisco, April 1989.

Day, P., Macy, H., and Jackson, E. *Social Working.* Englewood Cliffs, N.J.: Prentice Hall, 1984.

de Groot, A. D. *Thought and Choice in Chess.* The Hague, The Netherlands: Mouton, 1965.

de Tornyay, R., and Thompson, M. *Strategies for Teaching Nursing.* New York: Wiley, 1987.

DeCotiis, T. A., and Steele, W. W., Jr. "The Skills of the Lawyering Process: A Critique Based on Observation." In American Law Institute–American Bar Association Committee on Continuing Professional Education (eds.), *Continuing Legal Education and Professional Competence and Responsibility: Since Arden House II.* Philadelphia: American Law Institute–American Bar Association Committee on Continuing Professional Education, 1984.

Derber, C. (ed.). *Professionals and Workers.* Boston: Hall, 1982.

Derber, C., Schwartz, W. A., and Magrass, Y. *Power in the Highest*

Degree: Professionals and the Rise of a New Mandarin Order. New York: Oxford University Press, 1990.

Derr, C. B., Jones, C., and Toomey, E. "Managing High-Potential Employees: Practices in Thirty-Three U.S. Corporations." *Human Resources Management,* 1988, *27* (3), 273–290.

Dewey, J. *How We Think.* Lexington, Mass.: Heath, 1933. (Originally published 1910.)

Dillman, D. A. "The Social Impacts of Information Technology in Rural America." *Rural Sociology,* 1985, *50* (1), 1–26.

Dinham, S. M. *Between Academe and Professional Practice: Initial Reflections on Analyzing the Role of Professional Practice in Higher Education.* Report No. HE-020-857. Tucson: University of Arizona, 1987. (ED 289 398)

Dinham, S. M., and Stritter, F. T. "Research on Professional Education." In M. C. Wittrock (ed.), *Handbook of Research on Teaching.* (3rd ed.) New York: Macmillan, 1986.

Dowie, J., and Elstein, A. (eds.). *Professional Judgment: A Reader in Clinical Decision Making.* New York: Cambridge University Press, 1988.

Durlak, J. A. "Comparative Effectiveness of Paraprofessional and Professional Helpers." *Psychological Bulletin,* 1979, *86,* 80–92.

Edwards, H. T. "The Role of Legal Education in Shaping the Profession." *Journal of Legal Education,* 1988, *38* (3), 285–293.

Eggert, G. R. "Why Certify?" Unpublished manuscript, Institute for Certification of Computer Professionals, Chicago, 1991.

Eisner, E. W. *The Enlightened Eye: Qualitative Inquiry and the Enhancement of Educational Practice.* New York: Macmillan, 1991.

Eisner, E. W. "A Slice of Advice." *Educational Researcher,* 1992, *21* (5), 29–30.

Eison, C. L. "The Measurement of Satisfaction in Departmental Association at Western Kentucky University Testing the Holland and Biglan Models." Unpublished doctoral dissertation, Department of Higher Education, University of Kentucky, 1976.

Elbaz, F. *Teacher Thinking: A Study of Practical Knowledge.* New York: Nichols, 1983.

Elson, J. S., "The Case Against Legal Scholarship, or, If the Professor Must Publish, Must the Profession Perish?" *Journal of Legal Education,* 1989, *39* (3), 342–381.

Elstein, A. S., Shulman, L. S., and Sprafka, S. A. *Medical Problem Solving: An Analysis of Clinical Reasoning.* Cambridge, Mass.: Harvard University Press, 1978.

Engel, J. D., Wigton, R., LaDuca, A., and Blacklow, R. S. "A Social Judgment Theory Perspective on Clinical Problem Solving." *Evaluation and the Health Professions,* 1990, *13,* 63–78.

Epstein, A. M. "The Outcomes Movement—Will It Get Us Where We Want to Go?" *New England Journal of Medicine,* 1990, *323,* 266–270.

Escovitz, G. H., and Davis, D. "A Bi-National Perspective on Continuing Medical Education." *Academic Medicine,* 1990, *65,* 545–550.

Eurich, N. *Corporate Classrooms: The Learning Business.* Princeton, N.J.: Carnegie Foundation for the Advancement of Teaching, 1985.

Faver, F. A., Fox, M. F., Hunter, M. S., and Shannon, C. "Research and Practice: Orientations of Social Work Educators." *Social Work,* 1986, *31* (4), 282–286.

Federal Rules of Evidence for United States Courts and Magistrates. Saint Paul, Minn.: West, 1989.

Feiman-Nemser, S., and Floden, R. E. "The Cultures of Teaching." In M. C. Wittrock (ed.), *Handbook of Research on Teaching.* (3rd ed.) New York: Macmillan, 1986.

Feldt, L. S., and Brennan, R. L. "Reliability." In R. L. Linn (ed.), *Educational Measurement.* (3rd ed.) New York: American Council on Education and Macmillan, 1989.

Feltovich, P., Spiro, R., and Coulson, R. "Learning, Teaching, and Testing for Complex Conceptual Understanding." In N. Fredrickson, R. Mislevy, and T. Bejar (eds.), *Test Theory for a New Generation of Tests.* Hillsdale, N.J.: Erlbaum, forthcoming.

Fenstermacher, G. "The Place of Science and Epistemology in Schön's Conception of Reflective Practice?" In P. P. Grimmett and G. L. Erickson (eds.), *Reflection in Teacher Education.* New York: Teachers College Press, 1988.

Fielding, S. L. "Organizational Impact on Medicine: The HMO Concept." *Social Science and Medicine,* 1984, *18* (8), 615–620.

Firestone, W. A., and Bader, B. D. "Professionalism or Bureaucracy? Redesigning Teaching." *Educational Evaluation and Policy Analysis,* 1991, *13,* 67–86.

Fisher, T. "P/A Reader Poll Education." *Progressive Architecture,* 1989, *2,* 15–17.

Fitzpatrick, A. R. "Social Influences in Standard Setting: The Effects of Social Interaction on Group Judgments." *Review of Educational Research,* 1989, *59,* 315–328.

Flexner, A. *Medical Education in the United States and Canada: A Report to the Carnegie Foundation for the Advancement of Teaching.* Bulletin no. 4. Princeton, N.J.: Carnegie Foundation for the Advancement of Teaching, 1910.

Forsythe, G. B., McGaghie, W. C., and Friedman, C. P. "Construct Validity of Medical Clinical Competence Measures: A Multitrait-Multimethod Matrix Study Using Confirmatory Factor Analysis." *American Educational Research Journal,* 1986, *23,* 315–336.

Fox, R. D., Mazmanian, P. E., and Putnam, R. W. *Changing and Learning in the Lives of Physicians.* New York: Praeger, 1989.

Frederiksen, N. "The Real Test Bias: Influences of Testing on Teaching and Learning." *American Psychologist,* 1984, *39* (3), 193–202.

Freidson, E. *The Profession of Medicine.* New York: Dodd, Mead, 1970.

Freidson, E. "The Theory of the Professions: The State of the Art." In R. Dingwall and P. Lewis (eds.), *The Sociology of the Professions: Lawyers, Doctors, and Others.* New York: St. Martin's, 1983.

Freidson, E. "The Reorganization of the Medical Profession." *Medical Care Review,* 1985, *42* (1), 11–35.

Freidson, E. *Professional Powers: A Study of the Institutionalization of Formal Knowledge.* Chicago: University of Chicago Press, 1986.

Freidson, E. "The Future of the Professions." *Journal of Dental Education,* 1987, *51,* 140–144.

Freund, P. "The Legal Professions." *Daedalus,* 1963, *92,* 689-700.

Frey, K. "Do Curriculum Development Models Really Influence the Curriculum?" Paper presented at the annual meeting of the American Educational Research Association, San Francisco, April 1989.

Friedman, R. B. "Fantasyland." *New England Journal of Medicine,* 1983, *308,* 651–653.

Frye, S. J. "Mandatory Continuing Education for Professional Relicensure: A Comparative Analysis of Its Impact in Law and Medicine." *CLE Journal and Register,* 1990, *36,* 5–21.

Frymier, J. "Bureaucracy and the Neutering of Teachers." *Phi Delta Kappan,* 1987, *69,* 9–14.

Gagne, E. D. *The Cognitive Psychology of School Learning.* Boston: Little, Brown, 1985.

Gallagher, E. B., and Searle, C. M. "Content and Context in Health Professional Education." In H. E. Freeman and S. Levine (eds.), *Handbook of Medical Sociology.* (4th ed.) Englewood Cliffs, N.J.: Prentice Hall, 1989.

Gangler, B. B., Rosenthal, D. B., Thornton, G. C., and Bentson, C. "Meta-Analysis of Assessment Center Validity." *Journal of Applied Psychology,* 1987, *72,* 493–511.

Gentner, D., and Stevens, A. (eds.). *Mental Models.* Hillsdale, N.J.: Erlbaum, 1983.

Giamatti, A. B. *A Free and Ordered Space: The Real World of the University.* New York: Norton, 1988.

Gies, W. J. *Dental Education in the United States and Canada: A Report to the Carnegie Foundation for the Advancement of Teaching.* Bulletin no. 19. New York: Carnegie Foundation for the Advancement of Teaching, 1926.

Gillers, S., and Simon, R. D., Jr. *Regulation of Lawyers: Statutes and Standards with Recent Supreme Court Decisions.* (Rev. ed.) Boston: Little, Brown, 1991.

Glass, G. V. "Standards and Criteria." *Journal of Educational Measurement,* 1978, *15,* 237–261.

Glazer, J. S. *The Master's Degree: Tradition, Diversity, Innovation.* ASHE-ERIC Higher Education Reports, no. 6. Washington, D.C.: Association for the Study of Higher Education, 1986.

Glazer, N. "The Schools of the Minor Professions." *Minerva,* 1974, *12* (3), 346–363.

Goldman, W. *Hype and Glory.* New York: Villard Books, 1990.

Goodlad, J. I. *Teachers for Our Nation's Schools.* San Francisco: Jossey-Bass, 1990.

Grabowski, S. M. "How Educators and Trainers Can Ensure On-the-Job Performance." In S. M. Grabowski (ed.), *Strengthening Connections Between Education and Performance.* New Directions for Adult and Continuing Education, no. 18. San Francisco: Jossey-Bass, 1983.

Griswold, A. W. *Liberal Education and the Democratic Ideal and Other Essays.* New Haven, Conn.: Yale University Press, 1962.

Hacker, A. "The Decline of Higher Learning." *New York Review,* Feb. 13, 1985, pp. 35–42.

Hall, B. P. "Clergy Assessment in Roman Catholic Applications." In R. A. Hunt, J. E. Hinkle, Jr., and H. N. Malony (eds.), *Clergy Assessment and Career Development.* Nashville, Tenn.: Abingdon Press, 1990.

Hall, R. H. "Theoretical Trends in the Sociology of Occupations." *Sociological Quarterly,* 1983, *24,* 5–23.

Halmos, P. "Professionalism and Social Change." *Sociological Review Monographs,* 1973, (entire issue 20).

Halpern, S. C. "On the Politics and Pathology of Legal Education." *Journal of Legal Education,* 1982, *32* (3), 383–394.

Hambleton, R. K., and Swaminathan, H. *Item Response Theory: Principles and Applications.* Boston: Kluwer-Nijhoff, 1985.

Hammond, K. R., Hursch, C. J., and Todd, F. J. "Analyzing the Components of Clinical Inference." *Psychological Review,* 1964, *71,* 438–456.

Harris, I. B. "Forms of Discourse and Their Possibilities for Guiding Practice: Towards an Effective Rhetoric." *Journal of Curriculum Studies,* 1983, *15,* 27–42.

Harris, I. B. "An Exploration of the Role of Theories in Communication for Guiding Practitioners." *Journal of Curriculum and Supervision,* 1986, *1,* 27–55.

Harris, I. B. "Communicating Educational Reform Through Persuasive Discourse: A Double-Edged Sword." *Professional Education Research Quarterly,* 1987, *9,* 3–7.

Harris, I. B. "A Critique of Schön's Views on Teacher Education: Contributions and Issues." *Journal of Curriculum and Supervision,* 1989, *5,* 13–18.

Harris, I. B. "Implications of Deliberative Curriculum Inquiry for Research and Practice in Professional Education." Paper presented at the annual meeting of the American Educational Research Association, Boston, April 1990.

Harris, I. B. "Deliberative Inquiry: The Arts of Planning." In E. Short (ed.), *Forms of Curriculum Inquiry*. Albany: State University of New York Press, 1991.

Hattie, J. A., Sharpley, C. F., and Rogers, H. J. "Comparative Effectiveness of Professional and Paraprofessional Helpers." *Psychological Bulletin,* 1984, *95,* 534–541.

Haug, M. R. "Deprofessionalization: An Alternative Hypothesis for the Future." *Sociological Review Monographs,* 1973, *20,* 195–211.

Haug, M. R. "The Deprofessionalization of Everyone?" *Sociological Focus,* 1975, *3,* 187–213.

Haug, M. R. "Computer Technology and the Obsolescence of the Concept of Profession." In M. R. Haug and J. Dofny (eds.), *Work and Technology*. Newbury Park, Calif.: Sage, 1977.

Hegarty, E. "The Problem Identification Phase of Curriculum Deliberation: Use of the Nominal Group Technique." *Journal of Curriculum Studies,* 1971, *9,* 31–41.

Heim, M. *Electric Language: A Philosophical Study of Word Processing.* New Haven, Conn.: Yale University Press, 1987.

Herbers, J. E., and others. "How Accurate Are Faculty Evaluations of Clinical Competence?" *Journal of General Internal Medicine,* 1989, *4,* 202–208.

Hesseldenz, J. S., and Smith, B. G. "Computer-Prepared Questionnaires and Grouping Theories: Considerations for Mail Surveys in Academic Settings." *Research in Higher Education,* 1977, *6,* 85–94.

Hirsch, E. D. *Cultural Literacy: What Every American Needs to Know.* Boston: Houghton Mifflin, 1987.

Holahan, J. "Make-Believe Flying: Real-World Proficiency." *Aviation International News,* Jan. 1, 1991, pp. 42–47.

Houle, C. O. *Continuing Learning in the Professions.* San Francisco: Jossey-Bass, 1980.

Hughes, E. C. "The Study of Occupations." In R. K. Merton, L. Broom, and L. S. Cottrell, Jr. (eds.), *Sociology Today: Problems and Prospects.* New York: Basic Books, 1959.

Hughes, R. R. *Consulting/Practice Survey Response Sampling.* Atlanta: Georgia Institute of Technology College of Architecture, 1986.

Hunt, R. A., Hinkle, J. E., Jr., and Malony, H. N. (eds.). *Clergy Assessment and Career Development.* Nashville, Tenn.: Abingdon Press, 1990.

Huston, M. M. "Extending Information Universes Through Systems Thinking." *College and Research Libraries News,* 1990, *51,* 692–695.

Ibister, N. "The Christian in the Professions: Some Questions." *Spectrum,* 1986, *18,* 143–156.

Ide, T. R. "The Technology." In G. Friedrichs and A. Schaff (eds.), *Microelectronics and Society: A Report to the Club of Rome.* New York: New American Library, 1982.

International Gymnastics Federation. *Code of Points.* Indianapolis, Ind.: International Gymnastics Federation, 1989.

Irby, D. M., and Milam, S. "The Legal Context for Evaluating and Dismissing Medical Students and Residents." *Academic Medicine,* 1989, *64,* 639–643.

Jaeger, R. M. "Certification of Student Competence." In R. L. Linn (ed.), *Educational Measurement.* (3rd ed.) New York: American Council on Education and Macmillan, 1989.

Jang, R., and Solad, S. "Teaching Pharmacy Students Problem-Solving: Theory and Present Status." *American Journal of Pharmaceutical Education,* 1990, *54,* 161–166.

Jencks, C., and Riesman, D. *The Academic Revolution.* Chicago: University of Chicago Press, 1977.

Johnson, D. W., Johnson, R. T., and Smith, K. A. *Active Learning: Cooperation in the College Classroom.* Edina, Minn.: Interaction, 1991.

Johnson, T. J. *Professions and Power.* London: Macmillan, 1972.

Jonas, H. S., Etzel, S. I., and Barzansky, B. "Educational Programs in U.S. Medical Schools." *Journal of the American Medical Association,* 1991, *266,* 913–920.

Jones, T. V., Gerrity, M. S., and Earp, J. "Written Case Simulations: Do They Predict Physicians' Behavior?" *Journal of Clinical Epidemiology,* 1990, *43,* 805–815.

Kahn, K. L., and others. "Measuring Quality of Care with Explicit Process Criteria Before and After Implementation of the DRG-Based Prospective Payment System." *Journal of the American Medical Association*, 1990, *264*, 1969–1973.

Kane, M. T. "The Validity of Licensure Examinations." *American Psychologist*, 1982, *37*, 911–918.

Kanter, R. M. *The Change Masters: Innovation and Entrepreneurship in the American Corporation*. New York: Simon & Schuster, 1983.

Kaplan, S. H., Greenfield, S., and Ware, J. E., Jr. "Assessing the Effects of Physician-Patient Interactions on the Outcomes of Chronic Disease." *Medical Care*, 1989, *27*, S110–S127.

Kaufman, I. R. "The Role of the Advocate: The Court Needs a Friend in Court." In American Law Institute–American Bar Association Committee on Continuing Professional Education (eds.), *Continuing Legal Education and Professional Competence and Responsibility: Since Arden House II*. Philadelphia: American Law Institute–American Bar Association Committee on Continuing Professional Education, 1984.

Keeves, J. P. (ed.). *Educational Research, Methodology, and Measurement*. Elmsford, N.Y.: Pergamon Press, 1988.

Kennedy, M. "Inexact Sciences: Professional Education and the Development of Expertise." *Review of Research in Education*, 1987, *14*, 133–167.

Kenyon, R. A. "The Future of Engineering Science and Technology: Collision or Convergence?" *Engineering Education*, 1985, *75* (8), 706–712.

Kets de Vries, M.F.R., and Associates. *Organizations on the Couch: Clinical Perspectives on Organizational Behavior and Change*. San Francisco: Jossey-Bass, 1991.

Kimball, B. A. "Review Essay." *Journal of Higher Education*, 1988, *59* (4), 456–468.

Kirk, S. A., and Rosenblatt, A. "The Contribution of Women Faculty to Social Work Journals." *Social Work*, 1984, *29* (1), 67–69.

Kirschenbaum, S. S. "Influence of Experience on Information-Gathering Strategies." *Journal of Applied Psychology*, 1992, *77*, 343–352.

Knitter, W. "Curriculum Deliberation: Pluralism and the Practical." *Journal of Curriculum Studies*, 1985, *17*, 383–396.

Koen, B. V. "Toward a Definition of the Engineering Method." *Engineering Education,* 1984, *75* (3), 150–155.

Kolb, D. A. *Experiential Learning: Experience as the Source of Learning and Development.* Englewood Cliffs, N.J.: Prentice-Hall, 1984.

Korcak, M. "American Family Physicians Battle HMOs." *Canadian Medical Association Journal,* 1985, *133,* 483–484.

Krathwohl, D. R. (ed.). *Taxonomy of Educational Objectives: Affective Domain.* New York: McKay, 1964.

Kremer, B. K. "Physician Recertification and Outcomes Assessment." *Evaluation and the Health Professions,* 1991, *14,* 187–200.

LaDuca, A., Staples, W. I., Templeton, B., and Holzman, G. B. "Item-Modelling Procedure for Constructing Content-Equivalent Multiple-Choice Questions." *Medical Education,* 1986, *20,* 53–56.

LaFrance, A. B. "Clinical Education and the Year 2010." *Journal of Legal Education,* 1987, *37,* 352–363.

Lampert, M. "Teaching About Thinking and Thinking About Teaching." *Journal of Curriculum Studies,* 1984, *16,* 1–18.

Langsley, D. G. "Medical Competence and Performance Assessment." *Journal of the American Medical Association,* 1991, *266,* 977–980.

Larson, M. S. "Proletarianization and Educated Labor." *Theory and Society,* 1980, *9,* 131–177.

Lave, J. *Cognition in Practice.* Cambridge, England: Cambridge University Press, 1988.

Leigh, T. M. "Computerized Office Record Review." In J. S. Lloyd and D. G. Langsley (eds.), *Recertification for Medical Specialists.* Evanston, Ill.: American Board of Medical Specialties, 1987.

Lesgold, A., and others. "Expertise in a Complex Skill: Diagnosing X-Ray Pictures." In M.T.H. Chi, R. Glaser, and M. J. Farr (eds.), *The Nature of Expertise.* Hillsdale, N.J.: Erlbaum, 1988.

Levenson, J. A. *Circa 1492: Art in the Age of Exploration.* Washington, D.C.: National Gallery of Art, 1991.

Levine, M. "The Academic Achievement Test: Its Historical

Context and Social Functions." *American Psychologist,* 1976, *31,* 228–238.

Liaison Committee on Medical Education. *Functions and Structure of a Medical School.* Chicago: American Medical Association, 1991.

Linn, R. L. (ed.). *Educational Measurement.* (3rd ed.) New York: American Council on Education and Macmillan, 1989.

Linn, R. L., Baker, E. L., and Dunbar, S. B. "Complex, Performance-Based Assessment: Expectations and Validation Criteria." *Educational Researcher,* 1991, *20* (8), 15–21.

Liston, E. M., Yager, J., and Strauss, G. D. "Assessment of Psychotherapy Skills: The Problem of Interrater Agreement." *American Journal of Psychiatry,* 1981, *138,* 1069–1074.

Lloyd, J. S. *Oral Examinations in Medical Specialty Board Certification.* Evanston, Ill.: American Board of Medical Specialties, 1983.

"Local Doctor Shortage." *Macomb Journal,* Jan. 19, 1992, pp. 1–2.

Loftus, E. F., and Schneider, N. G. " 'Behold with Strange Surprise': Judicial Reactions to Expert Testimony Concerning Eyewitness Reliability." *University of Missouri–Kansas City Law Review,* 1987, *56,* 1–45.

Lohr, K. N. "Outcome Measurement: Concepts and Questions." *Inquiry,* 1988, *25,* 37–50.

Lohr, K. N. (ed.). *Medicare: A Strategy for Quality Assurance.* Washington, D.C.: National Academy Press, 1990.

Lortie, D. C. *Schoolteacher: A Sociological Study.* Chicago: University of Chicago Press, 1985.

Lynton, E. A., and Elman, S. E. *New Priorities for the University: Meeting Society's Needs for Applied Knowledge and Competent Individuals.* San Francisco: Jossey-Bass, 1987.

McAuliffe, W. E. "Studies of Process-Outcome Correlations in Medical Care Evaluations: A Critique." *Medical Care,* 1978, *16,* 907–930.

McClelland, D. C. "Testing for Competence Rather Than for Intelligence." *American Psychologist,* 1973, *28,* 1–14.

McClosky, M. "Naive Theories of Motion." In D. Gentner and A. Stevens (eds.), *Mental Models.* Hillsdale, N.J.: Erlbaum, 1983.

MacDonald, K., and Ritzer, G. "The Sociology of the Professions: Dead or Alive?" *Work and Occupations,* 1988, *15* (30), 251–272.

McGaghie, W. C. "Evaluation of Learners." In W. C. McGaghie and J. J. Frey (eds.), *Handbook for the Academic Physician.* New York: Springer-Verlag, 1986.

McGaghie W. C. "Perspectives on Medical School Admission." *Academic Medicine,* 1990, *65,* 136–139.

McGaghie, W. C. "Educational Criticism as a Component of Professional Competence Evaluation." *Professions Education Researcher Quarterly,* 1991a, *12* (4), 10–13.

McGaghie, W. C. "Professional Competence Evaluation." *Educational Researcher,* 1991b, *20* (1), 3–9.

McGrath, W. E. "Relationships Between Hard/Soft, Pure/Applied, and Life/Nonlife Disciplines and Subject Book Use in a Public Library." *Information Processing and Management,* 1978, *14,* 17–28.

McGuire, C. H. "Medical Problem-Solving: A Critique of the Literature." *Journal of Medical Education,* 1985, *60,* 587–595.

McGuire, C. H. "The Curriculum for the Year 2000." *Medical Education,* 1989, *23,* 221–227.

McGuire, C. H. "Professions Education." In M. Alkin (ed.), *Encyclopedia of Educational Research.* (6th ed.) New York: Macmillan, 1992.

McGuire-Masserman, C. H., and Masserman, J. H. "Social Medicine and World Health." In J. H. Masserman and C. M. Masserman (eds.), *Social Psychiatry and World Accords.* New York: Gardner Press, 1992.

Machlup, F. *The Production and Distribution of Knowledge in the United States.* Princeton, N.J.: Princeton University Press, 1962.

Mackenzie, R. S. "Symposium: Addressing the Negative Impact of Scholarship on Dental Education." *Journal of Dental Education,* 1984, *48* (9), 496–499.

McKinlay, J. D. "Toward the Proletarianization of Physicians." In C. Derber (ed.), *Professionals as Workers: Mental Labor in Advanced Capitalism.* Boston: Hall, 1982.

McNeece, C. A. "Faculty Publications, Tenure, and Job Satisfaction in Graduate Social Work Programs." *Journal of Education for Social Work,* 1981, *17* (3), 13–19.

"Madison Shuns Journalism Accrediting, Stirring a Curriculum Debate." *Chronicle of Higher Education,* Dec. 18, 1991, p. A19.

Mager, R. F. *Preparing Instructional Objectives.* Palo Alto, Calif.: Fearon, 1962.

Maggs, P. B., and Morgan, T. D. "Computer-Based Legal Education at the University of Illinois." *Journal of Legal Education,* 1975, *27* (2), 138–156.

Malanga, M. L., and others. "Too Much Sun." Unpublished manuscript, Guided Design Project, West Virginia University School of Pharmacy, 1987.

Mantei, M. M., and others. "Experiences in the Use of a Media Space." In S. P. Robertson, G. M. Olson, and J. S. Olson (eds.), *Proceedings of CHI '91.* New York: Association of Computing Machinery Press, 1991.

Marlatt, G. A. *Relapse Prevention: Maintenance Strategies in the Treatment of Addictive Behaviors.* New York: Guilford, 1985.

Marsh, P. T. (ed.). *Contesting the Boundaries of Liberal and Professional Education: The Syracuse Experiment.* Syracuse, N.Y.: Syracuse University Press, 1988a.

Marsh, P. T. "Preface." In P. T. Marsh (ed.), *Contesting the Boundaries of Liberal and Professional Education: The Syracuse Experiment.* Syracuse, N.Y.: Syracuse University Press, 1988b.

Marshall, J. G. "Diffusion of Innovation Theory and End-User Searching." *Library and Information Science Research,* 1990, *12,* 55–69.

Matarazzo, I. D. "Higher Education, Professional Accreditation, and Licensure." *American Psychologist,* 1977, *32,* 856–857.

Menges, R. J. "Assessing Readiness for Professional Practice." *Review of Educational Research,* 1975, *45,* 173–207.

Messick, S. "Validity." In R. L. Linn (ed.), *Educational Measurement.* (3rd ed.) New York: American Council on Education and Macmillan, 1989.

Metzger, W. P. "The Spectre of 'Professionism.' " *Educational Researcher,* 1987, *16* (8), 10–21.

Miller, A. R. *Meat Hygiene.* Philadelphia: Lea and Febiger, 1958.

Miller, D. I. *Experience in Decision Making for Students of Industrial Psychology*. Lanham, Md.: Unipub, 1981.

Millman, J. "If at First You Don't Succeed: Setting Passing Scores When More Than One Attempt Is Permitted." *Educational Researcher*, 1989, *18* (6), 5–9.

Millman, J., and Greene, J. "The Specification and Development of Tests of Achievement and Ability." In R. L. Linn (ed.), *Educational Measurement*. (3rd ed.) New York: American Council on Education and Macmillan, 1989.

Mohrman, A. M., Jr., and others. *Large-Scale Organizational Change*. San Francisco: Jossey-Bass, 1989.

Mooney, C. "Crowded Classes, Student-Advising System Are Targets of Report on Liberal Learning." *Chronicle of Higher Education*, Jan. 9, 1991, pp. A1, A40.

Moskos, C. C. *The American Enlisted Man: The Rank and File in Today's Military*. New York: Russell Sage Foundation, 1970.

Muffo, J. A., and Langston, I. W. "An Empirical Model for the Use of Biglan's Disciplinary Categories." Unpublished manuscript, University of Illinois, 1979.

Munby, H. "Metaphor in the Thinking of Teachers: An Exploratory Study." *Journal of Curriculum Studies*, 1986, *18,* 197–207.

Munger, B. S., and Reinhart, M. A. "Field Trial of Multiple Recertification Methods." In J. S. Lloyd and D. G. Langsley (eds.), *Recertification for Medical Specialists*. Evanston, Ill.: American Board of Medical Specialties, 1987.

Naisbitt, J. *Megatrends*. New York: Warner Books, 1982.

Nathanson, S. "The Role of Problem Solving in Legal Education." *Journal of Legal Education*, 1989, *39* (2), 167–183.

National Board for Professional Teaching Standards. *Report to the U.S. Senate Committee on Labor and Human Resources and the U.S. House of Representatives Committee on Education and Labor*. Detroit: National Board for Professional Teaching Standards, 1991.

National Board of Medical Examiners. "Development of the Comprehensive Part I and Part II Examinations." *National Board Examiner*, 1990, *37* (1), 1–8.

National Board of Medical Examiners. "Standard Setting and

Score Reporting for the Comprehensive Part I and Part II Examinations." *National Board Examiner,* 1991, *38* (3), 1–8.

National Council for Accreditation of Teacher Education. *Standards, Procedures, and Policies for the Accreditation of Professional Education Units.* Washington, D.C.: National Council for Accreditation of Teacher Education, 1987.

National Institute of Education. *Involvement in Learning: Realizing the Potential of American Higher Education.* Washington, D.C.: National Institute of Education, 1984.

Newell, L. J. "The Healing Arts and the Liberal Arts in Context." In R. A. Armour and B. S. Fuhrmann (eds.), *Integrating Liberal Learning and Professional Education.* New Directions for Teaching and Learning, no. 40. San Francisco: Jossey-Bass, 1989.

Nolan, J. F., and Huber, T. "Nurturing the Reflective Practitioner Through Instructional Supervision: A Review of the Literature." *Journal of Curriculum and Supervision,* 1989, *4,* 126–145.

Norcini, J. J., and Dawson-Saunders, E. "Issues in Recertification in North America." In D. Newble (ed.), *The Certification and Recertification of Doctors: Issues in the Assessment of Competence.* New York: Cambridge University Press, forthcoming.

Norcini, J. J., and Swanson, D. B. "Factors Influencing Testing Time Requirements for Written Simulations." *International Journal of Teaching and Learning in Medicine,* 1989, *1,* 85–91.

Norcini, J. J., and others. "A Comparison of Knowledge, Synthesis, and Clinical Judgment Multiple-Choice Questions in the Assessment of Physician Competence." *Evaluation and the Health Professions,* 1984, *7,* 485–500.

Nowlen, P. M. *A New Approach to Continuing Education for Business and the Professions.* New York: Macmillan, 1988.

Oakeshott, M. *Rationalism in Politics: And Other Essays.* New York: Basic Books, 1962.

Ogden, G. L. "The Problem Method in Legal Education." *Journal of Legal Education,* December 1984, pp. 654–673.

O'Neill, J. P., and Murphy, R. T. "Changing Age and Gender Profiles Among Entering Seminary Students: 1975–1989." *Ministry Research Notes,* ETS Occasional Report. Princeton, N.J.: Educational Testing Service, 1991.

Oppenheimer, M. "The Proletarianization of the Professional." *Sociological Review Monographs*, 1973, *20*, 213–227.

Ozar, D. "Patients' Autonomy: Three Models of the Professional-Lay Relationship in Medicine." *Theoretical Medicine*, 1984, *5*, 61–68.

Ozar, D. "Social Ethics, the Philosophy of Medicine, and Professional Responsibility." *Theoretical Medicine*, 1985, *6*, 281–294.

Ozar, D. "The Demands of Profession and Their Limits." In C. Quinn and M. Smith (eds.), *The Professional Commitment: Issues and Ethics in Nursing*. Philadelphia: Saunders, 1987.

Ozar, D. "Professional Values in Engineering." In N. Warren and M. Rogers (eds.), *A Delicate Balance: Techniques, Culture, and Consequences*. Torrence, Calif.: Institute of Electrical and Electronic Engineers, 1990.

Ozar, D., Kelly, C., and Begue, Y. "Ethical Conduct of State Court Employees and Administrators: The Search for Standards." *Judicature*, 1988, *71*, 262–276.

Ozar, D., Kelly, C., and Begue, Y. "Ethical Conduct of Nonjudicial Court Employees: A Proposed Model Code." *Judicature*, 1989, *73*, 126–137.

Ozar, D., Schiedermayer, D., and Siegler, M. "Value Categories in Clinical Dental Ethics." *Journal of the American Dental Association*, 1988, *116*, 365–368.

Panel on the General Professional Education of the Physician. *Physicians for the Twenty-First Century: The GPEP Report*. Washington, D.C.: Association of American Medical Colleges, 1984.

Parsons, T. "Professions." In D. L. Sills (ed.), *International Encyclopedia of the Social Sciences*. Vol. 12. New York: Macmillan, 1968.

Patel, V. L., Evans, D. A., and Groen, G. J. "Biomedical Knowledge and Clinical Reasoning." In D. A. Evans and V. L. Patel (eds.), *Cognitive Science in Medicine*. Cambridge, Mass.: MIT Press, 1989.

Pereira, P. "Deliberation and the Arts of Perception." *Journal of Curriculum Studies*, 1984, *16*, 347–366.

Perelman, C., and Olbrechts-Tyteca, L. *The New Rhetoric: A Treatise on Argumentation*. South Bend, Ind.: University of Notre Dame Press, 1971.

Perry, W. G., Jr. *Forms of Intellectual and Ethical Development in the College Years.* Troy, Mo.: Holt, Rinehart & Winston, 1970.

Perry, W. G., Jr. "Cognitive and Ethical Growth: The Making of Meaning." In A. W. Chickering and Associates, *The Modern American College: Responding to the New Realities of Diverse Students and a Changing Society.* San Francisco: Jossey-Bass, 1981.

Petersdorf, R. G., Turner, K. S., Nickens, H. W., and Ready, T. "Minorities in Medicine: Past, Present, and Future." *Academic Medicine,* 1990, *65,* 663–670.

Petrusa, E., and others. "A Multi-Institutional Trial of an Objective Structured Clinical Examination." *Teaching and Learning in Medicine,* 1991, *3,* 86–94.

Picton, J. "How Forecasters of 1950s Have Fared: Microwaves Abound but No 3-D TV." *Toronto Star,* Sept. 11, 1988, pp. A1, A10.

Podgers, J. "The Practice of Law: What Does the Future Hold?" *American Bar Association Journal,* 1980, *66,* 267–269.

Polanyi, M. *The Tacit Dimension.* New York: Doubleday, 1967.

Porat, M. I. *The Information Economy: Definition and Measures.* Washington, D.C.: Government Printing Office, 1977.

Porter, L. W., and McKibbin, L. E. *Management Education and Development: Drift or Thrust into the 21st Century?* New York: McGraw-Hill, 1988.

Pulakos, E. D. "The Development of Training Programs to Increase Accuracy with Different Rating Tasks." *Organizational Behavior and Human Performance,* 1986, *38,* 76–91.

Rader, H. "Bibliographic Instruction of Information Literacy?" *College and Research Libraries News,* 1990, *51,* 18–20.

Ramsey, P. G., and others. *Assessment of the Clinical Competence of Certified Internists.* Final Report to the American Board of Internal Medicine. Philadelphia: American Board of Internal Medicine, 1990.

Ramsey, P. G., and others. "Changes Over Time in the Knowledge Base of Practicing Internists." *Journal of the American Medical Association,* 1991, *266,* 1103–1107.

Raskin, I. E., and Maklan, C. W. "Patient Outcomes Research: AHCPR Highlights." *SGIM News: Research and Education in Primary Care,* 1991, *14,* 1, 4.

Reed, A. Z. *Training for the Public Profession of Law.* New York: Carnegie Foundation for the Advancement of Teaching, 1921.

Reed, R. R., and Evans, D. "The Deprofessionalization of Medicine: Causes, Effects, and Responses." *Journal of the American Medical Association,* 1987, *258,* 3279–3282.

Reibstein, L., and Springer, K. "Spotting the Write Stuff." *Newsweek,* Feb. 17, 1992, p. 44.

Reid, W. A. *Thinking About the Curriculum: The Nature and Treatment of Curriculum Problems.* New York: Routledge & Kegan Paul, 1978.

Reid, W. A. "Deliberative Curriculum Theory: A Manifesto." Paper presented at the annual meeting of the American Educational Research Association, Los Angeles, 1981.

Relman, A. S. "Assessment and Accountability: The Third Revolution in Medical Care." *New England Journal of Medicine,* 1988, *319,* 1220–1222.

Resnick, L. *Education and Learning to Think.* Washington, D.C.: National Academy Press, 1987a.

Resnick, L. "Learning in School and Out." *Educational Researcher,* 1987b, *16,* 13–20.

Rest, J. "A Psychologist Looks at the Teaching of Ethics." *Hastings Center Report,* 1982, *12,* 29–36.

Rest, J. "Morality." In P. Mussen (ed.), *Manual of Child Psychology.* Vol. 3. New York: Wiley, 1983.

Riesman, D. "Professional Education and Liberal Education: A False Dichotomy." In J. N. Burstyn (ed.), *Preparation for Life? The Paradox of Education in the Late Twentieth Century.* Philadelphia: Falmer, 1986.

Roberts, N. (ed.). *The Use of Social Science Literature.* London: Butterworths, 1977.

Roby, T. W. "Habits Impeding Deliberation." *Journal of Curriculum Studies,* 1985, *17,* 17–35.

Roid, G. H., and Haladyna, T. M. *A Technology for Test-Item Writing.* San Diego: Academic Press, 1982.

Rosenthal, D. E. "Evaluating the Competence of Lawyers." In American Law Institute–American Bar Association Committee on Continuing Professional Education (eds.), *Continuing*

Legal Education and Professional Competence and Responsibility: Since Arden House II. Philadelphia: American Law Institute–American Bar Association Committee on Continuing Professional Education, 1984.

Roskens, R. W. "Implications of Biglan Model Research for the Process of Faculty Advancement." *Research in Higher Education,* 1983, *18* (3), 285–297.

Rothman, R. A. "Deprofessionalism: The Case of Law in America." *Work and Occupations,* 1984, *11* (2), 183–206.

Royal Colledge of Physicians London. *By-Laws of the Royal Colledge of Physicians.* London: Royal Colledge of Physicians, 1693. Microfilm.

Rubenstein, L. V., and others. "Changes in Quality of Care for Five Diseases Measured by Implicit Review, 1981–1986." *Journal of the American Medical Association,* 1990, *264,* 1974–1979.

Russell, T. "Beginning Teachers' Development of Knowledge-in-Action." Paper presented at the annual meeting of the American Educational Research Association, San Francisco, 1986.

Ryle, G. *The Concept of Mind.* London: Hutcheson, 1949.

Sackett, P. R., Burris, L. R., and Callahan, C. "Integrity Testing for Personnel Selection: An Update." *Personnel Psychology,* 1989, *42,* 491–529.

Samson, G. E., Graue, M. E., Weinstein, T., and Walberg, H. J. "Academic and Occupational Performance: A Quantitative Synthesis." *American Educational Research Journal,* 1984, *21,* 311–321.

Schaffer, N. D. "Methodological Issues of Measuring the Skillfulness of Therapeutic Techniques." *Psychotherapy: Theory, Research, and Practice,* 1983, *20,* 486–493.

Scheffler, I. *The Language of Education.* Springfield, Ill.: Thomas, 1960.

Schön, D. A. *The Reflective Practitioner: How Professionals Think in Action.* New York: Basic Books, 1983.

Schön, D. A. *Educating the Reflective Practitioner: Toward a New Design for Teaching and Learning in the Professions.* San Francisco: Jossey-Bass, 1987.

Schön, D. A. (ed.). *The Reflective Turn: Case Studies in and on Educational Practice.* New York: Teachers College Press, 1991.

Schuck, P. H. "Why Don't Law Professors Do More Empirical Research?" *Journal of Legal Education,* 1989, *39* (3), 323–336.

Schuller, D. S., Strommen, M. P., and Brekke, M. L. (eds.). *Ministry in America.* New York: HarperCollins, 1980.

Schwab, J. J. "The Practical: Arts of the Eclectic." In I. Westbury and N. J. Wilkof (eds.), *Science, Curriculum, and Liberal Education: Selected Essays.* Chicago: University of Chicago Press, 1978a. (Originally published 1971.)

Schwab, J. J. "The Practical: A Language for Curriculum." In I. Westbury and N. J. Wilkof (eds.), *Science, Curriculum, and Liberal Education: Selected Essays.* Chicago: University of Chicago Press, 1978b. (Originally published 1969.)

Schwab, J. J. "The Practical: Translation into Curriculum." In I. Westbury and N. J. Wilkof (eds.), *Science, Curriculum, and Liberal Education: Selected Essays.* Chicago: University of Chicago Press, 1978c. (Originally published 1971.)

Shadish, W. R., Cook, T. D., and Leviton, L. C. *Foundations of Program Evaluation: Theories of Practice.* Newbury Park, Calif.: Sage, 1991.

Shavelson, R. J., Mayberry, P. W., Li, W., and Webb, N. M. "Generalizability of Job Performance Measurements: Marine Corps Rifleman." *Military Psychology,* 1990, *2,* 129–144.

Shavelson, R. J., and Webb, N. M. *Generalizability Theory: A Primer.* Newbury Park, Calif.: Sage, 1991.

Shaw, B. F., and Dobson, K. S. "Competency Judgments in the Training and Evaluation of Psychotherapists." *Journal of Consulting and Clinical Psychology,* 1988, *56,* 666–672.

Shaw, K. E. "Skills, Control, and the Mass Professions." *Sociological Review,* 1987, *35* (4), 775–794.

Shea, J. A., and others. "An Adaptation of Item Modeling for Developing Test Item Banks." *Teaching and Learning in Medicine,* 1992a, *4,* 19–24.

Shea, J. A., and others. "A Comparison of Video and Print Formats in the Assessment of Skill in Interpreting Cardiovascular Motion Studies." *Evaluation and the Health Professions,* 1992b, *15,* 325–340.

Shimberg, B. "What Is Competence? How Can It Be Assessed?" In M. R. Stern (ed.), *Power and Conflict in Continuing Professional Education.* Belmont, Calif.: Wadsworth, 1983.

Shuchman, H. L. *Information Transfer in Engineering.* Glastonbury, Conn.: Futures Group, 1981.

Shuell, T. J. "Cognitive Conceptions of Learning." *Review of Educational Research,* 1986, *56,* 411–436.

Shulman, L. S. "Paradigms and Research Programs in the Study of Teaching: A Contemporary Perspective." In M. C. Wittrock (ed.), *Handbook of Research on Teaching.* (3rd ed.) New York: Macmillan, 1986.

Shulman, L. S. "Knowledge and Teaching: Foundations of the New Reform." *Harvard Educational Review,* 1987, *57* (1), 1–22.

Shulman, L. S. "The Dangers of Dichotomous Thinking in Education." In P. P. Grimmett and G. L. Erickson (eds.), *Reflection in Teacher Education.* New York: Teachers College Press, 1988.

Siegel, D. H. "Defining Empirically Based Practice." *Social Work,* 1984, *29* (4), 325–331.

Simon, H. A., and Newell, A. "Human Problem Solving: The State of the Theory in 1970." *American Psychologist,* 1971, *26,* 145–159.

Smart, J. C., and Elton, C. F. "Goal Orientations of Academic Departments: A Test of Biglan's Model." *Journal of Applied Psychology,* 1975, *60* (5), 580–588.

Smart, J. C., and Elton, C. F. "Administrative Roles of Department Chairmen." In J. C. Smart and J. R. Montgomery (eds.), *Examining Departmental Measurement.* New Directions for Institutional Research, no. 10. San Francisco: Jossey-Bass, 1976.

Smart, J. C., and McLaughlin, G. W. "Reward Structures of Academic Disciplines." *Research in Higher Education,* 1978, *8,* 39–55.

Smith, C. "How Will the Corporatization of Health Care Influence Health Professions Education?" Paper presented at the annual meeting of the American Educational Research Association, New Orleans, April 1988.

Smith, K. A. "The Nature and Development of Engineering Expertise." *European Journal of Engineering Education,* 1988, *13,* 317–330.

Smith, M. D., DeWeaver, K. L., and Kilpatrick, A. C. "Research

Curricula and Accreditation: The Challenge for Leadership." *Journal of Social Work Education,* 1986, *22* (2), 61–70.

Soder, R. "On Lemmings in Higher Education." *Metropolitan Universities,* 1991, *1* (4), 19–28.

Solomon, D. J., and others. "An Assessment of an Oral Examination Format for Evaluating Clinical Competence in Emergency Medicine." *Academic Medicine,* 1990, *65,* S43–S44.

Spiro, R., Feltovich, P., Jacobson, M., and Coulson, R. "Cognitive Flexibility, Constructivism, and Hypertext: Random Access Instruction for Advanced Knowledge Acquisition in Ill-Structured Domains." *Educational Technology,* 1991, *31* (5), 28–38.

Starfield, A. M., Butala, K. L., England, M. M., and Smith, K. A. "Mastering Engineering Concepts by Building an Expert System." *Engineering Education,* 1983, *4* (2), 104–107.

Stark, J. S., and Lowther, M. A. *Strengthening the Ties That Bind: Integrating Undergraduate Liberal and Professional Study.* Ann Arbor: Professional Preparation Network, University of Michigan, 1988.

Stark, J. S., Lowther, M. A., and Hagerty, B.M.K. *Responsive Professional Education: Balancing Outcomes and Opportunities.* ASHE-ERIC Higher Education Reports, no. 3. Washington, D.C.: Association for the Study of Higher Education, 1986.

Stark, J. S., Lowther, M. A., and Hagerty, B.M.K. "Faculty Perceptions of Professional Preparation Environments: Testing a Conceptual Framework." *Journal of Higher Education,* 1987, *58* (5), 530–561.

Stark, J. S., Lowther, M. A., Hagerty, B.M.K., and Orcyak, C. "A Conceptual Framework for the Study of Preservice Professional Programs in Colleges and Universities." *Journal of Higher Education,* 1986, *57* (7), 231–258.

Starr, P. *The Social Transformation of American Medicine.* New York: Basic Books, 1982.

Steig, M. "The Information Needs of Historians." *College and Research Libraries,* 1981, *42,* 549–560.

Sternberg, R. J., and Wagner, R. K. (eds.). *Practical Intelligence: Nature and Origins of Competence in the Everyday World.* New York: Cambridge University Press, 1986.

Stevens, R. *Law School: Legal Education in America from the 1850s to the 1980s.* Chapel Hill: University of North Carolina Press, 1983.

Steward, W. C. "Influences from Within the Academy upon Architectural Education." Unpublished manuscript, School of Architecture, University of Nebraska, Lincoln, 1988.

Stewart, A. L., and others. "Functional Status and Well-Being of Patients with Chronic Conditions: Results from the Medical Outcomes Study." *Journal of the American Medical Association,* 1989, *262,* 907–913.

Stiggins, R. J. "Design and Development of Performance Assessments." *Educational Measurement: Issues and Practice,* 1987, *6* (3), 33–42.

Stillman, P. L., Rutala, P. J., Stillman, A. E., and Sabers, D. L. "The Use of Patient Instructors to Evaluate the Clinical Competence of Physicians." In J. S. Lloyd (ed.), *Evaluation of Noncognitive Skills and Clinical Performance.* Evanston, Ill.: American Board of Medical Specialties, 1982.

Stillman, P. L., and others. "Assessing Clinical Skills of Residents with Standardized Patients." *Annals of Internal Medicine,* 1986, *105,* 762–771.

Stufflebeam, D. L., and Shinkfield, A. J. *Systematic Evaluation.* Boston: Kluwer-Nijhoff, 1985.

Sullivan, R. "City Expanding Use of Computers to Monitor Pediatric Care." *New York Times,* Feb. 29, 1984, p. B24.

Swanson, D. B., Norcini, J. J., and Grosso, L. J. "Assessment of Clinical Competence: Written and Computer-Based Simulations." *Assessment and Evaluation in Higher Education,* 1987, *12,* 220–246.

Swanson, D. B., Webster, G. D., and Norcini, J. J. "Precision of Patient Ratings of Residents' Humanistic Qualities: How Many Items and Patients Are Enough?" In W. Bender, C. M. Metz, H. J. Van Rossum, and M. G. Ver Wijnem (eds.), *Proceedings of the Third International Conference on Teaching and Assessing Clinical Competence.* Groningen, The Netherlands: BoekWerk, 1989.

Tamir, P. "Effects of Different Curriculum Process Models on the Outcomes." Paper presented at the annual meeting of the American Educational Research Association, San Francisco, April 1989.

Tarlov, A. R., and others. "The Medical Outcomes Study: An Application of Methods for Monitoring the Results of Medical Care." *Journal of the American Medical Association,* 1989, *262,* 925–930.

Thorndike, R. L. *Personnel Selection: Test and Measurement Techniques.* New York: Wiley, 1949.

Thornton, G. C., and Cleveland, J. N. "Developing Managerial Talent Through Simulation." *American Psychologist,* 1990, *45,* 190–199.

Thornton, G. C., and Zorich, S. "Training to Improve Observer Accuracy." *Journal of Applied Psychology,* 1980, *65,* 351–354.

Thyer, B. A., and Bentley, K. J. "Academic Affiliations of Social Work Authors: A Citation Analysis of Six Major Journals." *Journal of Social Work Education,* 1986, *22* (1), 67–73.

Tomain, J. P., and Solimine, M. E. "Skills Skepticism in the Postclinic World." *Journal of Legal Education,* 1990, *40* (3), 307–320.

Torstendahl, R., and Burrage, M. (eds.). *The Formation of Professions: Knowledge, State, and Strategy.* Newbury Park, Calif.: Sage, 1990.

Truxal, J. "Learning to Think Like an Engineer: Why, What, and How." *Change,* 1986, *18* (2), 10–19.

Tyler, R. *Basic Principles of Curriculum and Instruction.* Chicago: University of Chicago Press, 1949.

Tziner, A., and Dolan, S. "Validity of an Assessment Center for Identifying Future Female Officers in the Military." *Journal of Applied Psychology,* 1982, *67,* 728–736.

Underwood, B. J., and Schultz, R. W. *Meaningfulness and Verbal Learning.* Philadelphia: Lippincott, 1960.

United Methodist Church. *Book of Discipline of the United Methodist Church.* Nashville, Tenn.: United Methodist Church, 1980.

van der Vleuten, C.P.M., and Swanson, D. B. "Assessment of Clinical Skills with Standardized Patients: State of the Art." *Teaching and Learning in Medicine,* 1990, *2,* 58–76.

Vogt, L. M., Silverman, W., White, T. W., and Scanlon, J. W. "Field Test Results of Peer Review Quality Assessment of

Legal Services." In American Law Institute–American Bar Association Committee on Continuing Professional Education (eds.), *Continuing Legal Education and Professional Competence and Responsibility: Since Arden House II.* Philadelphia: American Law Institute–American Bar Association Committee on Continuing Professional Education, 1984.

Vogt, R., Cameron, B., and Dolan, E. *Economics.* Troy, Mo.: Holt, Rinehart & Winston, 1992.

Vu, N. V., and others. "Six Years of Comprehensive, Clinical, Performance-Based Assessment Using Standardized Patients at the Southern Illinois University School of Medicine." *Academic Medicine,* 1992, *67,* 42–50.

Wagner, R. K., and Sternberg, R. J. "Tacit Knowledge and Intelligence in the Everyday World." In R. J. Sternberg and R. K. Wagner (eds.), *Practical Intelligence: Nature and Origins of Competence in the Everyday World.* New York: Cambridge University Press, 1986.

Wainer, H. (ed.). *Computerized Adaptive Testing: A Primer.* Hillsdale, N.J.: Erlbaum, 1990.

Wales, C. "Does How You Teach Make a Difference?" *Engineering Education,* 1979, *69,* 394–398.

Wales, C., Nardi, A., and Stager, R. *Professional Decision-Making.* Morgantown: Center for Guided Design, West Virginia University, 1986.

Wales, C., Nardi, A., and Stager, R. *Thinking Skills: Making a Choice.* Morgantown: Center for Guided Design, West Virginia University, 1987.

Wales, C., Stager, R., and Long, T. *Guided Engineering Design Project Book.* Saint Paul, Minn.: West, 1984.

Walker, D. "A Study of Curriculum Deliberation in Three Curriculum Projects." *Curriculum Theory Network,* 1971, *7,* 118–134.

Walsh, D. C. *Corporate Physicians: Between Medicine and Management.* New Haven, Conn.: Yale University Press, 1987.

Watson, S., Meyer, A., and Wotman, S. "Factors Affecting Applications to Professional Schools of Six Professions: Medicine, Dentistry, Nursing, Law, Social Work, and Public Health." *Journal of Dental Education,* 1987, *51* (3), 130–136.

Weaver, F. S. *Liberal Education: Critical Essays on Professions, Pedagogy, and Structure.* New York: Teachers College Press, 1991.

Webb, N. B. "From Social Work Practice to Teaching the Practice of Social Work." *Journal of Education for Social Work,* 1984, *20* (3), 51–57.

Webb, N. M., Shavelson, R. J., Kim, K., and Chen, Z. "Reliability (Generalizability) of Job Performance Measurements: Navy Machinist Mates." *Military Psychology,* 1989, *1,* 91–110.

Webster, G. D. "Some Aspects of Scoring and Standard Setting for Recertification by the American Board of Internal Medicine." In American Board of Medical Specialties, *Proceedings of the Conference on Recertification.* Evanston, Ill.: American Board of Medical Specialties, 1979.

Webster, G. D. "Computer Simulations in Assessing Clinical Competence: A Fifteen-Year Perspective." In J. S. Lloyd (ed.), *Computer Applications in the Evaluation of Physician Competence.* Evanston, Ill.: American Board of Medical Specialties, 1984.

Wells, K. B., and others. "The Functioning and Well-Being of Depressed Patients: Results from the Medical Outcomes Study." *Journal of the American Medical Association,* 1989, *262,* 914–919.

Wennberg, J. E. "Outcomes Research, Cost Containment, and the Fear of Health Care Rationing." *New England Journal of Medicine,* 1990, *323,* 1202–1204.

Wergin, J. F. "The Faculty as Change Agents." *Journal of the American Podiatric Medical Association,* forthcoming.

Whalley, P. *The Social Production of Technical Work: The Case of British Engineers.* London: Macmillan, 1985.

White, L., Jr. *Medieval Technology and Social Change.* Oxford, England: Oxford University Press, 1962.

Whitehead, A. N. *The Aims of Education and Other Essays.* New York: Macmillan, 1929.

Wiggins, J. S. *Personality and Prediction: Principles of Personality Assessment.* Reading, Mass.: Addison-Wesley, 1973.

Wilensky, H. L. "The Professionalization of Everyone." *American Journal of Sociology,* 1964, *70,* 137–158.

Williams, G. *Western Reserve's Experiment in Medical Education and Its Outcomes.* New York: Oxford University Press, 1980.

Wingard, J. R., and Williamson, J. W. "Grades as Predictors of Physician's Career Performance: An Evaluative Literature Review." *Journal of Medical Education,* 1973, *48,* 311–322.

Wiser, M., and Carey, S. "When Heat and Temperature Were One." In D. Gentner and A. Stevens (eds.), *Mental Models.* Hillsdale, N.J.: Erlbaum, 1983.

Worzel, R. "What the Next Ten Years May Bring." *Globe and Mail,* Mar. 3, 1992, p. C2.

Wurman, R. S. *Information Anxiety.* New York: Doubleday, 1989.

Zeidenberg, J. "Special Report: Office Technology." *Financial Times of Canada,* Mar. 11–17, 1991, pp. A1–A7.

Zuboff, S. "New Worlds of Computer-Mediated Work." *Harvard Business Review,* Sept.-Oct. 1982, pp. 142–152.

Zuboff, S. *In the Age of the Smart Machine: The Future of Work and Power.* New York: Basic Books, 1988.

NAME INDEX

363

SUBJECT INDEX

Subject Index

Continuing medical education
(CME), 269; innovative program in, 325–326
Continuing professional education
(CPE): change agents in, 263,
271–275; and experience, 263,
266–268; future of, 276–278;
learning and change in, 263,
268–270; and performance, 262,
263–265; self-directed curricula
in, 263, 275–276
Coprofessionals, relationships
among, 170
Corporate education, 212–215;
practices of, 218–226
Council on Social Work Education,
300
Crafts, as type of practice, 25
Criterion problem, in competence
evaluation, 237–240
Critical thinking, and liberal
learning, 134–135. *See also*
Thinking
Critical view, of professionals, 264–
265
Curriculum: and education-
practice discontinuity, 114; in
engineering, 38–39; integration
of, 112–113; in law, 39–40; in
medicine, 36–38; and reflective
practice, 41–47; self-directed,
263, 275–276; technical and
practical knowledge in, 319–320

D

Dalhousie University, 325–326
Data collection and analysis,
information technologies for,
65–68
Datastar, 63
Decision making: Guided Design
exercise on, 193–204; steps in
process of, 190–191
Deliberative curriculum theory,
and curriculum planning, 42–45
Demographics, and competence
evaluation, 253–254
Dentistry: Gies report on, 280, 302,

323; scholarship in, 296, 302;
scholarship/practice relationship in, 314
Diagnostic tests: to assess potential
to practice, 91–93; methods of,
93–96
Dialog, 63
Discovery: and practice, 295–298;
with purpose, 306–307; scholarship of, 285
Division of labor, 8–9
Document creation, information
technologies for, 61–62

E

Educating the Reflective Practitioner
(Schön), 26, 182
Education: continuing, 225–226,
259; corporate, 212–215, 218–
226; engineering, 38–39; legal,
39–40; and liberal learning,
140–141; medical, 36–38; and
reflective practice epistemology,
51–52; and scholarship, 296,
298, 299, 312. *See also* Continuing medical education (CME);
Continuing professional
education (CPE); Professional
education; Professional ethics
education
Education program evaluation,
120–122
Educational methods, and reflective
practice, 45–47. *See also* Teaching and learning
Educators, and information
technologies, 54–55. *See also*
Teachers
Electronic mail, information
technologies for, 64–65
Engineering: curriculum for, 38–
39; and liberal learning, 141–
142; and scholarship, 296,
297–298; teaching thinking in,
180
Ethics, assurances of, 148–149. *See
also* Professional ethics education

reflective, 182–185, 210–211; Schön on process of, 185–189; Wales, Nardi, and Stager's process of, 189–204

Time, incorporating value of student, 222. *See also* Response time

Toronto, University of: Centre for Computing in the Humanities, 76–77; health services administration program at, 44

U

United Methodist Church, 230

United Way (Toronto, Canada), information technologies of, 68–69

U.S. National Library of Medicine, 63

V

Validation research, and competence evaluation, 257, 260. *See also* Research

Value(s): central, of profession, 165–166; formation of, 135–136; of student time, 222

Virginia Commonwealth University, general/professional education integration at, 145

W

West Virginia University, teaching thinking at, 204–206

Western Michigan University, 120

Wisconsin, University of, at Madison, journalism accreditation at, 236

Women: and competence evaluations, 254; and scholarship in professional schools, 294